The Art of Soul

D1245181

The Art of Soul

An Artist's Guide to Spirituality

Regina Coupar

NOVALIS

© 2002 Novalis, Saint Paul University, Ottawa, Canada

Cover painting: *Birthing* by Regina Coupar

Business Office:
Novalis
49 Front Street East, 2nd Floor
Toronto, Ontario, Canada
M5E 1B3

Phone: 1-800-387-7164 or (416) 363-3303
Fax: 1-800-204-4140 or (416) 363-9409
E-mail: cservice@novalis.ca

National Library of Canada Cataloguing in Publication

Coupar, Regina
    The art of soul : an artist's guide to spirituality / Regina Coupar.

Includes bibliographical references.
ISBN 2-89507-299-X

    1. Spirituality. 2. Art and religion. 3. Art–Technique. 4. Creation
(Literary, artistic, etc.) I. Title.

N72.R4C66 2002   291.4   C2002-902968-6

Printed in Canada.

All rights reserved. No part of this publication may be reproduced, stored in a retrieval system, or transmitted in any form, or by any means, electronic, mechanical, photocopying, recording, or otherwise, without the written permission of the publisher.

We acknowledge the financial support of the Government of Canada through the Book Publishing Industry Development Program (BPIDP) for our publishing activities.

10 9 8 7 6 5 4 3 2 1   10 09 08 07 06 05 04 03 02

for John, my husband and soulmate

*"…art should speak its own truth,
and in so doing it will be in harmony
with every other kind of truth – moral,
metaphysical, and mystical."*[1]

Thomas Merton

ACKNOWLEDGMENTS

I would like to thank Michael and Rosemary O'Hearn for their curiosity about my work after a brief encounter at a Boston book display, and also Kevin Burns and Anne Louise Mahoney for their expert guidance in the final shaping of the manuscript. A special thanks to Todd Hyslop for his assistance in photographing the demonstrations.

There are many students and teachers who have contributed to my understanding of both art and soul over the years. I appreciate their support and their challenges. I am grateful to my friends Terry, Joanne, Christene, Lesa, Marlene, Sharon, Susan and Liz for their constant encouragement as I worked on this book, and to my family – especially my children, Jennifer, Erin and John – for their continuing love.

And, finally, I am deeply indebted to my husband, John Schellenberg, without whom I literally would not have completed this work. An analytical philosopher, he offered input during the editing process that helped me untangle twenty-five years of experience and insights and make them accessible to others. His personal support kept me writing when I would have preferred to be painting.

Some of the poems, stories and images are taken from my earlier books. They are reprinted here because they help to fill out the story.

CONTENTS

PREFACE

Sex, politics and religion have traditionally been unacceptable topics for polite social or family gatherings. While sex and politics have managed to work their way out of the closet, religion remains a taboo subject for small talk, perhaps because such conversations can quickly turn into heated debates. Everyone, whether they practise religion or not, seems to have an opinion about its virtues and vices! The very word sparks hostility in some, anxiety in others. But whatever we may think of it, and no matter how we may seek to ignore it, religion has been part of our heritage since the dawn of human civilization, and continues to exert its influence in ways none of us can escape. From disputes in the Middle East to bans on Sunday shopping, religion shapes our culture and customs to this day, fuelling both war and relief efforts simultaneously.

For many, religion is more than an external commitment to a specific group; it is a set of personal beliefs and practices that provides a structure for everyday life. This broader approach may be called *spirituality*. Spirituality need not be wed to one religious tradition, but is cousin to all — sometimes, but not always, walking along one or more of these paths.

It is in this context that religion can be linked to art. Art, as we shall see, provides a vehicle for stimulating and nurturing our spiritual development. Three main connections between art and spirituality are visible in this book. First, by learning the practical skills of artmaking we learn a new way of seeing the actual world, which has important spiritual implications. Our enhanced observations enable us to see differently from before — literally. Part One helps to facilitate this new approach to seeing. Parts Two, Three and Four include a 'beginners' course' in art, which introduces the reader to basic art principles and use of media. These lessons provide striking metaphors that are useful for understanding and promoting self-awareness and spiritual growth. Finally, this book is written by an artist seeking to develop spiritually. Art and spirituality are ingrained in me, and so they — and the relationship between them — cannot help but be present in everything I say, perhaps especially in certain stories drawn from my personal experience.

It is my claim that by exercising our creativity through artmaking we become more spiritual. It should be noted that a basic common thread between these two aspects of human life is self-discipline. Neither will develop well without a commitment of time and effort, and both will mature more quickly when consciously and deliberately pursued. Without discipline, ideas for artistic creations spin about in our heads but never fully develop. By making our images concrete, we can move beyond them to further growth. Likewise, spiritual self-discipline helps us to ride the sea of life so that we are not destroyed by its storms. Without such discipline, spiritual growth is erratic — mediated by chance and ruled by emotions, like a ship tossed about on an unpredictable sea. Disciplined spirituality connects us with our soul, providing the means for inner peace regardless of exterior circumstances. Of course, it moves outward from here to interaction with others. But both art and spirituality must be grounded in personal experience and both need a balance between disciplined, solitary activity and community participation.

While the language of this book is meant to be inclusive and clear, it cannot help but be provocative at times. The matter of inclusivity is easily solved by alternating pronouns: odd-numbered chapters use feminine pronouns, and even-numbered chapters, masculine ones. References to God are gender neutral. More difficult is the problem of 'soul' language. Any attempts to communicate matters of spirituality will necessarily run into problems: How does one describe that which is by nature indescribable? What follows is a map that will help the reader plot the 'characters' of spiritual development as they are revealed in the book.

For me, the term *soul* represents that inner part of every person that is directly connected to God – whatever we perceive God to be. Our soul is already fully developed within; we need only uncover it to strengthen our everyday connection with the divine. But even with this divine connection, the human person is not and cannot become God. While God is infinite, we are finite; while we hold something of God within, we cannot contain the fullness of God. The soul is our bridge, allowing something of divinity and humanity to merge during our human journey. Our main obstacles in making this connection to God through our soul are the self-interested or unenlightened tendencies of the *ego*. (We can think of the ego as what

in most everyday interactions we would call our self, or name 'I.') As we learn to resist the desires and illusions of the unenlightened ego, our lives can be guided by our soul to a deeper reality, thus enabling our true self, or enlightened ego, to emerge. Artmaking, when done as a spiritual discipline, provides a catalyst for this transformation. Through it we are also able to share the contents of our soul with others.

I believe that one of the greatest shortcomings of organized religion in the past century has been the unwillingness to ask new theological questions, binding us to a religious past that cannot always meet the needs of the present. On the other hand, an understanding of God that engages our imagination enlivens our faith, awakening that part of ourselves through which optimism is restored. In the wake of the horrific terrorist attacks on the United States in 2001, the need for optimism has never seemed greater. If religion – any religion – is to help us through not only our day-to-day routine, but also our darkest hours, it must put us and keep us in touch with the vision of our soul. Asking new questions and allowing ourselves to find new answers strengthens our spirituality so we can meet the challenges of our time. Deep within we already have all we need for a relationship with God that nurtures our selves and the world around us. *The Art of Soul* seeks to provide a bridge, one of many, whereby we can reach what is already within our grasp.

Regina Coupar
Chester Basin, Nova Scotia
Spring 2002

PART ONE

ART AS A
SPIRITUAL DISCIPLINE

The practice of art can put us in touch with our soul. The creative process engages our intuition and opens doors for dialogue between our inner and outer selves. Because anyone, regardless of age or ability, can learn art, it provides an accessible and reliable vehicle for spiritual development. Learning the skills of drawing and painting expands our vision – both literally and metaphorically. Not only do we see the actual world differently, noting things that previously escaped our attention, but through cultivating our imagination we sense interrelationships and possibilities we've never seen before. As we develop creatively, our spirituality finds roots – and wings.

I will meet you
where you are
and bring you
where I am

and I will travel
with you
and guide you
and hold you
when you need to be held

I will give you
all you need
and I will be
all you want

and when you reach the place
that is your destiny
you will look back
and see
that you were never
lost

Chapter 1

RECONNECTING

RECONNECTING WITH OUR CREATIVE SELVES

Beginning again

My favourite art classes are the ones where people have little or no experience in art, have registered because they want to learn something new, and have no purpose for showing up each week except that they want to be there. Often such students are a bit self-conscious during the first class. When asked what kind of art they have done in the past and why they decided to take an art class, they often say, "I did some drawing when I was younger, but I haven't touched it in years." They admit to almost nothing in terms of prior experience, perhaps hoping to keep expectations (mine and theirs!) low. But often by the end of a short series of classes they let down their defences and admit to having tried drawing (or even painting) before, or at least to being more attracted to artmaking than they initially appeared to be. At this point a reconnection with their creative selves is well underway.

Most people today recognize the value of art for children. Activity centres in banks, department stores, restaurants and the like often include an art 'studio' that is outfitted with crayons, pencils, markers and paper for kids who accompany their parents on errands or outings. No preschool or daycare would be considered properly equipped without such supplies. Children, for their part, have no qualms about making art, whether they have had lessons or not. They dive right in, proudly showing each completed creation to anyone who will look (Figure 1.1). Most of us had this

Figure 1.1 Pastel drawings by sisters, Kirsten, 8 (left), and Rachel, 6 (right).

freedom of artistic expression as children, yet at some point along the way, many of us became detached from it. As we grew older and more susceptible to criticism, we stopped sharing our art, and sometimes even stopped making it, putting away our 'childish things' as we followed the example set by the adults in our lives. Especially during adolescence, with its heightened insecurities and peer pressure, we turned away from expressing ourselves through art. Those of us who continued to be interested in art during this time were probably channelled by well-meaning adults and agencies towards 'acceptable,' professional artistic disciplines such as graphic design or architecture. And so we emerged as adults who are uncomfortable giving artistic expression to our vision. In fact, many of us have even forgotten we have a vision! Our culture's attitude towards images produced after childhood doesn't make it easy to remember this vision. How often do you find pictures by adults on your refrigerator or office bulletin board?

It is no wonder, then, that adults initially feel a little uneasy in art classes. It takes a while to recall childlike anticipation, and to give yourself permission to play without expecting specific results. But this is where you need to start if you are to rekindle your creative fires. The least satisfied adult students of art are those who begin the process with specific expectations and objectives. Thinking that perhaps they will paint 'something nice' for their living room, or make Christmas presents, or learn to paint birch trees "like the guy on TV," they want to learn tricks and techniques that will fulfill preconceived objectives. But beginners must first learn to engage the *process* of art. The product will eventually take care of itself. As we often remind our children, playing the game is more important than winning or losing. Our success in art is measured by our ability to let the process become part of us – to *become* artists, seeing the world in a whole new way. As we remember the anticipation of our childhood explorations, our imagination will ignite and a wealth of possibilities will be reawakened within us. Once again, anything is possible! The success of the long-running Canadian children's television show *Mr. Dressup*

was due to this attitude. Children loved the character played by Ernie Coombs because he related to them from his world of make-believe in ways that stimulated their imaginations and respected their intelligence. A box could be a castle, a sock could be an exotic animal, and a change of clothes from his Tickle Trunk could invite children into a whole new world. While *Sesame Street* was seducing parents with its elaborate costumes and set designs, Mr. Dressup continued to be popular with kids who could identify with his simple but creative process of discovery.

For most of us, art classes at school were linked to other subject areas. The idea of art for its own sake was neglected or lost. When learning about early settlers and native culture in social studies class, we made tiny birchbark canoes or designed primitive buildings. When studying the solar system in science, we drew the planets in their paths. We illustrated poems for English class, designed patterns for math, and so on. Few of us were introduced to art as a worthy discipline of its own. As a result, many of us grew up understanding art as purely functional. It is true that cars and houses are artistic designs, as are wallpaper, newspapers, clothing and dishes. But design, like craft, is a category within art. It is the *fine artist*, the person who makes art for its own sake and provides the discoveries upon which other artistic disciplines build, who will be the mentor in this book, helping you to tap your inner resources for creative and spiritual growth, which are natural elements of the fine art process.

A certain level of narcissism is essential if you want to begin artmaking in this spirit. You will need a childlike attitude: tell yourself that "anything I do will be great!" Believe in yourself; dedicate the time and energy you need to bring forward a vision that is uniquely your own. The process of art, when applied as a spiritual discipline, teaches us the secret of originality: to be completely and truly ourselves. No one stands where you stand; no one sees the world exactly as you do. While being yourself may seem simple enough, it is the most difficult of tasks. Our culture has taught us repeatedly that conformity is more important than individuality. When we are young we adopt this attitude without knowing it – even when we think we are asserting our individuality. Continuing the trend today, young people dye their hair, pierce their bodies, and do a host of other things which, while making them appear very different from their parents, initiate them into a new generation with new sets of rules for conformity. And so the cycle is repeated, generation after generation. Finding our original selves in the midst of all this is no easy task, but it can be done.

Reconnecting with our intuitive, creative nature begins, as suggested above, when we give ourselves permission to play without expectation. In doing so, we encourage a sense of self-discovery that connects us with our soul. By directing some of our valuable time and resources to nurturing our creativity, we will gradually uncover our soul, revealing and meeting its deepest yearnings. We will learn more about who we really are than any resumé could show.

To make the most of this creative-spiritual experience, you must reject your preconceived notions about the kinds of images you will make, your misconceptions about your lack of skill or ability and, most of all, your fear of what others might think about what you are doing. Making art means becoming vulnerable. An artist friend once told me that, at the opening of her first solo exhibition, she felt as if she were standing naked in front of strangers. The creative process has the power to strip away the layers of ego that separate us from our soul, leaving us bare. Sharing this with the world can be a bit daunting! But art will also prepare you for sharing yourself with others by promoting self-discovery and a love of life. The human pilgrimage on which we find ourselves, regardless of the path we have chosen, is a sacred, one-time event in which we are privileged to participate. The process of art can help us savour and celebrate the journey.

Physical environment

While many inadequacies in our environment can be overcome by a positive attitude, it is good to pay attention to our physical surroundings as we begin deliberately to nurture our creative, spiritual selves. Because painting and drawing are sensory activities, born of sensory response, it is helpful if all the senses can be recruited to aid us in our concentration. Attention to visual surroundings, smells, sounds, physical comfort and even taste will help to generate, especially in the beginner, the attitude of anticipation and excitement needed for a positive experience. Creativity that has been dormant for long periods of time needs to be gently and respectfully summoned from its rest. Taking care to create an artist's nest for ourselves also demonstrates, in a way visible to ourselves

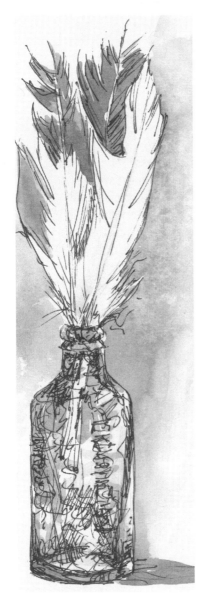

Figure 1.2 I am better able to set the tone for my artmaking session when I have feathers nearby.

and to others, the level of our commitment to the creative, spiritual process in our lives. While you may not be able to have a formal studio, or even a room or section of a room dedicated to your artmaking, you can find ways to create an environment that will address your needs. One student I know kept all her supplies in a large basket. She brought it to class each week as her portable studio. However you decide to create your work environment, it should reflect your personality and your commitment to the process.

When your creative spirit begins to stir, it can feel awkward, as if you are meeting an old friend for the first time in many years. You need to let this 'friend' know that you welcome and appreciate her. Directing your full attention to this fragile part of yourself, ask yourself what you need to feel comfortable and safe in your creative pursuits.

Where would you like to create your art? In which room or chair do you feel most comfortable? Can you position yourself near a window to have natural light? Are there favourite objects or colours that help to stimulate you? Over the years I have collected bouquets of feathers, which I keep in bottles in almost every room of my house. Perhaps they remind me of the freedom of birds in flight, or maybe their colour or texture stimulates me; I'm not sure. But I know that I am better able to set the tone for my artmaking session when I have feathers nearby (Figure 1.2). Different people have different needs; what is important is not to decide right away what you need, but to develop a habit of observing your reactions to your environment so that what you need will be revealed to you. These things you already know deep inside; the task is to allow them to become conscious.

Timing

The experience of making art differs from person to person. As you begin to be aware of your natural work patterns, you will understand that the speed at which you work is less important than whether you connect or click with the process itself. Because we are taught to work within timetables developed from averages and governed by the clock, most of us have become far removed from our own sense of rhythm. We tend to focus on completing a task within a given time. As a beginner in art, think instead in terms of a rhythm of exposure and practice. As you learn new things and absorb them into your unconscious mind through practice, pace yourself according to your inner clock, taking seriously the time you need for assimilation.

For beginners, starting an image is more important than finishing one. Focusing on the experiential element instead of the result helps you form a solid base that will eventually allow you to move forward in the process with confidence. Images are not so much made as born. As midwives to our artistic creations, we need to respect the gestation period required to give them form – not the time required to complete a specific work of art, but something more complex. We are not machines pumping out images or filling in colours numbered by someone else; we must spend time becoming familiar with the process of making art if we are to tap our inner intuitive resources. Learning art is not only about the manipulation of materials, but about the creative process itself, which changes us over the course of time. Through the art process we begin to see the world from the level of soul. Our attitudes, opinions and goals become modified to express this new vision. As we develop respect for our inner processes, we will be less inclined to force ourselves to meet deadlines imposed from the outside. Instead, we will learn to recognize the symptoms that tell us the time is right for our images to come to life and to push them gently into the external world.

Rhythm can also be applied to when we make our art. Some people work best in the morning; others, in the evening. Some like to work a little every day; others like to work in blocks of time. In the beginning stages it is especially important to find a balance between the duties of your every-day world and your creative, spiritual develop-ment. If you have not integrated your creative needs into your daily life, you may try to do too much at first, as if making up for lost time, and upset the balance. Your enthusiasm will likely fizzle if your expectations and time commitments are not realistic. It is more helpful to work slowly and consistently, building yourself up over time, allow-ing your creativity to seep into other parts of your life as a steady stream of constantly renewing inspiration.

One last note on timing. The routine that you find works for you at first may not always work for you. Just as we must constantly adjust to the ever-changing sleeping and eating habits of our children when they are infants, so we must learn to adjust to changes in our evolving creative needs. Over the years I have had to make many adjust-ments to my artmaking schedule. At one time, when my children were young and caught an early bus for school, I found mornings to be a highly productive and nurturing time for spiritual reflection and creative production. I soon let friends and family know that mornings were a bad time for them to call or visit me, and I protected those times as best I could. Later, life changes made it more difficult for me to devote those morning hours to creativity. For a long time, I tried to cling to my old routine because it had worked so well for me. But because I resisted change and contin-ued working during the mornings as I always had, my artwork began to suffer, and along with it, the connection to my soul. My creative spirit did not feel the freedom it had once felt. The more I forced myself to work in a situation in which my soul was denied a voice, the greater the internal conflict that prevented access to my creative spirit. My natural inner rhythm was lost to desires and structures of the ego.

This kind of inner stress blocks creativity and shuts out access to our soul. Creativity cannot be forced to emerge at certain times. Once I realized that I had become more concerned about using my time productively than about tapping the natural resources of my soul, I conceded and gave myself the opportunity to explore new patterns for a work schedule. For several years after this, I did my best creative work during the early afternoons, and then evenings, adjusting and harmonizing my responsibilities to myself and to others accordingly. Recently, I discovered that what I need are chunks of time instead of a certain number of hours each day. This means booking off retreat-like periods of two or more days when I take no phone calls, do no unnecessary non-art work, and give myself fully to the experience. Allowing myself time to engage in the process of art without expectations (which can be difficult for a professional artist with exhibition commitments!) provides the kind of freedom that ensures the return of my creative flow every time. There is always a way to find time for your art: finding that time may be your first creative challenge.

EXERCISE

Keep a journal as you work through this book. Throughout the week, note times when you feel the most creative and times when you feel the least creative. Note what encourages your creativity and what hinders it. Record as much as possible about your attitude and your physical surroundings for each instance. Consider where you want to be physically as you embark on this process, and 'mark' your territory so that you feel a sense of stimulation and familiarity in your 'art and soul' studio. Buy a few simple art supplies, such as charcoal and pencils of different grades. On a blank page in your journal, make as many different kinds of marks with them as you can. Try using them together to create new effects. Record how you feel as you do this exercise.

RECONNECTING WITH OUR SPIRITUAL SELVES

New wine and old skins

Most of us don't think of ourselves as spiritual. Perhaps we are not attached to a specific religion or church – or if we are, we do not attend regularly. We may give to the poor, but not as often or as much as we think we should; we may not read the Bible or pray daily. Or maybe we have quirky personality traits (such as a bad temper or negative attitudes that are hard to control) that we feel would disqualify us from being spiritual even if we did those other things. We recognize that we don't have the answers to many of life's difficult questions and that sometimes we feel a bit anxious, whereas we think of spiritual people as being more at peace. Comparing ourselves to those whose spirituality shines – say, Mother Teresa – we conclude that we are not even on the same page.

But where did our ideas about what it takes to be spiritual originate? Somewhere along the line, we may have been taught that being spiritual meant being 'good.' As children many of us had a sense of cosmic goodness and even felt that we were good, but the adults in our lives may have disagreed. "God alone is good," we may have been taught. We may further have been told that by denying ourselves in service to God and others – like the saints – we could compensate in a small way for our innate defectiveness. As we grew, we allowed others to define spirituality for us and forgot the goodness we originally sensed.

As a very young child I had such a sense of goodness about life. I have a vivid memory of lying in my crib at age three or four, my brother sleeping in a crib nearby and the sun shining through our grey printed curtains. I also remember thinking about the transience of human life. Although I didn't have the ability to express it, I thought about the fragility of the human body and our inevitable death. As a child, I was quite fascinated by death and spent many hours trying to figure out what it would feel like to be dead. I was more curious than frightened by the prospect. Always I felt it to be the natural result of living; I did not feel that my own death would separate me from the reality of my existence, although I certainly had no vocabulary (or theological framework) to explain this. Many children wonder about death. When they ask their parents about it, religion often supplies the answers. Adults use terms like 'God' and 'heaven' to help soften what they see as a harsh reality. Sometimes those who use such terms to explain death to children don't really know what the children are wondering about. They likely don't know what the terms they use have meant historically, even in their own religious denomination, and they may not have grasped the meaning of the terms for themselves. And so, half understood, they are passed to the next generation, resulting in growing dependence on the religious authorities who are thought to know the meanings of such concepts. This hand-it-down-without-thinking-about-it tradition teaches children to associate spirituality with specific religions, and holiness with people who practise them.

At age 13 I had another experience that has helped to shape my understanding of spirituality. I was daydreaming during a lecture in a high school English class. This time the daydream became more intense than usual. I felt myself being drawn out of my body through the 'holes' of my eyes. I felt transformed into a state of being that I had never read or heard about before. I was not afraid during the experience, but felt a sort of caution about this perceptual switch and about 'getting back' to the physical reality of my English class. The encounter felt something like what I have since read about near-death experience. I'm not sure how long it lasted; I seemed to be outside time. During the experience I felt the presence of an overwhelming goodness much like the one I had felt years before. Again, I felt myself to be part of that goodness. When the class ended, I excitedly told one of my friends what had happened. She was not terribly interested and suggested I keep the whole thing to myself lest others think me a little crazy. She said I should spend my time thinking about boys, and being 13, I agreed!

During my youth I attended church regularly with my family; nothing was ever said there of such experiences. I learned stories from the Bible as interpreted by the clergy and through the literature supplied by Sunday School. I took religion seriously and wanted to be a religious person as I understood that notion from the Church's teaching. At 17 I was invited to teach Sunday School, and although I didn't think I knew enough to do

so, was convinced by the superintendent that I could do the job if I followed the curriculum provided by the church. For some time I taught the classes as requested – until I came to the story of Jonah and the whale. I had been led to think that the Bible had to be taken as literal truth, so I felt I had to reason my way into believing the story. But I couldn't. I tried to explain to the superintendent that because I did not believe the story, I could not teach it. Being in the midst of a shortage of Sunday School teachers, she did not have much sympathy for my situation. "Do it anyway!" she replied in exasperation. While today I can understand her frustration, at the time I felt crushed. I left the church that Sunday feeling lost.

The conflict between what I felt as a result of personal experience and what I was taught by religious authorities caused me great anxiety. While I sensed something good within myself, everything I was taught by my religion seemed opposed to it. It insisted that I (and everyone else) was basically sinful by nature. Within a year of the Sunday School debacle I ended up in the hospital after taking an overdose of prescription drugs. Deeply confused, I felt religion had won: I must indeed be a sinful person – so sinful that I was responsible for the unhappiness of those I met. I did not really want to die; I only thought my death to be reasonable compensation for the harm I must have caused. When I read the statistics of teen suicides today, I remember what it feels like to think oneself more a burden than a blessing to the world. After having my stomach pumped and intravenous fluids sent through my body, I was released from the hospital on the third day. (This was significant to me even then, because of what I remembered of Jesus' resurrection.) I felt strangely invigorated as I left. It seemed to me that I couldn't go any farther down. I had reached the bottom and could only go up from there.

I walked home from the hospital with a friend, feeling cautiously optimistic. I didn't know what I was going to do with my life, but I felt that I had been spared and that perhaps there was a purpose to living that I did not yet know. I did not run to a church with this new revelation. I decided instead that I would pay more attention to what was happening inside me than to what others told me about how I should feel or what I should think. At that time my spirituality began to separate from traditional religion, a separation that continues to this day.

It is not my intention to advocate a new spirituality, but to reconnect with an old one in a new way. The spirituality that guides my life, I have come to learn, is also a vital, forgotten undercurrent in the Christian tradition. While some of what has troubled me about my religion remains, what I have found within the Christian tradition gives me hope that it will continue to evolve more fully towards its purpose, which is the purpose of all religion: to provide a true connection with God. The famous words of the Christian theologian Augustine, written in the fourth century, echo the yearning I have felt in my spiritual journey: "My soul can know no rest, until it rests in thee." Religion understood in a broader sense speaks to this yearning for rest – a yearning that must be addressed if we are to find fulfillment in our lives. By measuring the level of this kind of rest in our lives we can learn something of the innermost part of ourselves – our soul. If we sense an absence of inner peace when we examine our spiritual condition, we can take steps to build a spirituality that will fill this important need. This does not mean denouncing everything we have learned from religious teaching, but asking whether what we have learned feeds us spiritually in our everyday lives.

Recognizing spiritual experience

Eventually, after the awakening experience precipitated by my suicide attempt, I found my way back into a traditional church community. I even convinced my parents, who had stopped going to church, to join me for Sunday services. One morning, soon after they had started attending, I stood in line with my father to greet the priest as we left the building. My father had been moved by the sermon, which was about feeling the presence of God, and wanted to express his appreciation. As we were leaving the church, he briefly told the priest how much he loved spending time alone in the woods. He talked about strong feelings that nature evoked in him and their effect on his outlook. A few words from the priest about the profundity of nature as a revealer of the divine would have validated my father's experience and helpfully widened the parameters of what is considered spiritual. Instead, the priest responded with something like, "Well, if feeling God's presence were *really* important to you, you'd be in church more often!" I felt a knot tighten in my stomach as I heard him speak these words. For the priest it may have been only one brief comment among many made at the end of a busy morning, but for my father (and me) it was a slap on the wrist for not conforming to house rules.

Many of us have had profound experiences like my father did. The sight of the horizon dividing sky and sea, the diamond-like sparkles on new-fallen snow, and the distant sound of gulls as I fill my lungs with salt air in the spring touch me deeply. I call any such moment – whether it occurs in nature or not – a *petite rapture*. It is a moment filled with insight, exciting and calming at the same time. This label is borrowed from the medical term *petit mal*, which means 'small seizure' and is meant to bring to mind the latter's relationship to *grand mal*, which means 'large seizure.' A *petit mal* has all the qualities of a *grand mal* – it is complete in itself, but fleeting, so that it often goes unnoticed by the one experiencing it, showing up only on medical tests devised to identify it. Likewise, *petites raptures* are complete and fleeting – intense moments of profound insight that tend to vanish as quickly as they appear. These moments are noticeably different from our ordinary states of consciousness; they instruct us or give us peace from a source that seems at once immanent and transcendent. Sometimes the resulting feelings affect us for long periods of time, and sometimes we dismiss them immediately, bringing ourselves back to ordinary consciousness as if we had been in a daze.

For many, the introduction to spiritual experience is made up of brief moments that stand out because they seem so different from our normal state. Thomas Merton, the prolific Trappist monk of the last century, wrote about such an encounter from his own experience in a crowd of strangers: "In Louisville, at the corner of Fourth and Walnut, in the center of the shopping district, I was suddenly overwhelmed with the realization that I loved all those people, that they were mine and I theirs, that we could not be alien to one another even though we were total strangers."[2] Merton calls this sense of all things coming together and imploding upon the soul *le point vierge* (the blank point). He understands this as "a point of pure truth, a point or spark which belongs entirely to God, which is never at our disposal, from which God disposes of our lives, which is inaccessible to the fantasies of our own mind or the brutalities of our own will. [It] is the pure glory of God in us."[3] These overwhelming intrusions make us feel as though we have discovered a link to whatever might lie beyond the boundaries of physical life; they make us feel at once very important and very small.

Such common experiences, however brief or infrequent, are indeed a form of spiritual experience. They are moments in which we make contact with our soul. Such moments are not tied to specific religions, but all religions refer to them. The awareness granted in these moments – of ourselves as part of a greater intricate design from which we may draw strength and wisdom – is the result of our soul making its way into consciousness. The Psalms are filled with insights from *petites raptures*: "My soul finds rest in God alone" (Psalm 62), "My help comes from the Maker of Heaven and Earth" (Psalm 121), and "Be still and know that I am God" (Psalm 46) are but a few examples. And while we may not all write psalms, we have all probably stood in the psalmist's shoes, even if only for a moment. Few lives are devoid of such experiences.

If we have been confined by archaic and inadequate definitions of spirituality, we may fail to see the many ways in which we are already spiritual. We may forget what we saw as children. But now we can review our lives to see where and when our soul has broken through the layers of everyday consciousness to make itself known to us. Religion does not cause us to be spiritual; rather, it can be a vehicle to express our spirituality. If, however, the vehicle becomes more important than what it carries, the balance is upset and the connection to our soul suffers. Our soul does not need a specific religion to express itself, nor can spiritual insight be claimed exclusively by any religion or sect. By recognizing that we have had spiritual experiences in our everyday life and that such experiences are not extraordinary but are part of the human journey, we can begin to understand ourselves as the spiritual beings we are.

Finding our spiritual community

Finding the right community to help nurture, sustain and guide us in our spiritual development is not always easy. Belonging to a church, meeting on Sundays for services and again at mid-week for Bible study, and working together on community projects to address social issues is one way of exercising community. I have a community within my immediate circle of friends that supports, sustains and nurtures me, while also offering guidance and demanding accountability. I have an ongoing community of students with whom I have shared a

great deal and from whom I continue to learn. In addition, I have found an historical community with which I am closely connected. Like the "Dead Poets' Society" brought to life on film by Robin Williams, this community continues to nurture me from beyond the grave. Through books and ongoing meditation I am linked to like minds stretching across boundaries of time, religion and culture.

I first noticed this alternative to traditional community when I began to read the Bible upon being released from the hospital after my teenage suicide attempt. Rather than reading the text as back-up for theological interpretations presented by church leaders, I read only to learn more about what was written there. Approaching the Bible with an open mind was a new experience for me. While I understood the phrase "seek and you shall find," I came to appreciate an alternative to it, best expressed for me by Picasso: "I do not seek, I find." So often seeking is influenced by specific objectives: we are looking for a particular answer to a particular question. But when we stop seeking in this directed manner, we allow ourselves to find whatever presents itself to us; this is a small but important difference for artistic growth and spiritual development. It is the difference between looking for a heart-shaped rock on the beach and unexpectedly finding a gull's feather in the seaweed. Sometimes concentration on the former prevents us from experiencing the latter. By freeing our creative spirit to wander and express itself, we open ourselves to be guided by our soul, which delights as much in questions as in answers.

As I read the stories in the Bible with this new mindset, the characters leapt to life, allowing me to make unexpected discoveries. I made ancestry charts to keep straight who was married to (and who begat) whom, and often tried to imagine myself in their culture and them in mine. It was as if I had found friends, many of whom shared emotions and dilemmas similar to my own. In those early days, the Bible was instrumental in uncovering my soul, offering me comfort and challenges I had never experienced in the physical community around me. And while my understanding and appreciation of the text has evolved dramatically since then, it continues to offer much of what I need for my spiritual growth.

The apostle Thomas became a member of my new form of community early on. Thomas' need for intimate knowledge mirrored my own, and he became my mentor. When Thomas heard that the risen Jesus had appeared to the other disciples, Thomas did not believe it. He said, "Unless I see the marks in his hands and put my finger where the nails were, and put my hand into his side, I will not believe it" (John 20:25). A week went by before Jesus finally appeared to Thomas, thus giving him what he needed in order to exclaim in faith, "My Lord and my God!" While Jesus' response extolls the benefits of believing without seeing, I take from this text that God will fulfill our deepest need if we are not willing (or able) to settle for less. Like Thomas, I am not moved by hearsay. In order to be satisfied, I need to hear God's word deep in my heart – no matter what others think of me. Thomas risked ridicule – and the wrath of God – by expressing his need, and he was rewarded. This gives me hope that my needs will also be met.

Over the years, another Thomas – Thomas Merton – has also become an important member of my spiritual community. While I do not get together with them each Sunday at a specific time and place, these individuals and others who will be revealed as this book unfolds are always with me. I have only to turn my thoughts to them to receive support and guidance. But I am also an extension of their communities, allowing their voices to be heard in the contemporary world through my words and deeds. Not all of our companions need to be alive – or even Christian – in order to nurture us on our spiritual path. They need not all be religious, either. Taking our cue from Jesus, who redefined family as all who share the human journey, we can look beyond traditional categories for members and forms of community.

Connecting art and soul

As we reconnect with our creative and spiritual selves, we will, among other things, come to understand the difference between image and concept. For example, we may use an image of a bird in flight to illustrate the concept of freedom. Such an image is not conclusive; it does not exhaust the meaning of freedom but merely sparks our imagination by providing an example related to our own experience. Replacing the bird in flight with a picture of ourselves driving alone in a convertible along a deserted highway on a bright sunny day gives us another image of freedom. Or we may imagine freedom as simply walking in our garden. Each of these images can express the same concept – freedom – but each affects us differently. While the concept is broad and inclusive, the images are specific and partial.

Images are dear to us because they simplify complex ideas in ways we can understand on a personal level. Concepts of art and soul and God generate different images for different people. Perhaps our main image of an artist is that of someone who paints bowls of flowers in oils. The soul we may picture as a heavenly part of ourselves that leaves the body upon death; we may see God as a fatherly figure who judges our actions. These are images, not concepts. They are born of specific and limited exposure and interpretation. Changing our images, therefore, does not always entail changing the associated concepts. We can easily see by the examples given above that there are many images we can use for a given concept: an artist might be a person who dresses flamboyantly, the soul a quasi-physical ghost, and God a motherly figure. During the course of evolution, both collective and personal, our images change. For example, many adult Christians no longer believe that God is best illustrated as a human male – a grey-haired man who looks down on us from above. Over time, some Christians have come to see falsehood and potential harm inherent in such an image and so have discontinued its use, while maintaining the relevant concepts – God as personal and all-knowing. By separating image from concept we can continue to value the concept while discovering images that reflect a more enlightened understanding. In art it is particularly easy to see that the image created is not the concept, but an illustration of it. For example, while 'balance' is a concept, artists' pictures can illustrate balance in a variety of ways and through diverse media. Likewise, religious concepts can legitimize a number of images beyond those to which we become accustomed.

Our personal experiences lead us to accept certain images and reject others, and intimately to connect our images with our beliefs. But by setting aside our dependence on (or preference for) specific images, we can move beneath their surface appearance to the underlying concepts they express. At this level we will find the connective tissue that ties seemingly different images together. For example, by releasing our preconceptions (or beliefs) about what it means to be creative or spiritual, we give ourselves freedom to explore areas we may have previously closed off. No one forces us to hold beliefs; we adopt or reject ideas as we are led by the evidence of experience to accept or reject their validity. We can (and do) change our minds about images and concepts as we evolve spiritually and creatively. When art and soul join forces within, we will become more conscious of the images we use, not only in our art but in our lives, and be led to make changes as they become necessary.

As our artistic and spiritual journeys merge, we allow each of these to feed the other: our creativity becomes more spiritual and our spirituality, more imaginative. Art gives us creative tools to express our thoughts, and our soul gives us inspired content for artistic expression. Time spent creating art is time spent on spiritual development. As we devote both time and space within our busy lives to discovering and expressing our innermost thoughts and feelings, we become midwives to our soul, bringing into the physical world the spiritual contents of what has been hidden inside us – as illustrated at the end of the book by Gallery Image 1, *Birthing*.

I have found that taking deliberate steps to make the connection between art and soul more concrete helps both enterprises. At one point in my life I used daily Bible or inspirational readings as a way of centring myself for each art session. This reading set the tone for my soul by marking my work time as sacred. More recently I have developed a different personal ritual. I begin by giving attention to my physical location by noting the directions of north and south, east and west. Using small symbolic objects such as stones, shells, candles and feathers, I identify each with the elements of earth, sea, wind or light, reminding myself that I am part of something bigger than my individual self, and that I contain these same elements within me, symbolically and literally. A few moments of quiet meditation before beginning to draw, paint or write allows me to reduce the distractions from my physical environment, quiet the desires of my ego and focus my attention on the voice I have come to recognize as that of my soul. I did not impose such a ritual upon myself to help me become more creative or spiritual, but allowed the ritual to evolve by listening to the needs expressed by my soul over many years.

By being sensitive to ourselves as spiritual beings, we will gradually come to know what will help and what will hinder our progress, so that we can construct our rituals accordingly. In Philippians 4:8 we find an additional clue for how we may begin the process of unravelling the needs of our soul. The writer suggests that we turn our thoughts to "whatever is noble, whatever is right, whatever is pure, whatever is lovely, whatever is admirable, excellent or praiseworthy." As we fill in the blanks for each category listed by the author, we will get an idea of what is valuable in helping us reconnect with our soul.

EXERCISE

Journalling is one of the most important aids to spiritual development. So many thoughts pass through our minds in the course of a day; it is impossible to remember all of them. Try to carry your journal with you so that you can record random thoughts (words, phrases, meaningful exchanges) as they arise, especially ones your conscious mind tries to dismiss as unimportant. Don't try to make sense of any of them – merely record them without judging them. They will begin to make sense later on.

A good starting point for reconnecting with your soul is to consider what you think of as noble, right, etc., as suggested by Philippians 4:8. After completing your list, consider whether the source of each answer comes from your soul or elsewhere. There are no right or wrong answers; the point of such exercises is merely to get to know yourself better, an important prerequisite for spiritual growth.

I saw a Van Gogh sky
etched into
a piece of driftwood

lines of grey and brown
swirled around
circles and holes

a monument
engraved by time
and the sea

I wondered
had Van Gogh
copied the driftwood

or had the driftwood
copied Van Gogh

Chapter 2

SEEING

THE ARTIST'S WAY OF SEEING

Opening artist eyes

Making art is more a matter of the eyes than of the hands. If we have the motor co-ordination to write our name legibly, we have the physical ability to learn the skills of drawing and painting. The ability to manipulate media is accessible to everyone and, like music perfected through practice, our success depends on the amount of time and effort we apply to the task. But technical skill is not all we need. What produces art is the combination of technical ability with the discipline of seeing as an artist sees. As we learn to see with our 'artist eyes' it matters less which media we use to make our statement; we will choose whatever helps to express our vision best. The ten art lessons in this book presuppose an understanding of seeing as an artist, and provide you with ample opportunity to practise with a variety of media. But seeing in this way requires a shift in how we think, so we need to give separate attention to it.

Modern studies of 'split brain' patients (people who have had the connection between the two main parts of their brain severed as a result of impairment or as part of treatment) show that most of us use the left and right hemispheres of our brains for different purposes. In common conversation, we talk about a person being 'left brain' and logical, or 'right brain' and creative. While this is an oversimplification, it reflects an important truth. Both approaches are needed for the making of art, but not at the same time. In the beginning stages of learning to make art, you will need to emphasize the exercising of your right brain and pay close attention to what you see in the natural world. Over time this will work its way into your unconscious mind, influencing your decisions by providing an information base from which you can draw – literally and metaphorically.

My introduction to the concept of right-brain thinking was experiential. Mainly self-taught as an artist, I grew up experimenting with various media as I tried to draw what I saw. I found that sometimes I had great success – my drawings looked much like the objects I tried to represent. But at other times, no matter how hard I tried, I could not represent the natural world as I saw it. At first I felt my lack of experience was to blame. I thought that if I had better control over the materials, my drawings would improve. This proved to be only partially true. For a long time, my drawings continued to be hit and miss; it seemed I could never count on being able to produce what I wanted.

Not knowing anything about right- and left-brain research, I was confused by this inconsistency. I began keeping notes in my journal about my artmaking sessions, trying to find something to distinguish between times when things were going well and times when they were not. I recorded not only what media I was using, but also the subject matter, what mood I seemed to be in, what music I was listening to, what time of day it was, what I had previously eaten, what I was wearing, and so on, trying to find what made the difference between a good and a bad session. Why was I able to do adequate work on some days and not on others? It seemed to me that if I could duplicate the environment of my good days, including my mood, I should be able to turn the bad days into good ones! While this worked occasionally, I continued to lack the consistency for which I had hoped.

However, I was on the right track. After several years of experimenting and list-making, I stumbled on the concept of right and left brain. Personal experience had prepared me to understand the differences between these two methods of perceiving. On the days when my art sessions went well, I had accidentally tapped into the right-brain way of thinking. On days when the session did not go well, I had not made that connection. It did not take long to realize that I needed a way to access deliberately the kind of thinking (right-brain) that would lead to the good sessions, leaving me less a victim of successful accidents. Let's look more closely now at the two different approaches involved here.

Left-brain approach

For our purposes, we will understand the left brain as involving a propensity towards linear and logical thinking. Such thinking is necessary for the artist in the overall evaluation of his work. This approach, however, must be avoided during cre-

ation of the work. Drawings dictated by left-brain thinking are concocted from memory and pre-existing knowledge of the objects drawn rather than from direct observation. Such drawings result in a generic look that lacks the specific features necessary to make our image resemble the objects we are viewing in the actual world. For example, if we are in left-brain mode we will draw the opening of a bottle – even when it cannot be viewed from our perspective – because we know it is there! Artists must develop methods of blocking or overcoming this very strong perceptual tool if they are to make representations that are believable to the viewer (Figure 2.1).

Figure 2.1 The effects of left- and right-brain dominance.

The left-brain way of thinking, which is highly valued in Western culture, is thought to be the primary source of verbal communication. Because the two sides of the brain co-operate but do not work simultaneously, it is not possible for an artist to carry on a conversation while using the right-brain method. The type and intensity of concentration required to draw prohibits this. If you are talking during drawing sessions, do not be surprised if your images are a bit off. When I demonstrate concepts and techniques in art class, I slip in and out of conversation as I switch back and forth between the right-brain 'showing' and the left-brain 'telling' of the demonstration.

Right-brain approach

The right-brain approach to artmaking is securely anchored in the present and does not rely on memory or previous knowledge. It allows us to imitate what we are seeing by clearing away all non-relevant judgments about the object we are trying to draw. The right brain does not think of 'cow' or 'sky' or 'book' as the left brain does. It is unaware of 'hard' or 'soft' or 'new' or 'pretty' or 'messy.' It doesn't know that a bottle has an opening at the top. It knows only what it sees and its judgments are determined by relationships between the parts and the whole of the composition to which its attention is directed at any given moment. The more you learn to use your right brain, the further you will be able to develop your pictures – because you will see more of what you are looking at. Most of us look at many things, but *see* very few of them. Instead of seeing a barking dog as it actually is – a specific dog among all other dogs – we remember it as a beagle or Dalmatian, not noticing how this particular beagle or Dalmatian is distinct from all others and unique in this particular moment in time and space. This inability to see specific details partly explains why many people have a difficult time drawing portraits. In order to create a likeness in a portrait, attention must be given to the minute details that distinguish one face from another. Generalities, which are adequate for other subjects, such as a forest or a field, will not produce the subtleties necessary for the likeness of a specific face.

Our right brain gives us full access to everything within our visual field at the time of looking. Rather than recollecting symbols from our memory, the right-brain method of seeing transports us fully into the present, allowing us to become ultra-aware of even the tiniest detail, movement or change. It is as if we experience objects rather than observe them. We begin to notice the effects of the present moment, such as proportion relationships, which change if our perspective or the light source is even slightly altered. Instead of connecting our thoughts with thoughts of the past and/or future, which is the custom of left-brain thinking, we are freed to participate in the world exactly as it is at the present moment. As we will see, it is this moment of right-brain experience, accessed and sustained through the artmaking process, that is also the natural habitat of the soul.

Our ability as artists to draw what we see in the exterior world depends on our capacity to see in this right-brain manner. Once we apply this method of perception to drawing, we are able to see more precisely what is before us and thus can judge which marks on our paper will allow us to copy accurately what we are looking at. This means that if we draw a book, we draw a specific book from a specific angle, exactly as it appears to us in the present moment. We come to know intimately the visual properties of the book from a particular point in time and space. (If we distort the object in our representation of it, we will do so to help express what we want to say about the object, not because we don't know how to draw it as we see it.) Three steps will help you recognize and activate the right-brain process for ourself.

Recognizing the differences between right- and left-brain thinking

While we can intellectually discuss and agree or disagree about right- and left-brain ways of perceiving information, it is more helpful in artmaking to experience them. I have developed a series of exercises to help students in my art classes recognize these modes of perception. We begin this exploration by making three separate drawings.

First, using pencil or charcoal, draw a tree, any tree, from memory. It can be coniferous or deciduous, any size, in any season. Take five to ten minutes to draw what you remember. When you are finished, put the drawing aside. Next, draw your hand, looking at it carefully as you draw. Draw what you see. Again, take five to ten minutes to do this. After completing the two drawings, write down how you felt during the process of making each one. While the answers in my classes vary, most students agree that the experience for each of the drawings was different (Figure 2.2).

Figure 2.2 The student drawing on the left exemplifies a left-brain approach, the one on the right employs the right-brain way of seeing.

The first exercise uses a primarily left-brain approach to drawing. Rather than drawing a specific tree, you drew from memories of your experience of trees. Whether the drawing was successful as a realistic representation of a tree will depend on how familiar you were with a specific tree, or with trees in general. Drawing from memory is difficult if we are not familiar enough with the objects we are trying to represent. For example, if I were asked to draw an elephant, it would be hard for me to draw from memory since I have spent very little time looking at or thinking about elephants. Without directly observing elephants, I would have to rely on the little I have seen and read about them. Since I have rarely observed elephants, and certainly not with the intention of duplicating their visual properties, I have little data in my memory with which to work. In this respect, our minds are like computer hardware: without software and memory files, they can do very little.

Direct observation helps the artist to enter visual data into his memory which he can then recall when necessary. This information does not substitute for the observations we make while drawing, but eventually works its way into the unconscious as knowledge that informs our intuition.

The second exercise, drawing your hand, requires you to use your right brain. Generalities and preconceptions about hands are replaced by direct observation. Comparing your drawing with your actual hand, you can probably see where the two differ. Proportions will be incorrect if the lines were not drawn in the right places. If your drawing does not look three-dimensional, you may not have given enough attention to the tonal changes you observed. (These topics will be explored in greater detail in Part Two.) The success of a representational drawing depends primarily on how well we are able to see what is before us.

For the third drawing, use your non-dominant hand to draw your dominant hand. This exercise always elicits at least a few groans from my students, but the results never fail to astound. Most students are surprised to see that these drawings are much better than they expected. The picture drawn with the non-dominant hand is often at least as good as, or better than, the previous two (Figure 2.3). This comparison helps to reinforce the awareness that drawing is not so much about using our hands, but more about how we see. This fact explains, for example, why people who have lost limbs are able to paint well with their feet or their mouth after achieving sufficient motor control. As my students reflect on the processes they used for each of the three drawings, they can detect differences in how they felt during the construction of each. They conclude that the last two drawings required a different kind of concentration from the first. This realization is the first step in identifying the difference between right- and left-brain thinking.

Transferring from left- to right-brain thinking

Once we are able to identify the difference between right- and left-brain processes, it will be easier to know whether the process we are using is appropriate to the task. While the left brain helps us to evaluate our artwork, a right-brain approach is necessary for creating the art. But since our left-brain collection of descriptive symbols often overshadows our right-brain observations, we need methods to overcome our natural tendency to focus on the former.

To begin, we must understand that the right brain processes information without evaluating its importance. It perceives the world from a perspective where all lines, shapes and colours are equally important. Where the left brain might acknowledge a woman wearing a red shirt, thus giving added importance to the named components, the right brain has no concept defined by 'woman' or 'shirt' and no name for 'red' without reference to

Figure 2.3 Student drawing using the non-dominant hand. Compare this to Figure 2.2, drawn with the dominant hand.

another colour. Instead, it sees only an arrangement of lines, shapes and colours that are related to each other by proportion and degree of darkness or lightness (called *tone* or *value* in art). The more we are able to forget the left-brain labels for lines and shapes, the easier it will be for the right brain to identify correctly their size and arrangement in relation to each other. While the left brain values such terms for communication purposes, the right-brain method of drawing is concerned only about communicating the relationship between lines and spaces, textures and colours within the boundaries of the frame in which we are reconstructing them.

One exercise for suppressing the left brain involves copying an upside-down image (Figure 2.4). This exercise is effective because the left brain is less able to identify and name the lines and spaces of the upside-down work. Several years ago, I asked a young man in one of my art classes who was having problems drawing objects as he saw them to try this. I suggested he copy an upside-down picture of John F. Kennedy as it appeared in Betty Edwards' book *Drawing on the Right Side of the Brain*. He worked diligently on his drawing, not once turning the photograph or his drawing right side up. After he had worked for over an hour, I showed his image to the class, turning it so that Kennedy's face was right side up to the viewers. I asked, "Does anyone recognize this face?" Everyone in the room immediately identified Kennedy as the subject of the portrait.

This exercise ignites the right-brain process by opening doors of perception that lead to an intimate understanding of the relationships among the components of the object or objects being rendered. The right brain's supreme concentration on what the object looks like at this particular moment in time and space allows the artist to imitate it more closely. Keeping in mind that the process by which we make the image is, at this stage, more important than the resulting product, we nonetheless use the outcome to evaluate our efforts. By checking to see how closely we have imitated our object we can tell how effectively we were able to access our right brain. If the student's drawing could not have been identified as being of Kennedy, we could have turned it upside down once more and compared it to the picture in the book (which is also upside down), looking for those places where the drawing and the photograph differed.

This constant interplay of right-brain *drawing* and left-brain *checking* allows us to develop our skills as artists and critics. However, it is important when beginning to give the right brain time to do

Figure 2.4 Drawing an upside-down image renders the left brain less able to identify and name the lines and spaces, thus making the task of seeing what is actually there much easier.

its work before you criticize the outcome. As you become accustomed to using your right-brain processes in this way, it will become easier to identify and to influence which process is used during your artmaking.

Learning to access right-brain thinking at will

A misconception about the art process is that an artist must wait for the right mood before beginning. If artists had to wait for moods to come over them in order to produce art, they would miss exhibition deadlines, commission sales and other opportunities for development. They do not rely on chance to produce good works, as I did in my earlier days. Instead, professional artists develop ways to trigger right-brain thinking at will. My list-making as a young artist revealed some personal triggers that continue to work for me today. For example, I can almost always access my right brain when I listen to Mozart, but I do not paint well when listening to Chopin. This is not to say that one composer's work is better than another for encouraging a right-brain experience, but that one works better than another for me. I suggest that you make lists, mental or written, to identify what stimulates your right-brain experience, so that you can include them, whenever possible, as part of your artmaking routine.

The aim is to create the mood for successful artmaking through a balance of self-awareness and self-discipline. Art books, art teachers and even art exhibitions offer suggestions on how to prepare to make art. While you should consider everything, you need to apply only what works best for you. You will learn your right-brain triggers by getting to know yourself better. Beginning by creating a harmonious work environment (as suggested in Chapter 1), you can help set the tone for a right-brain experience. Sometimes, however, in spite of your best efforts, it will simply not be possible to create such a mood; these times are better spent taking a reflective walk. Remember that assimilation is as important as practice. As you become more familiar with right-brain experience over time, you will find it easier to access this approach to artmaking. And since, as we will see, this is the home of the soul, you will simultaneously find yourself becoming more attuned to your spiritual needs.

Skills resulting from right-brain thinking

While the implications of right-brain thinking for the soul will be discussed later, the most important outgrowth for the artist is an ability to identify *positive* and *negative* space and to *measure visually* the relationships between them. An understanding of these concepts is key to constructing any image that seeks to imitate life. They are the staples of drawing. Once you understand them, they will provide you with skills you can count on for successful image-making every time. It is like riding a bicycle: once you learn these skills, you will never completely forget them.

Identifying positive and negative space

As we have seen, direct observation is paramount for representational art. The more conscious you become of the content of your observations, the easier it is to draw what you see. If what you are viewing is to be rendered in two dimensions, each of the lines and shapes you make on your paper must correspond to the lines and shapes as you perceive them in the natural world from a particular perspective. Together, these lines and shapes form *positive* and *negative* spaces. In art, 'positive' and 'negative' are not value judgments but names given to different spaces as a way of showing their relation to each other. While some of the components within a picture have left-brain names, such as 'branch' or 'tree,' others have no such proper names. They are the spaces between the branches and the shapes that form the background or shadows. Artists tend to call the shapes that can be identified with names positive spaces and those without names, negative spaces (Figure 2.5). While this is an oversimplification, these definitions will serve our present purposes. Translating three-dimensional space into positive and negative components of two-dimensional space is like flattening the world into the front of a jigsaw puzzle. These positive and negative visual pieces fit together perfectly, and all are equally important and necessary to the completion of the puzzle. The balance created by positive and negative space helps us understand the overall composition as a sum of all its separate units. The more closely we can duplicate each of the spaces, the more our artwork will resemble the objects we are drawing.

Figure 2.5 In this tracing of Iguana, *vertical lines indicate positive space and horizontal lines negative space.*

Visual measuring

For an image to imitate the natural world, all lines and shapes must be arranged so that their

proportions relate appropriately to each other, corresponding to your observations of the three-dimensional subject matter. The head of a figure must be in correct proportion to the rest of the body as it is seen from the artist's vantage point at a specific moment in time and space if the image is to look believable to the viewer. While there are formulas for calculating the actual proportions between the head and the body of a human figure,

Figure 2.6 Compare the relative size of the head in these images. Sometimes our left-brain knowledge of a figure's physical proportions (top) prevents us from drawing what we actually see.

these will sometimes be of little help in the creation of a work. For example, we may know that on average an adult body is seven times taller than its head, but this information does not help our drawing if our perspective is foreshortened by the viewer looking up at, or down upon, the figure (Figure 2.6). Limbs that we know to be a certain length look very different when viewed straight on. In such cases, give close attention to the relationship between the lines and spaces as you actually see them, not as you know them to be. You can make such measurements by using one of the lines or shapes within your image as a reference point, and visually measuring all other lines and shapes as they relate to it. To help see these lines and shapes more exactly, study the proportions of your subject material with one eye closed. By eliminating depth perception in this way you can more easily identify the lines that form the edges of each shape. The cliché of artists closing one eye and extending their thumb comes from this technique (Figure 2.7). While it is not advisable to go through life with one eye closed, it is sometimes helpful to screen out irrelevant information so that you can more clearly identify your choices.

Between drawing sessions, visual measuring can become a game that helps you see more of what you are looking at – to see as

Figure 2.7 By closing one eye and using an extended thumb as a reference, it is easy to measure differences in sizes as they will appear in a two-dimensional drawing of three-dimensional space.

Figure 2.8 Dark and light shapes created by sun and shade form patterns of positive and negative space.

an artist sees. For example, as I look at the pine tree outside my studio window, I am aware of the dark and light shapes created by sun and shade. Accessing my right brain, I compare the size of the shapes: the thickness of branches compared to the trunk, the length of the needles compared to the branches, and so on. As the breeze picks up, I can watch the shapes of shadows change as the sun is blocked and exposed (Figure 2.8). This observation game helps me practise seeing as an artist sees while giving me greater awareness of subtle, ongoing changes in the natural world.

EXERCISE

Choose a familiar scene, something you look at every day – perhaps the view from your kitchen window. Try to look at it as if you are seeing it for the first time. Imagine that what you see out your window is a two-dimensional photograph. Close one eye and use your finger to trace some of the lines on the glass as you see them in the natural world. Imagine the lines forming the edges of jigsaw puzzle pieces. Pay particular attention to the spaces created between the main objects you are looking at – the negative spaces. Look at the same scene from the same vantage point several days in a row, repeating the exercise each day, noting anything you hadn't seen before. Record thoughts and feelings about your observations in your journal.

THE SOUL'S WAY OF SEEING

Seeing in a new way

The shift in perception facilitated by right-brain thinking provides an avenue to the soul's way of seeing. For the soul, seeing is not about using one's eyes (although visual sight can stimulate the seeing of the soul); what we have here is perception as understanding. While the *petites raptures* described in Chapter 1 provide examples from ordinary life of this deeper kind of seeing, the right-brain processes of artmaking make available a more constant experience of this mode of perception. Not only can the process for making art be adopted at will, it can be sustained, thereby offering greater opportunity for spiritual development than the unpredictable encounters of *petites raptures*. Thus when, as artists, we train ourselves to apply right-brain methods through practice, we can at the same time be disciplining ourselves to see with the 'eyes of our soul.' All religions advocate some such discipline as a means of spiritual development; I believe artmaking, when approached in an appropriate way, can also become a spiritual discipline.

The right-brain way of seeing that artists employ involves a mindset that is very different from ordinary consciousness. It is as if the artist is swept away to another place. This is not a physical place, but a state of consciousness that allows for a unique perception of the everyday world. In this place the artist has knowledge by acquaintance, an intimate knowing that bypasses ordinary, deliberate learning processes. This is a kind of knowing through direct experience that cannot easily be explained by ordinary language. It is as if the artist's hands and eyes are directly connected, acting together to create an image as much from what is felt as from what is actually seen. During each of the steps in the drawing process, the artist draws as he sees without thinking about doing one thing after another in a linear, preconceived way. He focuses only on the step in which he is presently engaged, understanding the relationships between all things within his field of vision in what seems to be a sustained single moment. Such knowledge by acquaintance involves his accepting the unexplained mysteries that guide his work. But this is not a trance. At all times he is aware that he is in a perceptive mode that is different from everyday consciousness and that he must stay there if he is to find the solutions to his artistic problems.

As you begin consciously to engage the creative process by adopting the right-brain methods of artists, you will become familiar with what it *feels* like to be in this place. From here you will not only learn how to see in a way that leads you to create artistic works, but become more familiar with the environment of your soul. This happens because the state of consciousness that produces your art is also the milieu of the soul. Right-brain experience seems to suspend linear time as we understand it, replacing it with a holistic sense of time, understood as a continuing present that is both momentary and eternal. In addition, it exposes us to a kind of wisdom that is different from other sorts of knowledge to which we have been exposed. The source of this wisdom can seem internal or external, depending on our religious, cultural and personal dispositions. As artists, what we bring back from this place are visual images. But whether these images are representational, abstract or symbolic, they can never do justice to the experience itself: our colours will never be so bright or our lines so clean as those in our vision. After being in this place, the connection with our soul is renewed and strengthened and we are able to participate more joyfully and peacefully in the ordinary acts of daily life.

Mystical seeing

Extended awareness of the present, sometimes called the 'now' moment or eternal moment, is cultivated by both artists and mystics as a way of perceiving the world more clearly; mystical awareness is thus very similar to artistic seeing. In such moments, the artist engages intimately with the object of his image, and the mystic with God. Both experience a right-brain understanding that is intense and intuitive, seemingly independent of external learning. This way of perceiving connects art and soul; it is a holistic engagement of spirit, mind and body.

Mystics of all religions have long understood the value of remaining focused in the present moment. While we may learn from the past and plan for the future, the present is really all we have. By becoming more sensitive to the importance of the present and our participation in it, we strengthen the connection to our soul. Listening to our soul provides insights that will help us find balance and direction for everyday living. As we bring the contents of our soul to consciousness we acquire great power for shaping our lives and fulfilling our deepest yearnings, letting go of the dissatisfactions we have amassed by following the pursuits of our self-interested ego. The present, or *kairos* (God's time), is our lifeline to a more intimate participation in our human journey. It is the place from which we make our art, the place in which we actually live, and the place to which we must return time and time again to make contact with our soul.

William James, a philosopher who is still influential in the study of religious experience, lists four qualities that must be present for authentic mystical experience. These will help us understand more clearly what I have described. The first quality is *ineffability*: such experience defies adequate expression because it is beyond our ability to comprehend fully. He writes that "no adequate report of its contents can be given in words" and that "its quality must be directly experienced; it cannot be imparted or transferred to others." James also insists that mystical experience has a *noetic* quality: it provides insights into the depth of truth that cannot be attained through normal intellectual processes. In such experiences there is a flash of knowing or a moment of clarity in which all things come together instantaneously to provide knowledge of something that was not known before (at least not in the same way): "They are illuminations, revelations, full of significance and importance, all inarticulate though they remain; and as a rule they carry with them a curious sense of authority for after-time." Further, according to James' study, mystical experience is *transient*: it cannot be sustained for long periods of time. Even the greatest of medieval mystics did not live constantly in their mystical experience, but travelled back and forth between ordinary and extraordinary consciousness. Finally, James says that mystical experience is *passive*: though we may learn how to make ourselves more receptive to it, it does not come to us of our own will, but breaks into consciousness from a source over which we have no control. He writes that such states are "never merely interruptive. Some memory of their content always remains, and a profound sense of their importance. They modify the inner life of the subject between the times of their recurrence."[4]

Interestingly, according to the broad definition supplied by James, we have all had mystical experiences in some form. This parallels Evelyn Underhill's thinking in her classic work *Mysticism*, first published in 1911. She writes, "...where the mystic has a genius for the Absolute, we have each a little buried talent, some greater, some less; and the growth of this talent, this spark of the soul, once we permit its emergence, will conform in little, and according to its measure, to those laws of organic growth, those inexorable conditions of transcendence which we found to govern the Mystic Way."[5]

The *petites raptures* described in Chapter 1 provide an example of mysticism in everyday experience – moments that cannot be fully described, that give us deep insights, that are fleeting and that interrupt our everyday consciousness. While such encounters may be transitory and passive, as we develop our spirituality we will increase the likelihood of experiencing them. Just as an artist cultivates right-brain thinking, we can persuade our ego to become more sensitive to mystical experience in everyday life. While we may not be able to cause or sustain mystical experiences, through disciplined practices (such as artmaking) we can prepare ourselves to receive and appreciate them when they happen.

Becoming conscious of mystical experience allows us to participate more fully in our spiritual development. As we become familiar with such breakthroughs into consciousness, they will reveal what is needed for the soul to become more influential in shaping our lives. These breakthroughs are the soul's way of guiding us towards wholeness – by illuminating alternatives to the distortions we have adopted through our self-interested ego. If we continue to ignore the yearnings of our soul, we push it farther away from our conscious reality – and suffer the consequences. We may become ill, despondent, angry or just plain unhappy. As our lives move naturally and inevitably towards death we can decide consciously how we want to live each of our days. While ultimately we have no control over our birth or our death, we can contribute a positive attitude while we are alive. Time on earth is precious; becoming aware of our soul opens doors to the spiritual reality in which we already participate. If we integrate the physical and spiritual parts of ourselves, each will help the other to flourish.

Mystical experience

I began working with the inbreakings of soul into consciousness when I experienced a *petite rapture* that was more intense and longer lasting than others I had had. It began during a weekly Bible study session as we studied The Parable of the Sower (Mark 4:1-8). Listening to the conversation and readings centred around this story, I experienced a kind of flash in my mind. But unlike my other *petites raptures*, which were more feeling-oriented, this was a very brief and complete visual image. At first I didn't pay much attention, but as the morning progressed, the image kept presenting itself before my eyes, always the same, and always for brief moments. It was as if the image was stuck in my mind, like a transparent slide in a projector, clicking in and out. The interruption became so intrusive that I tried to share it with the group, but I couldn't articulate it. It was all very frustrating and yet exciting.

The image continued to present itself in the same way for several weeks following that initial experience. I tried to draw it as I saw it, but because I had only ever drawn representational images of the natural world, I had no idea how to go about it. Although the image in my mind was complete, I could not seem to translate it onto paper with my usual techniques. My frustration level grew as weeks passed and I seemed no closer to being able to imitate what I saw. Finally, in an act of desperation, I decided to adopt the attitude of "power in weakness" (2 Corinthians 12:9) and let go of my preconceptions about what this image should look like. I went to my studio and placed yet another clean sheet of paper on my drawing table. This time I did not concentrate on making the image I had seen in my mind. Rather, I allowed myself the freedom of not knowing what would happen. Trusting that my acquired skills as an artist would provide communication tools for my unconscious, I simply put my pencil on the page and made an offering of a single line. Following my intuition, I added line after line until there was a reasonable depiction on my drawing table of what I had seen in my mind. The drawing time was only twenty minutes – a remarkable contrast to the hours I had spent during the previous weeks. (Gallery Image 2, *The Parable of the Sower*, is a lithograph based on the original drawing.)

What I learned from this experience is that sometimes our conscious, rational mind prevents our more intuitive, creative and spiritual elements from emerging. Exercises such as those provided by artmaking, where we deliberately subdue our conscious intentions and submit to unconscious processes, help to reveal the part of ourselves that may be hidden deep inside, the part that reminds us there is a force more powerful than the conscious desires of our ego. Mystics and artists are both able to submit to the unknown in this way. Answers to questions about the source of (or reasons for) the information and feelings from mystical experience are less important than the experience itself. As we allow ourselves to find instead of deliberately seeking, many questions will eventually be answered. Like Thomas, we will have the chance to satisfy our needs, not from the experiences of others, but through a connection with the wisdom of our soul.

If we accept that there is a spiritual reality, we can further accept that mystical experience links us to it. And it links us to others as well: the insights that we receive through such experiences are helpful for us individually, but also collectively. Through it we can see the greater picture of human development and where we fit into it, and take seriously our responsibility to all other creatures (and the earth itself) in our journey through time.

Finding historical roots

Mystical experiences can leave us somewhat bewildered at first. In my quest to understand them, I looked to history and to my Christian heritage. I wanted to validate my experiences – and to prove that I wasn't crazy! I stayed open to synchronicities (meaningful coincidences) as they unfolded during my search.

Turning first to the Bible, I did not find answers to specific questions about what I was experiencing or why, but I did find people who seemed to have had similar experiences. From the curiosity of Eve to the wailing of the psalmist and the insights of Jesus of Nazareth, the Bible spoke to me metaphorically. Reading of Paul's conversion on the road to Damascus, I understood that when the scales fall from our eyes, we begin to see in a new way. The relationship of Martha and Mary became more than an ancient account of two sisters, and it provided insights into two very different parts of myself – the practical and the intuitive. And the entire Gospel of John began to make perfect sense. My understanding of the role of religion in everyday life moved in a new direction as I began to see that my experience of direct interac-tion with the divine was natural and acceptable within my own tradition. I learned that I had spent much of my time asking the wrong questions and that I would need a new frame of reference if awareness of my soul was to grow.

In this search for historical roots, it was the medieval mystics who captured my imagination most. Their accounts of bizarre experience, akin to the descriptions found in Ezekiel and Jeremiah, showed that revelation continued long after biblical times. I thought that if God could speak to people directly in the days of old, why not now as well? Perhaps it is that we do not recognize the signs of divinity around us. As a result of my encounters with Hildegard of Bingen, Julian of Norwich, St. Teresa of Avila, St. John of the Cross, Meister Eckhart and others, I came to know God in ways I had never dreamed of and to understand that the power of divinity crosses boundaries of time and culture. Although the experiences (and the interpretations) of mystics differ, I came to believe that each of them journeys in his or her own way to the same place and gazes upon the same eternal Truth.

Hildegard of Bingen and St. Teresa of Avila have become especially important members of my spiritual community. These women lived almost four hundred years apart: Hildegard was born in Germany in 1098, and Teresa was born in Spain in 1515. Both were nuns who, at a young age, dedicated their lives to God and the Church in the Benedictine and Carmelite orders, respectively. I discovered St. Teresa one summer afternoon while reading by the sea. I had purchased a copy of *The Interior Castle* some months before, probably having read of it in the bibliography of another book. I had no preconceptions about the content of her book; I did not even know who she was. What struck me first in this work was that because she was writing to nuns in her charge, she used the feminine pronoun extensively. It was comforting to read a book on a religious topic that recognized and valued the experience of women. While Teresa could not rightly be called a feminist according to today's understanding of the term, she offers a welcome oasis for the contemporary reader of historical theological texts.

As I read *The Interior Castle*, I felt as though, finally, someone understood the struggles of my spiritual journey. In this work St. Teresa leads her readers through the door of a metaphorical castle to seven mansions where our struggles to know the fullness of God begin. Starting with a conscious desire to progress spiritually through the practice of meditation and prayer, we leave behind the ways of the exterior world and enter the first mansion. Progressing steadily, but with great fluctuation, we move through successive mansions within the castle, each of which represents a stage of development in our progress towards union with God. Teresa insists that the journey is not smooth and linear, but sporadic. We sometimes moves in and out of several different mansions within a short time. But overall, the closer we move to the central mansion (the seventh), the more consistently we experience God directly. Using the metaphors of reptiles and marriage to represent worldliness and union, Teresa explains the process by which we can extricate ourselves from the desires of the ego and consummate our final union in God. Along the way, we will be given visions: some for comfort and some for direction. We do not initiate these; they are spontaneous gifts from God.

I met Hildegard of Bingen a few years later, also on the beach. Settling into *Scivias* (her first major work, written at age 42) in the warmth of an August sun, I found another sister who shared my inner world. In that book she records her visions, which she had been experiencing since childhood. (The fact that I was 40 when I began reading her wasn't incidental to my appreciation of her work.) Hildegard had received a vision in which she believed that God told her to "write what you see and hear." The impact of this simple statement on my life was enormous. For, six years earlier, I had experienced something similar. I was sleeping in my cottage by the sea and awoke at six o'clock in the morning feeling drawn to the front door. When I opened it I saw a red sun reflecting on the ocean. It was beautiful, but I had seen such a sight many times before. However, this time I also felt an unusual stirring in me that led me to find a pencil and paper. Writing spontaneously, I recorded a poem, line by line, as it was revealed in my mind. Included within the text was this simple message: "Write what you see and hear." Reading Hildegard's words affirmed my experience and offered relief that I was not alone – or crazy.

In her works, Hildegard distinguishes between two kinds of mystical experience. The first she calls "the shadow of the living light," by which she means a sense of the presence of God, a path of light emanating from a central, all-encompassing divine source. This was something of which she could be conscious at all times. The second type, which she calls "the living light itself" (her name for God), represents unsought mystical experiences that filled her with intense ecstasy or joy. The *petites raptures* of our own experience resemble this second type. However, many of Hildegard's visions extended over longer periods of time, like mini-dramas. She watched events unfold in her mind's eye, much as fiction writers allow their characters to develop themselves. She reports not only a metaphorical equivalent of seeing during her mystical experiences, but also hearing, touching, smelling and even tasting. These dramas presented themselves during Hildegard's waking hours. She did not go into a trance, but remained alert and in control of her faculties throughout, watching the figures, patterns and colours move and change. The significance of the symbolism in her visions was not readily apparent to her. It was only as she wrote the commentaries that followed the visions (which she also believed to be revealed by God) that she began to understand their meaning. The vision itself, which was relatively short and concise, would form the basis for her prophetic interpretation, which took longer to develop, sometimes a period of years. For example, elements of *Scivias* were picked up in the themes of subsequent works as part of an ongoing dialogue.

While I was initially attracted to Hildegard by the visual images attributed to her, it was the parallels between Hildegard's experience evident in her written accounts and my own that offered me the most stimulation and encouragement. I desperately needed to ground my experience in an historical community since I could not find a con-

temporary one. And although I had looked forward to finding out more about Hildegard's direct connection with the artistic process, I was not terribly disappointed to learn that most scholars believe she did not create the visual images for which she has become known. In fact, in her works Hildegard does not write of the art process at all. Even so, her descriptions arise from her experience of that place where visual art is born.

The experiences of Teresa and Hildegard and others like them provided me with an authentically Christian framework for understanding my own experience. By rooting myself in history, I was better able to see my role in the contemporary world: I was not experiencing a new phenomenon, but reconnecting with an old one. With roots firmly planted in the Christian tradition, I gained confidence to explore ways of bringing elements of my own heritage into a modern context. In the mystics I found role models whose undeniable link to Christianity gave me a contemporary sense of community, despite the differences of time and culture.

Contemporary application

Mystical experience is a highly subjective thing. While we can relate something of our experience to others, we must be careful not to make assumptions about what they mean when they try to describe theirs. All such descriptions are shaped by beliefs. Hildegard and Teresa described their experiences using the language of their times, as did Ezekiel and Jeremiah before them. But we do not need to adopt the attitudes of an archaic culture or theology in order to share something of such mystical journeys. Responding creatively to records left behind, we may add our own insights as a way of continuing the mystical tradition in contemporary culture and theology.

We can apply, for example, Hildegard's observation that mystical experience takes place on two levels. The first ("the shadow of the living light") we may think of as a kind of attitude that can be consciously initiated and cultivated by anyone with the desire to do so. At the outset such an attitude merely requires accepting that in addition to the familiar world of body and mind, there is a spiritual dimension to reality. As we become accustomed to an attitude of mysticism that takes for granted a spiritual component to life, we welcome our soul into the realm of everyday experience and gain a deeper appreciation of how various parts of our lives are interconnected. Such an attitude makes us less susceptible to the whims of our self-interested ego and provides tolerance and stability as we weave our way through life's ups and downs. Hildegard's second level, "the living light itself," we can understand as an intrusion into consciousness by *petites raptures*, experiences like the one recorded in my description of *The Parable of the Sower*. These spontaneous events result in overwhelming sensations of fear, joy or insight and bring to consciousness important messages from our soul.

The process of right-brain thinking necessary for artmaking helps acquaint us with both levels of mystical experience while providing a new language for their expression. As we become familiar with a state of consciousness that is markedly different from our ordinary way of thinking and feeling, we come to see the world in a new way and gain more power to include and maintain a spiritual attitude in our lives. While we may not be able to induce specific mystical experiences, by cultivating such an attitude through the practice of art we enter the place where such spontaneous eruptions are more likely to happen. Reciprocally, the intensity and growing frequency of these intrusions into consciousness will help us to sustain the very attitude we are trying to nurture. As we give more attention to connecting with our soul through spiritual practices such as art, our soul will respond by increasing our awareness of its presence in everyday life.

Let the last word be Evelyn Underhill's. According to her, "...artists stand in a peculiar relation to the phenomenal world, receiving rhythms and discovering truths and beauties which are hidden from other(s)," and the mystic "stands in a peculiar relation to the transcendental world...his consciousness is transfigured in a particular way."[6] When the artist and mystic unite within, we can expect nothing less than a radical transformation of how we view and relate to both the physical and the spiritual aspects of our world.

EXERCISE

Look at your reflection in a mirror. Notice the shape of your head, and the placement of your eyes, nose and mouth. Focus on your eyes, looking from one to the other. Direct your attention to one of your eyes. Notice its shape and colour. Now look more closely, paying careful attention to the reflections in your eye, including the pupil. Move closer to the mirror if you have to. Think about yourself as a mystic and continue to look, listening to your thoughts at the same time. Draw what you see and record your thoughts without trying to interpret them.

PART TWO

ILLUSION

No two people see the world in quite the same way. This warrants both celebration and caution. Each of us stands before the Truth and experiences it as best we can from our unique vantage point, but also within the limitations of our knowledge and abilities. Artists know that their interpretations are necessarily subjective – and partial. To mistake our expressions for the reality they seek to describe is to make a grave error; it is like confusing a portrait and a face. Thinking we have experienced the fullness of divinity as human beings is also a mistake. The practice of art helps us unmask such illusions and encourages humility.

Through our observations of the natural world we gain insights into why things seem the way they do. We come to understand the principles underlying illusions in both art and soul. Because life is a dynamic system of actions and interactions, everything we experience is constantly changing. Artists know that the best they can do is to make an image that expresses their response to the world at a single moment in time and space. By the time the image is created, the moment has long passed and remains only as a memory and in the illusion created as its testimony. Making art depends to some extent on the ability to create believable illusions; the development of soul depends on being able to see beyond them.

there is nothing new
it has been done before
it has been thought before
it has already been

I am all that is new
I have never been done before
I have never thought before
I have never been
I am

Chapter 3

ORDER

Lesson I

LINES AND SHAPES

Artist materials

Choosing materials that are easy to use simplifies the artmaking task for the beginner, allowing attention to be directed towards *seeing* the way an artist sees. Use soft charcoal in a thin stick or pencil form for exercises described in this chapter. Such an instrument will feel familiar; and because charcoal marks are darker than those of ordinary pencils you will be encouraged to be bold in your mark-making. Our explorations thus begin in black and white, but a few coloured pastels or crayons will also be useful along the way. Smooth, plain paper provides an adequate working surface. The still life pictured in Figure 3.1 provides a point of reference for the exercises described; if you wish to try the exercises, feel free to set up a simple still life of your own.

Beginning to draw

Like a thumbprint or a signature, your art is unique to you, as different from all other works of art as you are from all other people. Your personal style will be enhanced as you become more familiar with artist materials and more conscious of your right-brain processes. It is best to begin by trying to imitate the natural world as closely as possible. Students who are eager to draw from their imagination sometimes become impatient with an emphasis on drawing what we see, but really seeing what is before us is more involved than it might seem. By directing our attention to the order of the external world first, we acquire the information and discipline we need to make art that is representative of the natural world. By learning how to deconstruct what we see, we dive below surface impressions to the underlying substance on which our surface illusions depend. This process informs our intuition by supplying us with a repertoire of information from which we can eventually re-create anything we see in the natural

Figure 3.1 This still life will be the reference for demonstrations shown in Figures 3.5, 3.6 and 3.7.

world – or later develop fantasy images from our imagination if we wish. As your degree of skill in observation and in manipulating artist materials increases, you will find yourself accumulating an exciting personal language for self-expression.

As you begin each drawing session, consider your physical and emotional comfort level. Think of yourself as a committee of parts, and make sure that 'everyone within' is comfortable and motivated. Asking yourself whether the chair is comfortable, whether there is adequate light, whether you have all the materials you need, and so on, will prevent minor distractions once you begin. Like meditation, which requires a stilling of the body, artmaking is most successful if all your attention and energy are channelled towards the process. By adjusting your chair and lighting, putting on music to camouflage unwanted sounds, and arranging materials before beginning, you can more easily turn your thoughts to inner creative processes. As you become sensitive to the importance of all your needs, the creative, spiritual part of yourself will gradually re-emerge.

Before starting to draw on paper, you may find it useful to become familiar with the objects of the still life before you. You may want to handle them to get a sense of their substance and consider the still life from different angles before you decide which to adopt as your point of view. You can further ease into the drawing mode by making some preliminary decisions and observations. For example, will you draw all the objects in the still life or only parts of them? You will also want to note which objects are nearest and which are farthest from you. Consider how large or small

you would like the objects to appear in your drawing and where on the page they should be placed. As you begin to focus intently on the still life, you will find yourself noticing more about each object and its relationship to other objects. Try to construct the still life in your mind as it will appear on the paper: in two dimensions instead of three. The goal of this preparatory work is to help activate your right brain so that you can begin to see the still life not as a collection of individual objects, but as an arrangement of lines and shapes. By envisioning the still life in two dimensions (like an image on a jigsaw puzzle), you can more easily identify the edges of each object and the spaces between them (taking each to represent a separate piece of the puzzle). Shadows and highlights should be viewed as shapes in their own right, related to other lines and shapes in the drawing. The arrangement of lines and shapes thus created in your mind forms the blueprint of your drawing.

The illusion of lines and shapes

Trying to create the illusion of three dimensions in two-dimensional space, to locate the exact position of lines and shapes of objects in the actual still life, can be difficult. Reducing your depth perception by closing one eye while viewing the still life will help you to see more easily the lines around edges of the objects. You can become even more familiar with these lines by tracing around them with your finger as if you were drawing in the air. Notice that if you open your other eye you will be unable to locate the same edge with precision. If you move your head even slightly, or if you switch eyes, what you see is actually altered. Immediately you will begin to understand that from an artist's perspective, the certainty of edges in the three-dimensional world is called into question. There is no right or wrong line placement; what matters are the relationships and proportions among the lines we choose. And just as the outcome of our drawings is determined by the choices we make, so our lives are shaped by our decisions. Becoming more conscious of our choices before making a decision allows us to see the implications of what we decide early on.

Because the precise identification of lines and shapes is difficult, some students are led to believe that it is easier to reproduce a photograph than to draw from life. While this may seem to be the case – after all, photographs do not move, or change when we move, and the visual material supplied by them is already two-dimensional – it is actually more difficult to make objects in our images resemble the three-dimensional world if we use photographs as our only source material. It is experience gleaned through observation and accumulating in our unconscious that informs our intuitive understanding of the natural world and eventually enables us to draw anything we see. And it is through relating to the natural world with the heightened awareness born of direct observation that we tap our latent creative and spiritual resources. The development of both art and soul depends on our own authentic experience, not on the illusions presented by others. Since the intention in this book is to become attuned to our spiritual life through the practice of art, the emphasis will be on direct observation, which explains why serious readers are asked to set up their own simple still life to use as a point of reference. For the

same reason, I suggest you avoid pre-constructed design patterns or grids for drawing. An honest reaction to visual stimuli in the natural world coupled with a few basic artist techniques will open you to a process of soul-expression in the form of art. Once you have learned and absorbed the process of relating to the world as an artist does, you will be able to express yourself using whatever medium you choose – drawing, painting, photography, play dough or a computer!

Although we may think of an image produced by an artist as being much like a snapshot – expressing a single perspective representing the artist's specific point of view – the details of that point of view are sometimes not so easy to determine. You may feel uncertain initially as to where to position your lines on the page, finding it difficult to decide which lines to copy and which to leave out. Paul Cézanne, the French Impressionist painter of the late nineteenth century, explored these possible differences of viewpoint in his work. As a result, some of Cézanne's paintings reveal tabletops and other surfaces that don't line up from a single perspective. Figure 3.2, Marcel Duchamp's famous painting, *Nude Descending a Staircase*, can seem positively chaotic to the uninitiated viewer. Influenced by Cézanne and the Cubists who followed him, Duchamp's image shows, on a

Figure 3.2 This image shows, on a single plane, many perspectives of a woman as she descends a staircase. (Marcel Duchamp, Nude Descending a Staircase, 1912. © Estate of Marcel Duchamp/ADAGP (Paris)/SODRAC (Montreal) 2002)

single plane, many perspectives of a woman as she descends a staircase. These artists and others expanded the notion of an objective interpretation of reality by representing movement and the passing of time within a single image.

Although it may seem otherwise, nothing in the natural world is stagnant: everything is always in a state of flux. For this reason it is difficult to freeze-frame what you see in your moving, three-dimensional field of vision. But in order to begin drawing, this is what you must try to do. Leaving the concepts of multi-dimensional space to Cézanne, Duchamp and others, you must try to suspend time so that you can capture a single instance on paper. Time and movement must cease for you; you must move into the present moment as if it were eternity. This relates to the language of the soul as expressed by William Blake: "To see a world in a grain of sand/ And a heaven in a wild flower/ Hold infinity in the palm of your hand/ And eternity in an hour."[7] While positions of lines and spaces may at first glance seem to be certain, the more you observe, the more you understand that their placement depends on your decision, not on what is correct or incorrect. The lines you choose provide a foundation for your interpretation from a specific point of view at a specific moment. And while they may be chosen with certainty, you know that the certainty in your mind, or in the mind of the viewer later on, is ultimately an illusion.

Lines

In the drawing process, lines can be used in two different ways. First, they can be *gestural*, as in Figure 3.3, describing both location and move-

Figure 3.3 Without giving firm definition, gesture lines describe both location and movement, as in these charcoal lines drawn on newsprint.

ment of objects without giving them firm definition. These lines are frequently used for figure drawing and quick sketches; they are more suggestive than precise. Contour lines, on the other hand, give more definite edges to shapes. They are used to establish *proportions* of objects and shapes – as we perceive their relationships through observation. Like the outlines around objects and their parts in children's colouring books, they are a useful tool for identifying shapes and their placement on the page (Figure 3.4).

Figure 3.4 Contour lines cut the picture plane into positive and negative spaces with minimal complexity.

You begin your drawing of the still life by making a single contour line on the page to represent the edge of one of the objects you are viewing. This serves as a reference point from which you then develop all other lines on the page. Parts of objects that are hidden by other objects do not need to be drawn; draw only what you see, with each line forming a division between shapes. Using the right-brain method of divorcing what is known about objects from what is seen through direct observation, lines are measured visually. They intersect each other at various points, as dictated by our interpretation of what we see. Line after line is drawn on the page, gradually translating the outlines of objects in the still life onto the paper. You will be constantly measuring at this stage of the drawing process, trying to use lines that best imitate the proportions of the objects being viewed from your perspective. Try not to use an eraser. Soft, feathery lines will allow you to make decisions concerning final placement gradually. Working over mistakes rather than erasing them is recommended so that the drawing mood will not be lost in a perfectionist attitude.

As the drawing develops, it is good to stand back from it periodically in order to check its proportions. If they seem unnatural (unlike the proportions of the actual still life), alter your lines according to what you see, making sure your position in relation to the still life remains consistent. At this stage it is the still life, not the drawing, that holds the answers to your visual problems. All the information necessary to draw the still life can be gleaned from observing it, so observing time is as important as drawing time in creating your image.

Figure 3.5 The positive spaces have been identified with vertical lines, the negative spaces with horizontal lines, revealing the two more clearly.

The sketch is finished when the lines of all the objects, and the major lines within each object, have been placed on the paper. At this point you will notice that the lines are more dominant than the shapes.

Shapes

In the drawing of your still life, the *positive* spaces are the shapes of the objects and the *negative* spaces are the shapes between, around and within the objects. By comparing the negative shapes in your drawing with those viewed in the actual still life, you can determine where you may have made mistakes in proportion due to your pre-occupation with the more easily identifiable positive spaces. If the negative shapes in the image differ from your observations, adjust these lines so that both positive and negative shapes reflect what you observe. The drawing will appear realistic and natural when both the positive and negative spaces conform as much as possible to your observations.

After you have completed a line-drawing of the still life, a further exercise will help to facilitate your understanding of the relationship between positive and negative space. Choose two different coloured pastels or crayons. Use one colour to identify positive spaces by filling them with vertical lines. Fill in all the negative spaces with the other colour, using horizontal lines, as in Figure 3.5. Note that at this point the shapes are more obvious than the lines. Through experience, an artist learns to balance lines and shapes, moulding them as necessary to reflect and express the natural world. Note that the contour drawing shown in Figure 3.4 cuts the picture plane into positive and negative spaces with minimal complexity. Here, shape and line work together to suggest the image of a figure to the viewer. In this case, whether the line or the shape is dominant is a matter of viewer preference.

Patterns

Now you can compare your image once more to the still life you sought to imitate. With a greater understanding of the relationships among the lines and shapes generated by the exercise above, it should be easier to identify the positive and negative spaces as you view the actual still life. To develop your image further, turn your attention to the details within each of the individual spaces,

Figure 3.6 Note that a close-up of the bottle (itself a positive space in the larger drawing) reveals a pattern of positive and negative spaces within it. These can be referred to as figure and ground, respectively.

where you will find additional positive and negative spaces. At this more advanced level, spaces have no names, as the objects of the still life do; positive spaces are referred to as 'figure' and negative spaces are called 'ground.' Together they form patterns within each of the components of the still life. For example, a bottle might seem to be only a positive space in relation to the negative spaces that surround it, but an advanced rendering would reveal another pattern of positive and negative spaces within the bottle itself – the shadows, reflections and highlights. (See the close-up view in Figure 3.6.) Each negative space is also treated as its own little world, with both positive and negative spaces within it being identified and developed. Being able to recognize such patterns at successively deeper levels will guide you in the development and refinement of your image.

Like the alphabet, which contains only twenty-six letters from which all the words of the English language are constructed, there are only a few basic lines and shapes that make up our entire visual vocabulary. Lines can be straight or curved; shapes are open or closed. These, like letters, are used in different combinations to make images of everything we see in the natural world. Because lines and shapes are so limited in their basic forms, a trained eye can detect underlying patterns in nature which, when transferred to images, create a sense of order in the work, reflecting the harmony found in nature. Lines, shapes and patterns are not invented by an artist; they are discovered. Like our soul, they already exist, merely waiting to be recovered. By bringing them into consciousness, we gain insights into the order of both the natural and the spiritual worlds.

EXERCISE

With charcoal, make a simple drawing from life using contour lines to establish outlines and proportions. After comparing the placement of lines on the page with observations from life as discussed above, make whatever changes are necessary to bring the image closer to what you see.

Then choose two colours, using one to fill in positive spaces with vertical lines and the other to fill in negative spaces with horizontal lines. If necessary, add more charcoal to the original lines to clean up the edges of the image (as in Figure 3.7).

Figure 3.7 Charcoal has been used to redefine the edges.

CHOOSING THE SOUL'S PATH

The illusion of certainty

I first saw an original Van Gogh painting during a visit to the Metropolitan Museum of Fine Art in New York. Wandering through the gallery, not looking for any particular exhibit, I unexpectedly came face to face with one of his iris paintings. It literally took my breath away. I felt tears well up in my eyes and an overwhelming sensation that I could not name. I had seen reproductions of Van Gogh's work all my life – I had even used them as illustrations for classes. But I had no idea that I would be affected so strongly by the originals. Thoughts of the colours and textures can still raise goosebumps on my arms. I was not moved so much by Van Gogh's ability to represent the exterior qualities of irises in paint on canvas. Rather, I felt as if I had been transported to the place in Van Gogh's mind where he first encountered the irises, which caused him to want to paint them. The painting further seemed to serve as a mediator between myself and the 'irisness' of all irises that have ever been or will be in the natural world. Though I was conscious that I was viewing paint on canvas, Van Gogh's image led me beyond the surface illusion of blossoms and brush strokes to glimpse a unifying order from which both had emerged.

Artists, like magicians, are in the business of illusion, expressing themselves by translating ideas into concrete forms with paint or clay or any number of media. The artist knows that she is creating an illusion; it is a necessary condition of her communication as a visual artist. She also knows that the images she creates express her own perspective on the subject matter and that others will express the same concepts in different ways. She understands that all she can be certain of in relation to her creations is her own experience, which has resulted in a specific image. She needn't be bothered if others' experiences of the same material differ from hers or if they respond to her image in ways she would not have predicted. The artist's illusion is merely a representation of how she understands something at a specific moment in time and space. Her intention is not for viewers to mistake her image for the truth of the matter, but to reveal her reaction through the illusion she creates.

Illusions, when mistaken for reality, create stumbling blocks for the soul. This was made clear to me one day through a disagreement I had with a friend. During a conversation, I referred to something as being true. She became angry and informed me not only that I was wrong, but that she would tell me "the *real* truth" about the matter. If her truth was not the same as mine, what were the implications? One of us could be wrong, or we could both be wrong, but surely we could not both be right!

I worked on the problem by working on a piece of art. The process of creating the lithograph

Perception Spiral (Gallery Image 3) helped me understand what was going on. For this image I drew on a lithographic stone a single spiral vine, which I then printed on paper as a representation of truth. Because I used the process of lithography, I could then print the exact same spiral again, using a slightly different colour to represent the same 'truth' a second time. I turned the paper a quarter turn so that the second spiral would not be printed directly on top of the first, allowing the initial spiral to be exposed. To my surprise, when the second spiral was printed, the first faded into the background; only the top spiral was visible at first glance. I repeated the process twice more, printing each spiral in yet another colour and turning the paper another quarter turn each time. Again, each successive spiral disappeared into the background, leaving the top spiral the most noticeable.

The print provided a metaphor for the relationship between truth and our perceptions of it. It may seem to be objective truth that is represented in the work by the original spiral image drawn on the stone (the left half of *Perception Spiral*). But while it appeared in various, ever-darkening shades of green and was positioned differently on the paper, the image subsequently printed was nonetheless always the same spiral. Each of the spirals can represent a different interpretation of Truth, and together they form a much fuller rendering than any one of them does individually.

No one can know our perceptions with more certainty than we do. But our perceptions are necessarily limited and subjective because we are finite individuals. We cannot expect to understand fully the perceptions of others, nor can we expect them to understand ours fully. Nor can we expect that any of our perceptions will fully correspond to the truth. Imagine students working around a central still life, with each student painting from a particular location. No two images would be the same, but neither would they be equally true or 'correct.' Each would reflect the visual perspective, skill level and style of the artist. In this example, it is easy to recognize the limitations of each artist in relation to fullness of visual description within a single work. Each artist describes only the parts she sees; her perspective is translated into an illusion on paper or canvas. But an artist can be informed by the perceptions of others, learning more about the subject matter by looking from different angles and by viewing the works of those whose perspectives differ from her own. Even if she continues to prefer her initial perspective, her understanding of the still life will be more greatly enhanced by sharing with others than by clinging to her partial and isolated viewpoint.

Another lesson I learned from *Perception Spiral* was that, while each of us holds a certain perception of truth at a given moment, that perception may change. As we journey through the life cycle, our perceptions naturally mature in all areas of life. What we understand about love at 18 is different from how we perceive it at 35 or 70! This does not mean we abandon our past perceptions. Rather, like the leaf spirals on my print, they together form the background on which our present perceptions rest.

I have come to understand that the certainty with which my friend and I made our claims, not the claims themselves, caused a rift in our friendship. Our interpretations of truth differed, and we were unwilling to consider the other's views as valid as our own. We confused objective truth with our ego-centred interpretations of it. Recognizing that what we can know is always going to be subjective and partial is a tough blow to an ego that prides itself on certainty. But by admitting our limitations and respecting the differing views of others, we open ourselves to possibilities that are closed to us when we think we have already found all the right answers. Choosing the soul's path means moving beyond our ego-centred need for certainty to embrace the experience of life itself. The soul does not yearn to be right – it only yearns to be.

A certain kind of order

We are attracted to certainty because it provides a sense of order and control, which makes us feel secure. We like to know that what we do today will yield the same result tomorrow. Unfortunately, the cost of maintaining the illusion of certainty is high – especially where discovery of soul is concerned. The soul has no more need for absolute certainty than the artist does as she chooses which lines she will use to create an image. Any lines she chooses will make a fine painting, depending on how she relates the components within the frame. Being attached to a specific outcome at the beginning prevents order from emerging through the creative process. Likewise, when the self-interested ego convinces us that its kind of security is essential to our well-

being, it prevents us from exploring what our soul really needs. Our culture supports such distortions, encouraging power over others and the hoarding of material goods as primary means of security. The ego defends this kind of order, going to great lengths to maintain the illusions of certain health and prosperity. Thus, a great deal of creativity is channelled into service of the ego's desires, while the needs of the soul remain unfulfilled.

For the ego, order and security mean having as much control over our lives as possible; we fear that if we depend on chance, we will be at the mercy of whatever or whoever has power over us. We like making our own decisions and being in charge of our lives, and we tend to resent those whom we perceive as having control over us. Giving up control seems to necessitate giving up security. But there is a difference between *feeling* in control and *being* in control. We have very little actual control; human life is far more tenuous than most of us would like to admit. There is much we just cannot be certain of – no matter how hard we try to convince ourselves otherwise. While the ego goes looking for certainty in order to keep control, somewhere deep inside, the soul reminds us that few things are certain.

In its quest for security, the ego sometimes turns to religion, looking to belief in God as ultimate certainty. Of course, if we construe God as transcendent, that is, as ultimately beyond our knowing, and if we are also afraid of the unknown, then to some extent we will be afraid of God. The ego counters this fear by ascribing to God familiar, human-like characteristics that help make God more knowable – and make the ego more comfortable. Thinking that God is in control, even if we are not, we feel satisfied because *we* have constructed the image of something doing the controlling! But the soul leads us beyond the illusions of the ego and teaches us that certainty is not a prerequisite for security. In fact, the soul is quite at home with an unknowable God. So while the ego worships with certainty, the soul basks in mystery.

With our images of God firmly in place, all may seem right in the universe – for the ego. This continues as long as no one upsets the constructions. But when someone undermines such images of God, ancient pangs of insecurity resurface and the ego becomes afraid of losing the secure world it has so carefully assembled. Since for almost everyone in Western culture the undeveloped ego is more dominant than the soul – and since the ego's concept of God has been one of our biggest aids in fighting insecurity – we defend our images tenaciously and sometimes viciously, drawing on thousands of years of innate survival skills. Worse, because the ego feels certainty to be a necessity in maintaining security, we sometimes impose the certainty of our ideas onto others. The more others agree with us, the better our ideas seem to us and the more secure we feel in holding them. We can increase our security through their support. And because we recognize deep in our soul the possibility that we could be wrong, the ego is motivated continually to seek such affirmation from others.

The soul recognizes that certainty locks us into a closed system. When we are certain of something, we have little incentive to listen to arguments that challenge our views. This attitude, transferred to our images of God, results in arrogance, prejudice and war. All religions struggle with the problem of describing God with accuracy, whether by pictures or by words. In Judaism, it is not considered respectful even to utter God's name, for God is beyond what any name might imply. Islam prohibits visual images of God in recognition of the Divine Mystery. A Buddhist saying, "If you see the Buddha, kill him," implies that images mistaken for reality are dangerous. Once an understanding of God becomes a certainty, and interpretations that differ from this understanding become unacceptable, then we are worshipping a specific interpretation of God – an idol. Certainty eradicates the mystery of God by confining God to our limited perceptions. The God of St. Anselm – "that than which none greater can be conceived" – is not compelled to remain within our individual perceptions or conform to our particular understanding. Our perceptions of God cannot possibly define all that God is. As we come to understand this, we will see that in claiming certainty we pledge our allegiance to an illusion of our own construction. The humility resulting from this realization may lead us further to speculate that the fullness of God might be better expressed though a combination of perspectives (from within Christianity and also from other religions), and that choosing the path of the soul requires us to continue learning and growing.

Embracing wonder

Reluctance to release our grip on certainty is bound up with our collective world view. Credit for this situation is due, in part, to the English mathematician and physicist Sir Isaac Newton, who entrenched in our psyche the view that the physical world behaves in accordance with natural regularities or laws. His work led to a general acceptance of the universe as a giant machine that operates predictably. But as the masses adopted and adapted Newton's world view over the centuries, artists, scientists and philosophers continued to push the boundaries of predictability. At the turn of the last century, a new era began to dawn and the door to mystery and wonder was reopened. In art, Wassily Kandinsky, the Russian lawyer turned painter, began to portray in his paintings only the subjective qualities of the objects he viewed. He let the surface elements of objects recede in importance, concentrating on the *essence* of the objects he painted. The resulting images did not realistically imitate the exterior appearance of the objects rendered, leaving the viewer uncertain about the content of Kandinsky's work and invoking a sense of wonder. Meanwhile, Freud's pioneering work in the newly developed field of psychology showed that human individuals were not exactly as they appeared on the surface either; they often acted out of unconscious and unpredictable forces. In 1905 Albert Einstein published the first of his innovative theories that shook the world of Newtonian predictability. Einstein's theory of relativity showed that what was once thought to be certain in Newtonian physics was actually not certain at all! For example, Einstein showed that the measurements of clocks and rulers change at certain very high speeds. It appeared that Newton's 'machine' could not always be counted on to perform as predicted. But while the innovators continued moving forward in their discoveries, most of us settled comfortably into the certainty supported by Newton's world.

In contrast to predictability, wonder allows us to ignite our imagination. As we metaphorically pry our fingers from the ego's desire for certainty, we open our hearts and minds to explore what lies beyond the limitations of our already-formed beliefs. As the physics of Newton's time made way for quantum mechanics in the last century, our understanding of the physical world had to change significantly. The new physics has revealed an order that is in stark contrast to the one of Newton's time. For example, it has been determined that observations are affected by the observer: if an experiment seeks to detect light as a wave, waves will be observed; if the experiment is changed to seek light as a particle, particles will be detected. In a sense, we find what we are looking for. To extend the point, it has been discovered that a subatomic particle may perform a quantum leap at any time, which means that it can ignore the pattern that previous observations have predicted for it.[8] This uncertainty is also reflected in the processes of art and soul. In each case, unexpected eruptions into consciousness provide moments of clarity that may cause us to change direction in unpredictable ways. Unlike the unenlightened ego on its narrow path of self-interest, both artist and soul are flexible and resilient, excited and stimulated by new directions as they are presented. A sense of wonder turns life into an adventure!

The illusion of chaos

Many of us fear that chaos will take over our lives if we abandon the ego's concept of order. This view is supported by the traditional biblical interpretation of chaos as negative. Because God caused order to emerge from chaos, it has been assumed that chaos was undesirable. But what if chaos and order are not opposed to each other? Maybe they are better considered partners in a paradoxical dance, as expressed by the notion of positive and negative spaces in art or by the Taoist concept of yin and yang. Perhaps each is balanced by the other. Consider the relationship between sea and shore, where waves break apart rocks, grinding them into sand – and sand settles over time into new rocks. In contrast to the static, linear, and familiar phrase of Christianity, "as it was in the beginning, is now and ever shall be," such a cyclical understanding encourages growth, change and interaction through time.

Chaos is a natural part of our lives; the better we are able to accept this fact, the easier our lives will be. Meteorologist Edward Lorenz, in his study of what has become known as the 'butterfly effect,' revealed that small alterations in local weather have the potential to affect global weather patterns. What appeared to him at first as chaotic and unrelated events turned out to be components of a much larger order.[9] The underlying principle behind this observation is that chaos is not always in opposition to order, but may be incorporated within an order of a different kind. As a Nova Scotian I am accustomed to a high degree of inaccuracy in weather predictions. Because of our proximity to the coast, many variables must be considered in making forecasts. As a result of regular inconsistency, Nova Scotians accept a wide range of fallibility in weather forecasts. We adjust by keeping an umbrella, a jacket and a bathing suit in the car at all times! Rather than bemoan the inaccurate forecasts, we develop tolerance for change and adapt accordingly. The uncertainty of the weather for most of us simply becomes a way of life; we have a system of order that encompasses chaos.

Chaos theory (an offshoot of quantum physics) takes into account the constant changes that are part of our physical world. As we learn to adapt to such changes, we become more comfortable in our experience of life as it really is. In their book *Seven Life Lessons from Chaos*, authors John Briggs and David Peat illustrate the order of chaos by describing the process of boiling water. Before water is heated, its molecules are ordered in a certain way. As the molecules are stimulated by heat, their order begins to change. Most of us would consider this stage to be chaos. Part of this process of change involves the molecules exercising what the authors call the "maximum degree of freedom." To describe this freedom, Briggs and Peat use the metaphor of an orchestra in which each musician has tuned her instrument in a different key and plays a different song. But the authors tell us that this chaotic process is a natural and necessary step on the way to the formation of a new order. Once the molecules have reached a temperature just below boiling, called the bifurcation point, they redirect themselves into a new pattern of geometric vortices. As the water boils, the new order emerges, in the same way that new music may eventually emerge from the chaos of the orchestra.[10]

So it is with our lives. We go through many stages, some of which we would call ordered because of their familiarity and desirability from the perspective of our undeveloped ego, and others chaotic because of their apparent lack of order. Because the order of the ego is rigid, fixed on specific goals, we feel varying degrees of stress when it is challenged. But, unlike the ego, the soul is not deterred by chaos; it helps us readjust to each of the stages in our lives as they emerge, seeing them as a series of personal bifurcation points. As the evolution of our species continues, we will personally and collectively engage in many such sequences of chaos and order. The more we accept this natural rhythm by choosing the soul's path, the less energy we will expend fighting the inevitable.

Cycles are very much a part of our natural world: day moves into night and then day again, seasons repeat yearly, even our own circulatory and digestive systems go through cycles. By standing back from the short-sighted perceptions of our ego, we can see more clearly that chaos, together with familiar order, is part of an ongoing process. As we recognize the natural role of uncertainty in the transitional stages of this process, it becomes less frightening to accept uncertainty in everyday life. Thus we may be led peacefully to adopt the attitude expressed by a Zen proverb: "This, too, shall pass."

Embracing the soul's order

Our first step in choosing the path of the soul is to accept the soul's order for our lives. By admitting that we do not have all the answers and that some of the answers we do have are probably wrong, we will make progress in navigating our way through the ego's illusions. By permitting our soul a voice in decision-making, we will move more easily through cycles of chaos and order, certainty and uncertainty, in the never-ending transitions of life. As we learn to detach ourselves gently but surely from the outcome of each moment in our lives, we will be better able to enjoy the process of life itself, and thus participate in a new kind of order.

As we embrace the soul's order for our lives, we must be on guard that we are not deceiving ourselves, thinking we are letting go of the desire for certainty when we are not. Several years ago, a friend expressed concern over my theological views. For a time we had shared the same spiritual path, but she had become increasingly concerned about my spiritual health as I moved in a direction different from hers. After listening to her critique, I told her that I honoured her right to express her views and respected them – even though they were different from mine – and that I would like her to give me the same respect. On the surface this request seemed reasonable. But was I really willing to respect her views? This meant I had to accept the fact that she thought I was wrong. What's more, I had to allow for the possibility that she might be right!

The book of Isaiah states that our thoughts and ways are not God's (Isaiah 55:8). We can take from this that God's order is different from the order constructed by our unenlightened ego. Choosing to follow the path of our soul, accepting our fallibility and limitations as human subjects, is a step towards adopting God's order. This underlying order of the soul is based on love. Choosing this path means being motivated not by a desire for certainty, control or security, but by love. We are told that "Love is patient, love is kind. It does not envy, it does not boast, it is not loud. It is not rude, it is not self-seeking, it is not easily angered, it keeps no record of wrongs. Love does not delight in evil but rejoices with the truth. It always protects, always trusts, always hopes, always perseveres" (1 Corinthians 13:4-7). Soul-love is unconditional: love is the soul's vocation. When we choose love, we have chosen to walk the path of our soul; the reordering of our lives resulting from this decision will become visible in our daily interactions. This kind of love extends to any and all people within our range, regardless of race, gender, age, sexual orientation or religious affiliation. We respect those who are different from us because soul-love dictates that others be respected. And we respect each moment of our life for what it can teach us. This kind of love, which is central to the Christian message, is lost if the certainty of our beliefs separates us from others or from our authentic selves.

EXERCISE

Write in your journal your present understanding of God. Without discussing your own views, ask at least one other person for their thoughts. Record in your journal what they say without judging their statements. Later, compare your thoughts with the other person's to see where you agree and disagree. Note the strength of any feelings that arise over disagreements. Ask yourself why you are responding as you do. Try to determine which of your beliefs you are most certain about, and how important that certainty is to you. Record these thoughts in your journal for later reflection.

*the union of diversity
is the gathering
of the Many
into the
One
and the
sharing of the
One with the Many*

Chapter 4

DIVERSITY

Lesson II

TONE AND TEXTURE

Artist materials

Exercises in this chapter require thin, soft charcoal sticks that make marks that are easily smudged when touched, as in Figure 4.1. Pencil forms of charcoal are usually a bit harder than thin sticks, making them less suitable for our present purposes. Plain, smooth paper provides a good working surface. The still life in Figure 3.1 will be

Figure 4.1 Charcoal comes in diverse forms and in varying degrees of hardness. Thin charcoal sticks are easily smudged when touched, making them desirable for creating tones and textures.

used as a reference, but for best results you can set up a simple three-dimensional still life of your own.

Transcending the illusion of lines

Lines provide only a skeleton on which to build our representations of three-dimensional space; dependence on outline alone in a drawing results in a sketch-like image that does not realistically reflect the natural world. To develop the image further, lines are best understood as places where shapes meet. They need not be divisive, but rather can be used to draw attention to the relationship between the shapes they describe. For example, if you look at your hand with your fingers together, you see lines dividing the shape of your hand into separate fingers. If you spread your fingers, however, those lines disappear, seeming instead to separate the fingers from the background shapes between them. If you retain any of these lines in your drawing as dominant outlines, you will not be able to develop a realistic likeness of the hand as it appears in three-dimensional space.

In the natural world, as in the spiritual, there are no firm dividing lines. Lines are merely an illusion that give us language to describe the world from our perspective. Knowing that our perspective is only one of many, we learn not to focus on the divisions created by these lines but on the shapes that are given form by them. To achieve this effect visually, we must find additional ways to differentiate the spaces. We will continue to work in black and white at this point and not yet look to colour as a solution for this problem. Instead, we

Figure 4.2 Clustering objects of similar tone and texture results in a less interesting arrangement. Compare this arrangement to the one in Figure 3.1.

tones from dark to light. To create an interesting pattern for your drawing, you may want to avoid clustering objects of similar tone and texture in the still life (as in Figure 4.2). Considering the tone of both positive and negative spaces of the still life (the objects and the spaces between them) is important to the overall balance of a composition. Beginning the drawing process once more with lines, as described in Chapter 3, sketch the proportions of the objects in the still life on your paper. Once these lines are in place to your satisfaction, you may begin to develop the tonal range of the image, de-emphasizing the lines as you proceed.

Every line drawn on the page represents the observation of a difference in tone (or colour, but we will leave that until the next chapter). Since black lines on white paper do not imitate the natural world, drawn lines must be blended into their corresponding shapes so that they appear more as edges of objects than as lines. Figure 4.3 shows how charcoal can be used to create 'one-sided' edges from 'two-sided' lines. The smudging is directed towards the darker of adjacent shapes. Consider the tone of each space in your image in relation to what you see in the actual still life. Comparing your line drawing with the

will concentrate on differences in *tone* and *texture*. Together, these variations help develop the image into a more believable illusion of three-dimensional space.

Recognizing tone

As with positive and negative space, *tone* or *value* does not refer to a judgment of worth, but to a relationship between parts within an image. A change in tone is a change in degree of darkness or light. As you seek to imitate the natural world in your drawing, you will need to show as full a range of tone as you observe in the subject. To begin, view the still life with your eyes *squinted*, thereby reducing the emphasis on colour and allowing you to see more clearly the range of

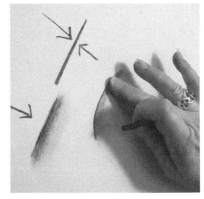

Figure 4.3 A one-sided line is created by smudging the charcoal toward the darker of adjacent shapes, creating the illusion of an edge .

still life before you – through squinted eyes – you will see that one side of each line you have drawn is almost always darker than the other in the actual still life. It is this tonal difference that enables us to see objects as three-dimensional. At first the change in tone may seem subtle, even difficult to recognize, but with practice you will become more adept at seeing these differences. We identify the darks as they relate to each line we have drawn and begin to create tonal differences by smudging the charcoal in the direction of the darker side, regardless of whether it is positive or negative space. Continue this process throughout the image as you compare every line you have drawn on the page with the corresponding lines of the actual still life, until the basic tonal differences have been established over the entire drawing. You will note that the darker tones may not always represent the positive spaces, or objects. Sometimes negative spaces, such as the background, will have the darker tones. Often there will be a variation of

Figure 4.4 Although the square on the left ('A') seems lighter than the square on the right ('B'), the two are the same tone. The illusion of a tonal change is created by differences in the external environment, not by changes in the squares themselves.

tone within a single object, depending upon its relation to other things. (Note that the squares in Figure 4.4, while of the same tone, appear lighter in 'A' and darker in 'B'.)

After you have recorded the basic tonal differences on your image, you can use a *grey scale* to determine the density of tone for each space. The scale in Figure 4.5 has been rendered in soft charcoal and in ink, showing a gradual change from black to white. By viewing the still life while squinting tightly, you can easily locate the extremes of black and white (that is, the darkest dark and the lightest light) and indicate these on your image. Note that under ordinary lighting conditions, very little within the actual still life will be pure black or pure white in tone. By keeping these extremes to a minimum in your drawing, you will be more successful in your attempt to imitate nature. (Moderation is the key – in art and in soul!) Your task is to identify and fill in the range of tones between the extremes on your image. Keeping the grey scale in mind, build tone in each of the spaces in relation to other spaces on the page. Working simultaneously over the entire image, you will develop the tone layer by layer. The more tones you are able to recognize and apply, the more the image will represent the natural world.

By comparing your drawings to a black and white photograph, you may see that you have used too few greys in developing your image, and that the changes within the tonal range are too abrupt. It is not uncommon for these changes to be more abrupt in a drawing than they are in a photograph. It seems the camera more easily

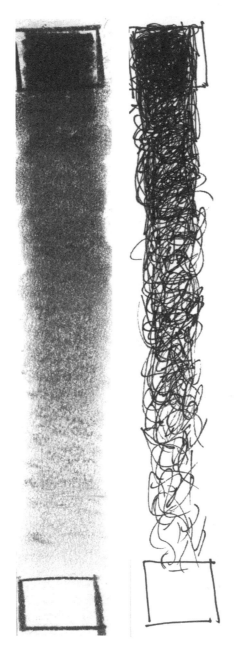

Figure 4.5 Grey scales in charcoal and ink show a range of possibilities between absolute black and absolute white.

copies the diverse range of tone in the natural world than an untrained eye. While the aim is not to make your work appear flat, like a photograph, the comparison lets you assess your success in recognizing tonal changes. By making and referring to a grey scale, you can easily check how many tones you have employed in your drawing simply by matching the greys in the image to those on the scale. If only a few greys have been used, you know you must train your eye to see more subtleties of tonal difference as they exist in the natural world. And, since tones blend into each other, each tone in the drawing must somehow merge into the tones around it. Large areas of undeveloped white space in a drawing usually mean the artist has not adequately considered these relationships. Note the difference between the images in Figure 4.6. Image A relies heavily on outline (which is black) and white space, with only one or two tones of grey. Image B shows more consideration to tone, while the black-and-white photograph in Image C demonstrates the greatest range of greys.

Creating texture

A natural extension of tone in the differentiation of spaces within an image is texture. While most people think of texture as being tactile, it is the visual illusion of texture that concerns us most in drawing. Physical textures can be incorporated into painting using thick paints and additives, but the nature of a drawing is to be flat. While some textures can be copied directly by placing the paper over a rough surface, such as a leaf, and applying drawing media on top, as in a rubbing

Figure 4.6 Note the tonal differences in these three examples. Image A, the drawing on the left, relies mainly on outline, Image B shows further development, and Image C (a photograph) shows the greatest range of tonal diversity, and thus gives the most accurate rendering of the objective physical world.

Figure 4.7 Creating texture by placing paper over a tactile object such as a leaf will not always result in the desired effect. Instead, an artist relies on tonal diversity to create the illusion of texture.

(shown in Figure 4.7), the overall patterns that these surfaces make do not always create the desired effects for the objects being depicted. What is needed are rendering techniques that interpret textures in such a way that the viewer will be encouraged to suspend disbelief while looking at the artwork. The possible differences in texture are as numerous as the tactile surfaces that exist in the world. Texture is essentially a pattern of dark and light; it is visible to the eye because of changes in tone, but the changes are arranged in such a way as to form patterns unique to each space in the image. All spaces in the drawing (positive and negative) have some kind of visual texture, which means we must treat each area accordingly.

Identification of tone in an image is the first step towards textural development; simply by smudging, a texture is created that is different from the untouched paper and the black outline sketch. Although this technique works well for establishing tone, it can be monotonous if it is the only rendering technique used to create texture in

an image. Layers of smudging can produce darker tones and some textural effects, but it is helpful to supplement with other methods. Adding lines in a parallel or cross-hatching fashion creates a pattern of light and dark that suggests texture to the eye; scribbles or short strokes (such as those that resemble fur) add further diversity to the work, as do erasing lines whose negative effect creates interest. *Stippling*, which is the use of small dot-like shapes, can be used to create patterns and suggest texture as well as tone. Other instruments, such as a toothbrush or sandpaper, can be used to apply or remove drawing material, adding variety to the image. Some examples of these techniques can be seen in Figure 4.8. The cat in Figure 4.9 shows a variety of techniques that help to relieve the overall dependence on outline. Here diversity of tone and texture is used to generate a more believable illusion.

Figure 4.8 Textures created with soft charcoal. Top row, left to right: smudging; layers of smudging; parallel lines over smudging; cross-hatching over smudging. Bottom row: scribbles and short strokes over smudging; tone lifted out by a kneaded eraser; stipples over smudging; smudging with sandpaper .

Figure 4.9 This lithograph, Christmas Cat, *uses lines to create shapes without depending solely on outline.*

EXERCISE

Look for similarities and differences in the textures of everyday objects. Try to duplicate textures as you see them, using some of the rendering techniques described above. Do not draw the thing that is textured, such as a dog, but only the texture itself, for example, the fur of the dog. To help narrow the field of vision so that you can focus more easily, cut a viewfinder opening out of paper that you can hold against an object, visually isolating the texture. Choose common objects, such as your skin, an accommodating animal, the wall or countertop, a tree trunk, and so on. Observe them carefully. After making a few sketches, compare your drawings for differences and similarities in the way you used the media to create the textures.

FOLLOWING THE SOUL'S PATH

The paradox of diversity

Just as the artist recognizes the need for differentiation in rendering an image of the natural world, the soul understands that diversity of expression presents a fuller account of ultimate reality. The fullness of God can never be sufficiently expressed by a single religious perspective, no matter how well-developed. As we transcend our ego-centred obsession with absolute correctness by choosing the soul's path, we are in a better position to acknowledge the various benefits of diversity. While the soul wants others to enjoy the experience of God, in its wisdom it understands that not everyone will experience God in the same way. Rather than insist that a particular path is the only legitimate one, the soul allows that many paths may lead to God, and that we may learn from the journeys of others.

From art we learn that if we use only lines in our drawing, our image remains a sketch, essentially undeveloped in its representation of three-dimensional space. Contrasts of tone and texture among spaces are necessary if we are to distinguish things from each other – and if we are to provide a more accurate account of the visible world. Lines focus our attention on the divisions themselves, not the spaces created by them. Dependence on outlines in our drawings reinforces these partitions, suggesting that each space is separate from the others. While this is useful for establishing proportions in the initial stages of drawing, it is only the first step in the process. The enhanced relationship between lines and shapes developed by the addition of tone and texture provides a metaphor for spiritual development. Our understanding of the spiritual life can remain in the sketch stage, but just as a multiplicity of tones and textures may be needed in a drawing to represent a single object from the natural world, so human diversity does not preclude an underlying unity. The soul knows that despite our differences as human beings we share the same properties and destiny: we are all beings of flesh and blood journeying towards physical death yet potentially in contact with aspects of divinity.

Each of us is a unique person; our thumbprint and DNA distinguish us from everyone else. While we may identify with categories of male or female, black or white, short or tall, Canadian or Norwegian, blond or bald, the combination expressed through our life is a one-time event peculiar to our experience. Even people who accept the concept of reincarnation would have to agree that each life is unique. But while each of us reflects a way of being that can be fully expressed by no other person, we are all of the same sort – we are, in Paul's words, individual jars of clay (2 Corinthians 4:7). Our 'jars' share the same basic organic and spiritual properties. And if, as Christians, we believe ourselves to be made in the image of God, we understand immediately why so many of us are needed if the fullness of God is to be expressed. If God is "that than which none greater can be conceived," then the diversity of all of us together may represent only a fraction of what is possible in God. Thus we are a paradox:

the same, but different. Following the path of the soul requires us to embrace others, respecting our differences while recognizing our common substance.

Learning about other images and concepts for God can be much like learning a new language. When we begin, we translate everything literally, using our own language as a reference point. But as we continue we find that not only are some words untranslatable, sometimes the very grammar is different from ours. It soon becomes clear that we will miss important nuances of the new language if we continue to funnel everything through our own. In this way we discover that language is not an end in itself, but a tool of communication, and that because people express things differently from us does not mean they are wrong or inferior. Different religious traditions likewise provide different vehicles for expressing our experience of God. The more we learn of both language and religion, the fuller our literal and metaphorical vocabularies will be, and the easier it will be for us to discern the voice of God in the communications of others.

The wider path

During a casual conversation, I once questioned a priest about the exclusivity of Christianity. Surely, I suggested, a loving God will not punish those who do not accept the Christian message. What kind of love would this be – certainly not the unconditional love to which Christians aspire! The priest responded by quoting Matthew 12:30: "Whoever is not with us is against us." While I didn't push the conversation further – by, for example, presenting a counter such as "Whoever is not against us is for us" (Mark 9:40) – it still didn't seem right to me. That particular passage (which also occurs in Luke) deals with the struggle between Jesus and Beelzebub. But my question did not refer to evil – or to people who might be considered evil. Rather, I was interested in the priest's understanding of the fate of caring individuals who don't accept traditional Christian doctrines. It seems to me that the omnipotent, omniscient God of traditional Christianity would see the bigger picture of people's lives and contributions and judge accordingly. A less literal reading of the Bible might show us that those who are not with us (in the limited sense of holding the same beliefs) are *not* necessarily against us!

The biblical text holds a wealth of historical information, expressions of human emotion and suffering, and advice for living – written in a variety of literary genres. For me, it is not a rulebook, but a guidebook for my life. While the intentions of the Jewish writers of the texts are important, our interpretation of the texts is crucial. The more we study and reflect on them, the more we can use our analytical thinking to enhance our understanding. Picking up threads from the text, we can weave a pattern for our present that respects both past and future.

One text that has caused much pain for our human family is found in the Gospel of John: "I am the way, the truth and the life; no one comes to the Father, except through me" (John 14:6). Understood from an exclusivist perspective, this text has caused splits among persons, families and nations, dividing us into categories of right and wrong, good and bad, chosen and rejected. Countless women burned as witches and Jews incinerated as inferior bear witness to this kind of thinking. And within our contemporary Christian community, Protestants and Catholics continue to wage wars – both militarily and personally – on similar grounds. I believe it is a history of which we should not be proud, and one that would greatly disappoint Jesus of Nazareth were he alive today.

But we needn't be prisoners of our past. Instead, we can learn lessons and move on in more humane and soul-oriented ways. Whatever the original writer of this text may have had in mind, it is not difficult to see the damage exclusivist interpretation has caused. Wrestling with it personally in order to find a place for myself in the Christian community, I have concluded that I do not accept the exclusivist's interpretation, but rather understand the text as a metaphor for following the soul's path. Thus the 'way of Jesus' is understood as the *direction of soul* in the human journey – a direction that reveals union with divinity. Movement in the direction of soul allows us to come to God (the Father, in patriarchal language), because that is the soul's natural home: the place where it finds rest.

Recently, many Christian denominations have grown in the direction of ecumenism, that is, an acceptance of the validity of other denominations. Recognizing that there is more than one appropriate way to express Christianity is a step off the path of arrogance towards the humility of the soul's way. Ecumenism allows us to participate in our chosen denomination with dignity while respecting our sisters and brothers whose theology differs from our own. Ecumenical services are becoming more common; participants are rewarded by an enriched understanding of their own path, much like the artist who views her subject matter from other angles. The soul naturally looks beneath the surface appearances to the motivation of the heart. If authentic love is present, it accepts that the path is a right way.

An even wider path

Once we have moved to accept those within other denominations of Christianity, how do we relate to those beyond our Christian boundaries? Here not only images but even concepts of God may differ. How does the path of our soul guide us through such unfamiliar terrain? While we may be able to resolve differences within our own camp, moving towards an ecumenism that embraces world religions puts us on altogether new ground.

It has been said that to understand our own religion properly, we need to understand others' religions too. In terms of art, it is the range of greys between black and white that makes the image visible. The greater the range of greys, the easier it becomes to identify the objects and the more realistic – and interesting – they look to the viewer. The more we learn about the religious concepts of others, the more we are able to understand what it means for a person to be on a religious path at all. Through our similarities and differences we can glean insights into the relationship between humanity and divinity.

But openness to other religions can be difficult. While Christianity shares historical roots (and concepts) with Judaism and Islam, few Christians understand either of these religions except through the lens of their own. It is as if we three are distant cousins, each knowing little of the other except what is learned through members of our own family (not always the most reliable source for an objective analysis). Even more puzzling for many are Eastern religions, including Hinduism, Buddhism and Taoism.

Given that religious groups know so little about each other, it is not surprising that misunderstandings arise. I was once part of a group that met weekly in a Roman Catholic church for Christian meditation as taught by Father John Main, an advocate of silent contemplative prayer as practised by the desert fathers. The group was ecumenical, welcoming all who wanted to join. Arriving a bit early one morning, I was surprised to find everyone waiting in the foyer outside the chapel. The door was slightly ajar; when I peeked in, I saw a woman kneeling on the floor with her head and arms extended towards a candle on a raised platform. Someone whispered to me that the woman was a Buddhist who sometimes used the chapel. No greetings were exchanged as she left. Much later I learned the woman was a practising Hindu, not a Buddhist. Sometime afterward, I shared this incident with the woman herself. She was amused and recounted an experience of her own. When someone once asked her whether she had read the Christian Bible, she had answered 'yes.' However, further conversation had revealed that what she had actually read was the Book of Mormon!

My introduction to Eastern religions has been spontaneous and synchronistic, a stream of events putting me in touch with people and writings that have served to stimulate an interest in traditions sharing few known cultural or historical ties with my own. Over the years, Hindu yoga, Buddhist meditation and Taoist Tai Chi have played significant roles in shaping my personal spiritual journey. As I have explored the texts, concepts and images of different religions, my understanding of the essential role of religion in people's lives has deepened. During my explorations I have had no thought of appropriating another religion and no fear that my new-found knowledge would jeopardize my own. Instead, I followed my soul's path along diverse religious trails, noting how frequently they overlapped. Learning about the religions of other cultures has helped me to fill out the tones in my personal picture of Christianity.

While there are many fine books available that describe Eastern religions, the best method of acquainting oneself with them is by reading translations of their sacred texts and interacting with their practitioners. By experiencing elements of other traditions in this way we can expand our notion of what it means to follow the soul's path. It turns out that the wider religious path is actually narrow, in that few find it and even fewer are able to follow it.

Unity in diversity

The prominent Jesus scholar John Dominic Crossan said in a recent lecture that he believes human beings are 'hardwired' for theology, that it is part of our nature to seek an understanding of God.[11] The historical art treasures of the world seem to support his hypothesis. Unknown to each other, primitive cultures with wide geographic and ethnic differences have left trails of relics that point to religious beliefs and practices. Most continue to astound us: the gigantic pyramids of Egypt, the massive formations of Stonehenge, and the enduring petroglyphs of North American first peoples are but a few well-known examples that show religious practice (albeit diverse) to be a common denominator in human evolution. With the development of systematic writing, which also shows cross-cultural diversity, peoples became able to refine and record their beliefs and to preserve them for future generations. As civilizations matured, religious forms developed independently in most cultures, diverse in expression but common in purpose: to answer questions about suffering and death and ultimate meaning. Religions grew as each culture addressed these dilemmas, each offering its own explanations and providing a specific path for development.

Gallery Image 4 depicts my understanding of the relationship between such diversity and unity. The title, *Ecclesiagenesis*, is borrowed from Matthew Fox. It means "birth of the Church." In this image, I am thinking of Church as something like a dynamic system of human energy in pursuit of transcendent wisdom. In the centre of the image is a red ring from which seven separate vines emerge. Each represents a different path, though the fact that there are seven represents completeness. Inside the red circle the roots of the vines intermingle as they fade into a common white. (In my work, white is often a symbol for God or transcendent reality.) Each of the seven vines represents a response to the question of transcendence. As the vines grow out from their common centre, they all first become green; but the farther they grow away from the centre the more each takes on a different colour. This represents the refinement of particular religious beliefs. On a Christian level, the undefined centre represents Christ, with the vines designating different denominations. On a larger scale, the centre symbolizes God (or ultimate reality), with each of the vines representing a different religious tradition. The overall composition of the image is dependent upon the diversity of the components. The artistic goal was not to merge the colours together as one, but to draw the viewer's attention to the diversity of colours, each of which contributes to the overall unity of the picture. Likewise, the diversity of religions expresses unity through the incorporation of each part into the larger whole.

Learning about other religions has filled out my understanding of Christianity by showing its place in the greater context of human spiritual evolution. The diversity of ways in which other religions approach questions about the ultimate meaning of life stimulates my imagination and nurtures my creativity. Each religion or religious tradition, like a masterpiece in a cosmic gallery, offers delightful insights in its own right; together they illustrate the paradox of diversity and unity. Spirituality benefits from diverse interaction, increasing our understanding of the relationship between religion and the transcendent reality to which it is directed. By becoming conscious of religion as an arrow, not as an end or goal in itself, we are freed to soar to a vantage point where we can see our own path in proper relation to the paths of others. As when tone and texture are added to an image, the resulting view will be fuller and richer, and will more adequately reflect the reality we seek to express.

EXERCISE

Take note of three objects around you at random. In your journal write what these objects have in common. Repeat the exercise, this time choosing objects as different from each other as possible. After focusing on the differences, turn your attention to the similarities and record them. Turn now to your personal conception of God. Write a short description of God from your own understanding, using words or drawing material. Think about how what you have written compares with traditional understandings. Note the similarities and the differences.

we are
unique and diverse
the greatest of things created
the least of things divine

we are
spiritual beings in bodies of flesh
imperfect by nature
made perfect in Christ

we are
a work in process
growing and changing
in constant transformation

we are
part of each other
woven into Creation's web
by a common thread

we are
light for the world
when we truly know who
we are

Chapter 5

SPECTRUM

Lesson III

COLOUR

Artist materials

Watercolour is a water-based paint that can be purchased in tubes or blocks, requires no solvents for thinning except ordinary tap water, and makes for easy clean-up. Combining pigments as you work with wet media will help clarify the theory behind mixing colours. A few brushes of synthetic fibres (#4, #8) will suffice to get you started; for these exercises, any thick white paper will do. You will need a palette or large white plate for colour mixing, a jar for water, and paper towels for clean-up. More specific information about supplies appropriate to watercolour will be given in Chapter 9, but at present, the emphasis is not on the medium; it is on mixing colours and exploring their relationships.

Individual families of colour are called *hues*, and each hue (e.g., red, green, blue) has an almost infinite range of possible variations. For example, tangerine, melon and peach are colours mixed from an orange hue. For the exercises in this chapter, the following hues are suggested: two reds (cadmium red light and alizarin crimson); two yellows (cadmium yellow light and yellow ochre); and two blues (ultramarine and cerulean). Other colours may be substituted, but it is important to have one light and one dark representative of each hue.

In preparation for the exercises that follow, lay out the palette by placing small blobs of paint on

Figure 5.1 The palette is laid out with small blobs of paint on the edges, with ample room being left for mixing colours.

the edges as in Figure 5.1. Leave the centre free for mixing colour and thinning the paint with water. Watercolours do not dry out like acrylics or tempera paint; they can be easily restored by adding a few drops of water to soften them before you use them. **(Figures in Chapter 5 also appear in colour at the end of the book, on pages 246-248.)**

A world of colour

The natural world, in addition to exhibiting a full range of tone and texture, is filled with every conceivable colour combination. While the tonal range can be captured in black and white, it is colour that really brings our images to life. Colour is born of light and changes according to differences in light. There are two systems of colour that affect our approach to its study. The *additive* system is at work as new colours are formed by the selective application of light. This allows lighting technicians and set designers to create visual illusions on stage. It also explains why the same colour can appear differently at different times. The *subtractive* system involves the process of mixing pigments to create colours. This system, which is employed by traditional visual artists, derives its name from reflecting rays of light that are not absorbed by objects. For example, objects that appear blue do so because they absorb, or subtract, all light rays but the blue ones – which are reflected back to the viewer. It is as if an object contains all colours within it, but as viewers we see only the surface. While artists use both systems, additive and subtractive, in various fields today (especially in the world of 'new media,' which employs computers), the subtractive system is used for the image-making described in this book.

Matching colours we see in the natural world poses a challenge – we must not only learn how to mix colours physically in different media, but also become familiar with their properties and relationships. When working in black and white, tone can be divorced from colour if you refer to a grey scale. However, the artist must also become sensitive to the tone – more commonly called 'value' – of each colour. The value of a colour refers to how light or dark it appears on the grey scale. Values for colours can be more difficult to determine than one might think. While some hues (for example, blue) naturally seem darker than others (for example, yellow), this is not always the case (sunflower yellow can be darker in value than baby blue). It is important, therefore, to make judgments of colour values based on direct observation.

The colour wheel

By creating a simple colour wheel in watercolour, you can become familiar with colour properties and relationships and the medium being used to explore them. For best results, watercolour paints are not mixed on paper but on the palette, where they can be thoroughly blended together (and thinned with water) before they are applied to paper. Beginning with the *primary* colours (red, yellow and blue), place one colour of each hue on your paper in the shape of a triangle, as in Figure 5.2. Primary colours are basic; they cannot be created by an artist, but all other colour is created through combining them. (Which red or blue or yellow you use for your colour wheel is not important for this exercise, but using the same colour for each step in the process will help you become more familiar with the characteristics of each of the colours you have chosen.) Next, *secondary* colours are created by mixing together *two primaries in equal quantities*. Position the resulting colour on your colour wheel between the colours used to produce it, as shown in Figure 5.3. For example, blue mixed with yellow results in green. Green goes between

Figure 5.2 Primary colours (see p. 246).

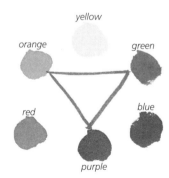

Figure 5.3 Secondary colours added by mixing primaries in equal quantities (see p. 246).

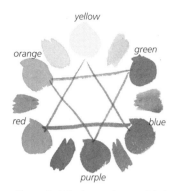

Figure 5.4 Tertiary colours added by mixing equal quantities of secondaries with their adjacent primary (see p. 246).

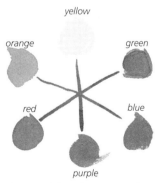

Figure 5.5 Complementary colours are located opposite each other on a colour wheel (see p. 246).

blue and yellow on your paper. Repeat the mixing process to create the other two secondary colours, orange and purple, and place them between their parent primaries. The result is a circle of six colours: three primaries and three secondaries. If desired, you can continue to mix colours using the same method: *tertiary* colours are mixed from equal quantities of a primary and its adjacent secondary. Each tertiary is located between the two colours used to create it. This fills out your colour wheel (Figure 5.4). You can easily see that if you were to continue this process, you would eventually have an even blend of colour, one fusing into another, all around the wheel. For ease of identification, it is helpful to draw lines to connect the primary and secondary colours on the colour wheel.

Another important colour concept for the artist to understand is that of *complementary* colour. Complementary colours are located directly across from one another on the colour wheel as shown in Figure 5.5: red and green; yellow and purple; blue and orange. Like black and white, complementary colours are polar opposites. In painting, these colours have two important functions. First, when juxtaposed, they help to balance the image visually by bringing out the intensity in the colour of their opposite. This contrast works in the same way as opposites of black and white, which also intensify each other when placed side by side. An example of how this might be helpful can be found in an image of a red barn on a field. If the barn has been rendered as red as the pigments will allow, its colour can be intensified further by adding green into the field directly surrounding the barn, as in Figure 5.6. The second useful function of complementary colours is found by mixing them together. Because they are opposites, they have the effect of neutralizing each other, thus creating colours known as *neutrals*. Red mixed with green results in brown, blue and orange make grey, and yellow and purple make taupe (Figure 5.7). Neutrals will vary according to which colours have been used to produce them, and how much pigment of each has been combined. Returning to our example of a red barn on a field, if either the barn or the field is too intense in colour, its colour can be neutralized by mixing its complement directly into the paint or by layering the complement overtop to subdue it.

Exact colour complements can be determined visually. To try this for yourself, stare intently at the coloured leaf (on p. 247) for two or three minutes, blinking as little as possible. Then, shifting your gaze to a blank white space, such as a wall, continue staring with the same intensity. Within a few seconds, the eye will adjust to the new visual field, and the shape of the leaf will seem to appear on the wall, but in its complementary colour! Applying this principle in a well-known lithograph, *Flag* (1968), artist Jasper Johns printed the

Figure 5.6 While these black-and-white renderings are similar in tone, when viewed in colour, the image with the greener field makes the barn appear redder. This illusion results from the juxtaposition of complementary colours, as seen on p. 247.

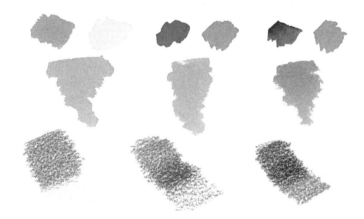

Figure 5.7 When mixed together, complementary colours produce neutrals. When layered, they subdue the intensity of their complement (see p. 247).

Figure 5.8 appears on p. 247.

American flag with green and orange pigments. The flag appears in its traditional red and blue if viewers use the method described above. Complementary colours remind us of important connections between opposites, which are vital to an understanding of balance in both art and soul.

Colour mixing

From my experience as a teacher, I have learned that not everyone sees colour in the same way. To encourage appreciation for one's own unique expression of the world and tolerance for differing opinions, I developed the following exercise. Using the colour wheel as a reference point, I ask my students to examine closely coloured objects found throughout the classroom. An object is selected, on whose colour students are agreed. Say it is purple. We note that purple is located between red and blue on the colour wheel. Given that few colours reflect a pure hue, the purple will tend to lean towards either blue or red on the colour wheel. Students stare at the purple object for a few seconds, giving their eyes adequate time to absorb the colour. Then, while continuing to stare at the colour, I ask them to say which way the purple leans. Even when the effects of light and shade which explain some of the differences in opinion have been removed, usually the students do not all agree. While we all perceive tone in the same way, the rods and cones of our eyes (peculiar to each of us) cause us to see colour differently, even when we view the same coloured objects as others under the same lighting conditions. In addition, many of us have devel-

oped preferences for a certain colour, which influence us to see it as leaning in one direction or another on the colour wheel. What is important to realize here is that no such identification is exclusively correct: our experience of colour will often legitimately vary from other people's.

An understanding of the basic concepts of colour relationships is all you need to begin matching and mixing colours. While the process can seem a bit daunting at first, if it is broken into steps, anyone can learn to do it. Begin by matching the colour in the natural world that you want to copy to a hue on a colour wheel (made of actual pigments from your palette) and take a close look at both. Asking some simple questions will help you become more conscious of the properties of the specific colour you are trying to mix. How does the colour on the colour wheel need to be altered so that it more accurately depicts the colour you want to copy? In which direction on the colour wheel does it lean? Is the colour of the object more or less intense than the hue on the wheel? Will it need to be neutralized by adding its complement? Such questions, asked consciously at first, become second nature as we persevere in mixing colour. When I was young, I played a mental game that sped up the learning process considerably. Imagining the pigments on my palette, during everyday activities I tried to visualize how I would alter them to create various colours around me. I also found that by staring intently at a colour, sometimes different colours within it would seem to glow, as if the components were separating. This helped me identify which colours from my palette needed to be mixed to give the colour I was viewing. Prolonged observation yields many insights – both in art and in soul.

Full spectrum

The understanding of relationships between colours allows an artist to depict the natural world more realistically. For an image to imitate the natural world, it must use the *full spectrum* of colour – that is, some colour from each family of primaries. For example, even when it seems that there is no red in the objects being rendered, red must be included somewhere in the image if it is to reflect the natural world. To the trained eye, the red is hidden in browns, purples or darks which, to the novice, seem devoid of other colours. We may think that an image of green grass with a blue sky does not need red to be realistic. But, as we observe more closely, we will see that not only do the greens need to include yellow or blue to diversify them, but they become appropriately less intense when their complement, red, which neutralizes them, is added. In the same way, the unrealistic intensity of blue may be reduced when its complement, orange, which is a combination of yellow and red, is added. The more you come to understand these relationships of colour and include in your images those colours that you do not immediately see on the surface, the more your images will project a natural balance. What you see on the surface is the result of unseen integration; your images will benefit from an understanding of this interrelatedness.

Finally, we should note that if an image has an area of isolated colour (that is, colour that has not been used elsewhere in the picture), that colour will stand out discordantly in the image. While this may be a desirable effect in advertising, in nature there is little discordant colour. A garden of the most diverse flowers with colours that might seem not to go together in other contexts are in perfect harmony in their natural setting (Figure 5.9). If an image is to imitate this balance, the isolated colour must be incorporated elsewhere in the painting; by keeping the colours of your palette to a minimum, you will be better able to ensure this harmony. As you develop your eye to identify colours present but not readily visible, you will decode nature's secrets, allowing you to apply them in your work.

Figure 5.9 A garden of diverse flowers (see p. 236). (Photo: Rose Caissie)

EXERCISE

Lay out watercolour paints on a palette or white plate, squeezing out a small amount of each colour. Watercolours are never used straight from the tube, so be sure to leave enough room for mixing – or get another plate for this purpose. Create a colour wheel, as shown in Figure 5.4, beginning with primary colours. Mix the primaries in equal quantities to make the secondary colours. Locate the primaries and the secondaries in triangles so that they are easier to find. Then identify complementary colours opposite each other on the wheel. Try mixing the complementary colours together to form neutrals. Now you are ready to experiment with colour mixing as described above. Mix several shades of each colour you are trying to match. Be sure to keep the paint thinned with water. Fifteen or twenty minutes a day will go a long way towards increasing your comfort level in mixing colour.

AFFIRMING THE SOUL'S PATH

The illusion of identity

While the study of tones and textures led us to consider our relationship with others, the spectrum of colour provides a metaphor that can be applied to our inner life. Each of us is like a ray of white light or a canvas covered in black pigment. Notice that seeming opposites of black and white have much in common: what appears on the surface as a single colour is actually the result of combining all the colours of the spectrum. Shone through a prism, white light separates into a rainbow of individual colours; mixing together all the colours in pigment form results in black. Either way, what we see on the surface is the result of unseen components. Similarly, when people interact, only the surface of their personality and character is immediately evident to others. And although we may get to know someone well, we still cannot claim to know them fully. More important, perhaps, we cannot even make that claim about ourselves! Each of us houses a mass of psychological material collected over a lifetime of experience, only a fraction of which is visible.

James Hillman, echoing the Gospel of Matthew, chapter 7, says that "character is revealed through actions."[12] But even this assessment seems inadequate. For example, we can appear generous if we give without complaint or apparent regret when asked. But on the inside, we may harbour resentment or wish to appear generous for some selfish gain. Alternatively, we can seem stingy to an observer if we do not give when asked. But perhaps we are refusing to give because we sense that some greater good will be achieved only by our *not* giving. In either case, we can agree that the tree is not always known by its fruit – sometimes the roots must also be checked!

When asked to describe ourselves, we may outline our physical appearance, identify a few personality traits or mention our occupation. However we do it, most of us have a self-image based largely on awareness of what we would like to be and of what we do not want to be. Knowing what we really are can be difficult given the confusing mixture of our needs, wants and emotions. The ego's response to our problem of self-identification is to create personae. These are like masks that allow us to present ourselves differently to the external world in different situations. For example, we do not usually act the same way at a social gathering as when we are home alone watching television. This does not necessarily mean that we are dishonest in presenting ourselves to others, but it can sometimes cause us to be unsure of who we are at the deepest level.

Gallery Image 5, *Persona Distortions*, is a lithograph illustrating the relationship between ego and soul in our struggle for awareness of personal identity. The central image in each section is a black drawing of the same face (this is possible through the medium of lithography). Layered over each of the three faces is an arrangement of tissues. Each is a torn piece of a coloured print made from the original face drawn on the litho stone and positioned differently in relation to the black image, and each offers a unique distortion of the underlying drawing. The black drawing (combination of all colour) represents identity according to soul – a holistic unit. The coloured tissues, printed in the three primary and three secondary colours (and thus representing the combination of all colour in another form), symbolize the attempts of the ego to create different arrangements for different situations. Taken together, the six colours that represent the ego are symbolically equal to the black, representing the soul: both represent a distinct method of arranging the raw material of our self. The difference is that while the ego routinely lops off some parts and retains others, the soul integrates all parts into a whole.

Identifying with the constructions of our ego leaves us vulnerable to external influences. This is especially evident in young people whose insecurities prevent them from making decisions for themselves. Disengaged from their soul, in part as a result of a culture that has not taken spiritual matters seriously, many adolescents look to others to determine who they are. Fashion preferences turn out to be more about designers than design, music is appreciated more for its popularity than its quality, and so on. The young rely more on what they perceive to be acceptable by their peers than on their own inner responses. Because they have not learned to trust the inner workings of their soul, they are driven not only by their own ego desires, but by those of culture as well. This process of borrowing opinions to substitute for our own often continues into adulthood. Indeed, many of us hold values adopted from others. But in order to get in touch with our true identity it is important to get beneath such surface reactions, peeling back each layer we have allowed to substitute for the unity of our soul.

Here is a personal example of discovering a discrepancy between my own values and some I had adopted from others. One day, while I was ordering coffee in a local donut shop with a friend, a man whom I had known slightly a number of years before came through the door. We chatted briefly. After he left, I confided to my friend that I didn't like that man very much. When my friend asked why, I didn't have a good answer. Upon reflection I discovered that it was my ex-husband who didn't like this man. I had adopted his attitude without knowing it!

The blind acceptance of borrowed ideas prevents the soul from making itself known. Prevalent in adolescents, it is also quite common in women, especially those who grew up at a time when men's opinions were valued more than theirs. At mid-life such women often begin to reassess their values and goals, keeping the ones that are authentically theirs on a soul level and weeding out those they have unconsciously taken on over the years. All of us have a need for such reflection. By examining our habits, attitudes and reasons and pinpointing their origin, we decide consciously which opinions we will hold and why. Such critical thinking is invaluable if we are to overcome the ego's powerful illusions in our lives.

Self-awareness may feel dangerous at first, as if we are poking at a carefully constructed house of cards that threatens to fall down around us. Perhaps we fear that we will not like what we find underneath the veneer our ego has created as a shield to protect itself. Or we may fear that while we will like the self we find, others won't like us anymore. We must move past our fears, for self-discovery is a necessary condition for spiritual development. If we are to affirm the soul's path for our lives, we need to take stock of our raw material – and become accountable for it.

A house divided

In the first chapter of Jeremiah, God tells the prophet, "Before I formed you in the womb I knew you" (Jeremiah 1:5). Each of our lives embodies divine potential. Each of us can find at least a spark of divinity within – which we can choose to fan or to ignore. While the ego commonly turns its back on the spark, fearing its own destruction, the soul longs to be revealed for what it is. But because our culture encourages us to favour the goals of the ego, many of us lack even basic knowledge of our divine–human connection. We follow blindly the illusions created by our ego, trying to find meaning in our lives while ignoring our spiritual nature. But the unenlightened ego cannot lead us to ultimate satisfaction, because it cannot fulfill our deepest needs. Although our soul provides what is needed for this deeper fulfillment, its path does not always correspond with the superficial desires of our ego, and so we feel a tension within. While the ego's achievements of obtaining a new car, a better job or personal recognition may make us momentarily happy, our satisfaction will be short-lived if our spiritual needs have not also been met. We are completely fulfilled as human beings only through our divine connection – the path of soul that leads to God.

This struggle between ego and soul is described by St. Paul: "I have the desire to do what is good, but I cannot carry it out. For what I do is not the good I want to do, no, the evil I do not want to do – this I keep on doing" (Romans 7:18-19). We feel like a house divided, pulled one way and then the other, unsure of who we really are. While the ego may seem to be in charge, the voice of our soul is never completely silenced. What we need is an alignment of values that allows the ego and soul to work in harmony. Since it is our soul that is connected to God, we must find ways to adjust the desires of the ego in the direction of the soul if we hope to find inner peace. As the ego is encouraged to follow the path of the soul, it becomes enlightened. This transformation is felt as the emergence of a new self, and the tension is diminished. But the struggle is not over. Harmony is maintained only if a spiritual discipline is in place to affirm the soul's path and keep the ego motivated to follow.

Paul's struggle in Romans is echoed by Thomas Merton, who sought to understand the relationship between his false and true selves. Merton considered the self-interested ego to be his false self. He writes: "This is the man that I want myself to be but who cannot exist, because God does not know anything about him…. Thus I use up my life in the desire for pleasures and thirst for experiences, for power, honour, knowledge and love, to clothe this false self and construct its nothingness into something objectively real."[13] The illusion of identity created by our false self directly opposes the emergence of our true self, stealing time and energy from fulfillment of the soul's objectives. Of the true self Merton writes, "our inner self awakens, with a momentary flash, in the instant of recognition when we say 'Yes!' to the indwelling Divine Persons. We are only really ourselves when we completely consent to 'receive' the glory of God into ourselves. Our true self is, then, the self that receives freely and gladly the missions that are God's supreme gifts... any other 'self' is only an illusion."[14]

Scattered throughout the Bible is encouragement for us to be holy or perfect as we imitate God (who is described in these terms). The unenlightened ego or false self misunderstands, confusing perfection with the illusions it has created. The false self rejects whatever it feels to be in conflict with perfection as viewed from its own perspective. But the soul understands the call to perfection as a quest for wholeness. This requires acknowledging everything that makes us who we are; there is nothing intrinsically bad about us – the raw material of our lives is like a palette of colours accessible to both ego and soul. Neither is the true self perfect by the distorted standards of the ego, but it is complete when seen from the perspective of the soul. In this perspective, we acknowledge a full spectrum of qualities, all of which need to be integrated into the final work in a way that affirms the path of the soul.

As a young person, I remember being attracted to the biblical figure of King David. Religious leaders extolled the virtues of David as one who overcame his imperfections, but I preferred to think of him as one who loved God despite his imperfections. While David's affair with Bathsheba, and his role in the subsequent murder of her husband, Uriah, cannot be overlooked or condoned, the text reveals a real human struggle between desire and responsibility. Sometimes David was blinded by his ego, as we all are, but he never stopped loving God. That the David who murdered could be the same David who loved God in the Psalms is a truly remarkable testament to our complexity as human beings. Like David, sometimes we fail. But by admitting and accepting our shortcomings, we can weave what we learn from them into our ongoing story and continue along the path of the soul with integrity.

Claiming our true self

The number of major and minor adjustments that had to take place for us to be who we are is staggering. Not only did the universe have to evolve in a particular way to provide a solar system with a planet capable of supporting life, but also the genetic code that contributes to our individual physical, emotional and spiritual characteristics had to develop through a long ancestral lineage. Since our birth, we have had to manoeuvre through illness, accidents, the decisions of others, and the consequences of our own choices in order to be who we are right now. In many ways, our existence can be compared to surviving a stroll through traffic on a busy freeway at rush hour! The result of this mind-boggling series of events is a complex, one-of-a-kind individual. While the same might be said of trees and dogs, our evolution as human beings includes advanced consciousness – something unparalleled in the known universe. Considering our unique situation in this world, and the improbability of our existence, the least we can do is use what we have been given to the fullest. Whether we are bookworms or sky-divers, we must become more fully who we really are beneath the illusions of our ego. To be diverted by the ego desires of wealth and power for their own sake is to miss the fullness of what life offers us.

Because of our advanced consciousness, we have the capacity for a kind of love that can be called intelligent. As human beings we care whether children starve and suffer, even if we don't know them personally. Unlike adult wolves and rabbits, which may eat their young to protect them from predators, we can use intelligent love to find other ways to deal with such problems. While the ego is affected by our instinctual responses and genetic history, distorting our perceptions and distracting our attention, the soul recognizes our higher calling: to add intelligent love to the universe. Through our total commitment to this kind of love – not of things or power, but of truth, justice and mercy – our true self emerges.

The process of becoming our true self involves a painful weeding out of the false selves we have created in response to our ego's desires. Like Lucifer, who elevated himself to divine status, an inflated ego distorts love in grotesque ways. Taking without giving, we become 'full of our-selves,' and disrupt the natural flow between our-selves and divinity. The soul is a channel for divine love – not only *to* us but *through* us. As the soul's

path is affirmed, we discover the true purpose of our human journey.

Jesus of Nazareth understood the importance and priorities of love. Echoing the author of Deuteronomy, he condensed the ten command-ments into two. The first (and greatest, we are told) is to love God with all our heart, mind, and strength and soul (Mark 12:30). This requires us to align all our emotional, intellectual, physical and spiritual capacities in the service of God. While the soul is happy to pursue this objective, the ego often gets lost in its own illusions, confusing love for God with love for other things. But for the true self, the enlightened ego, loving God is essential; it opens the gates of love, allowing the energy to run both ways between God and itself. Thus we are able to fill ourselves with spiritual energy, which strengthens us to reflect God's love in the world as no other creatures can.

Jesus' second commandment is to love others as ourselves (Mark 12:31). We cannot fully love others if we do not also love ourselves. The process of loving and being loved provides a deli-cate balance necessary to sustain love. As human beings we have the capacity for physical acts of love that demonstrate the love of God in the world. As individual messengers of divine love, it is in our overall best interests (personal and collec-tive) to dispense God's love to others, allowing us to maintain the free-flowing connections between God, ourselves and others. In order to do this we must resist the self-interested desires of our ego. From the ego's perspective, loving oneself means loving the illusions of self the ego has created; love for God and others is then filtered through the lens of this distorted self-love. The soul, on the other hand, recognizes self-love as part of a process of self-acceptance that also enables us to love others.

Thomas Merton provides an analogy: "A tree gives glory to God by being a tree. For in being what God means it to be it is obeying [God]. It 'consents,' so to speak, to God's creative love. It is expressing an idea that is in God and that is not distinct from the essence of God and therefore a tree imitates God by being a tree."[15] In the same way, the very best we can do on our human journey is to affirm what we are meant to be: enlightened egos following the path of the soul in a way that incorporates all that is unique to ourselves.

Self-acceptance

Spirituality is the method by which we untangle the angels and demons within ourselves. While the ego may at times seem to seek to destroy the soul in its perverted quest for power, the reverse is never true. The path of the soul is not one of rejection or destruction, but of harmony and peace. These are achieved by accepting our multi-faceted identity as unfinished works in a divine creation. By affirming the soul's path, we agree to work with the rainbow of emotions and events that constitute our lives, continually reshaping them as our soul's awareness of what is needed grows in our consciousness. We do not have to wait (in

fact, we cannot wait) until we are perfect in order to advance spiritually. Like David and even the disciples of Jesus, who continually misunderstood him, we are not ultimately bad or evil, but merely human beings struggling to redirect our ego towards the objectives of our soul.

Accepting ourselves has not always been easy for those who have walked the traditional Christian path. If we were made to believe from a young age that we were sinful from birth, self-hatred may seem more palatable than self-love. Although we have been encouraged to love others regardless of their sinfulness – to hate the sin, but love the sinner – we may have received little direction for loving ourselves. And while various religious denominations offer procedures and practices (grounded in theology) that address the issue of our sinfulness, many people are psychologically wounded as a result of years of self-loathing and distrust.

The doctrine of original sin (the idea that we are sinful by nature) can be traced to St. Augustine's struggle with the question of infant baptism in the fourth century. And while hints of the not always benign influence of Augustine's personal psychology can be found in the formulation of his ideas,[16] Christianity nonetheless accepted and developed his thesis, firmly rooting original sin in the tradition. But the doctrine of original sin is not the only lens through which to interpret ourselves as Christians. The Genesis stories tell us that we are born in the image of God – and that we are *good*. Even though we make mistakes, our goodness is affirmed as we express God's love in the world through our actions. Rather than over-emphasizing the negative qualities of our ego's distortions, we can look to the positive possibilities of the soul – interpreting our existence as an 'original blessing.'[17] As human beings, we struggle with our raw material much as an artist struggles with an image, moving and shifting pigment until the colours of the composition are balanced. All the colours are needed if the best representation of the natural world is to be given. Likewise, as we accept the full spectrum of what makes us uniquely who we are, we can begin the process of consciously arranging our lives in ways that bring fulfillment and peace – both to ourselves and others.

EXERCISE

In your journal, make two columns, then list what you perceive as your positive and negative qualities. Assign different colours to each of the traits using coloured pencils or pastels or paint, then set the list aside. Later, make several arbitrary designs (doodles) using these same colours, with each image on a separate page. Let some time pass (at least an hour), then return to the coloured drawings and 'translate' the colours into the qualities you had linked with them earlier. Reflect in your journal on the relationships of colours and traits from the exercise and on how each contributes to an overall design.

you fill me
with your self
until I shine

I shine into
the darkness
and glow brightly
with your light

your light
permeates my soul
and overflows
into the world

the world
will know your love
because
you fill me

Chapter 6

REVELATION

Lesson IV

LIGHT

Artist materials

Exercises described in this lesson emphasize the visual qualities of light. Materials used include coloured paper, charcoal and light-coloured pastels. Images created from previous lessons provide a base for further experimentation.

Let there be light!

Most of us take light for granted. While our attention in this book has thus far been focused on the accurate depiction of the proportions and surfaces of natural objects through observation, without light this would not be possible. It is light that enables us to see at all, illuminating our physical world, creating illusions and helping us to create them. Just as the soul needs spiritual light to reveal its path, the artist relies on physical light to distinguish one object from another. Without the changes caused by reflecting and absorbing light, we would not see the words on a page, the table in our kitchen or a bird flying across the sky.

Magicians have long known the secret power of light in creating illusions. In art as well, the effects of light captured on our paper or canvas help to give our images the appearance of three-dimensional form in two dimensions.

One of the most beautiful sights in eastern Canada is the brilliant colour of the leaves in autumn. From deep crimson to bright yellow and almost fluorescent orange, they are breathtaking, no matter how often we see them. In every beginner painting class, at least one person chooses such a subject for his first painting. But unfortunately, this type of beauty is very difficult to capture in a painting (if the artist's intention is realism), because while there is great variety of colour in such subject matter, there is little change in tone: looking at the hills of Cape Breton in mid-October on a cloudy day reveals little contrast between the values of their individual colours. Only the addition of natural sunlight catching the tops of trees provides the contrast of dark and light that helps simplify the task for beginners.

The Renaissance term for the interplay of light and dark to create the illusion of volume and depth in painting is *charioscuro*. In the works of artists such as Rembrandt, this illusion is so masterfully crafted that it seems the people in the images are not painted, but are standing still before us. Careful attention to the properties of light as they appear in tone and colour in the natural world guides artists to create such realistic impressions. No gimmicks are needed to produce these effects, just laborious observation and reflective application.

The term 'light source' traditionally refers to the direction from which light emanates in a painting. The light source can be located within the frame of an image, or the image can record light flow from a source beyond its boundaries. Knowing the direction of light is an important step in helping the artist build a realistic image. Consistency in the direction of light not only makes the image believable, it can add drama when exaggerated. But direction is not the only important attribute of light in artwork, as one of my students discovered. As part of a project, he was to complete a series of drawings with a "light source clearly identifiable by the viewer," which meant that the direction of the light in his image should be apparent. He submitted his assignment with this note: "Light source – fluorescent bulb"! His mistake provided a natural segue into the next lesson – the effects of the quality of light.

Anyone who has painted an entire wall or room based on a sample selected from small paint chips will understand the influence of light quality on colour in three-dimensional space. A blue wall, for example, will look very different at different times of the day. For this reason, the effects of light on colour are important in an image. Light causes colour to take on different appearances, each of which must be treated as a specific colour in its own right in the painting process. If we look at grey rocks (rocks that we know to be grey in natural daylight) at sunset, they will appear to be a different colour than at high noon or sunrise due to changes in direction and quality of reflected light. While we may know with our left brain that the colour of the rocks is grey, it is important not

Figure 6.1 Rembrandt was truly a master in his handling of light, as can be seen in this image, The Blindness of Tobit. *(University of Michigan Museum of Art, Bequest of Margaret Watson Parker 1954/1.310)*

to let our knowledge of the rocks influence our rendering of what we see. This is an example of a left brain–right brain conflict in the mind of the artist. We must learn to let go of what we know in order to experience what we see, just as the soul must sometimes learn to release its understanding of spirituality in order to embrace more fully a spiritual experience. The effects of light are experiential and if we intend to capture the essence of the moment, colours must be perceived as they are. As artists, we are not making a diagram to describe objects but are recording our personal response from a particular moment in time and space. In the works of painters such as Rembrandt we see the result of careful consideration to the details of both aspects of light – direction and quality (Figure 6.1).

Light source

The direction of light affects what we see in the natural world. In broad daylight, direction may be difficult to discern because not only does light stream from above, it is reflected to some degree by every surface it touches. While a dull black surface absorbs much light, reflecting little, highly polished surfaces absorb almost none, reflecting light in various directions depending on the shape of the object. Observation of direct and indirect light teaches us to create images that better rep-

resent the natural world. Note the differences in the images of Figure 6.2. One image shows an object drawn to look like the object it represents, with little attention to a consistent light source. The second adds to the realism by incorporating a consistent source of light. This object appears more three-dimensional because an illusion of depth has been created. All light comes from a specific source; in creating images we need to be able to identify the direction. For example, if we are painting an image in a room lit by natural light from two windows, at first we may be unable to judge the direction of the light merely from observing objects in the room. If we close the curtains of one window, the direct source of light becomes more apparent to us, and by squinting as we view objects, we should have a clearer indication of the light's path. We also need to be aware of the reflection and absorption of the light by different surfaces throughout the room. Reflected light provides important secondary sources, which must also be considered if images are to look natural. By becoming more conscious of the interplay of light, we inform our intuition and acquire important information for rendering images. Of course, an artist can deliberately distort light sources to generate interesting images; his knowledge of light can give him better control over the effect he hopes to create in the mind of the viewer.

Figure 6.2 *The shell on the left concentrates on the shape without attention to a light source. The one on the right uses light to create an illusion of depth, translating the visual properties of three-dimensional space into two dimensions.*

In the last century, quantum physics revealed that light is experienced both as a wave and as a particle. This fact provides helpful metaphors for understanding the dynamics of light in the art-making process. While we can understand the direction of light by thinking of a wave following a prescribed path, we can also imagine light as a physical particle contained in our pigments. When I was young, an instructor in a painting workshop told us, "Cadmium yellow is an artist's sunshine." Thinking of a yellow pastel as sunshine in stick form, we can apply it to a drawing to help visualize the path of light. Using older drawings or paintings that we have set aside but saved, we can practise 'drawing light.' Deciding upon a specific light source we 'apply light' to the image by adding cadmium yellow (or some other light colour) to the areas that would come in direct contact with the light, given the angle we have chosen (Figure 6.3). Using another colour, such as blue, we can identify the reflected light and apply it to our image as well. Such awareness of light gives us power to bring our images to life by intensifying the illusion of three-dimensionality.

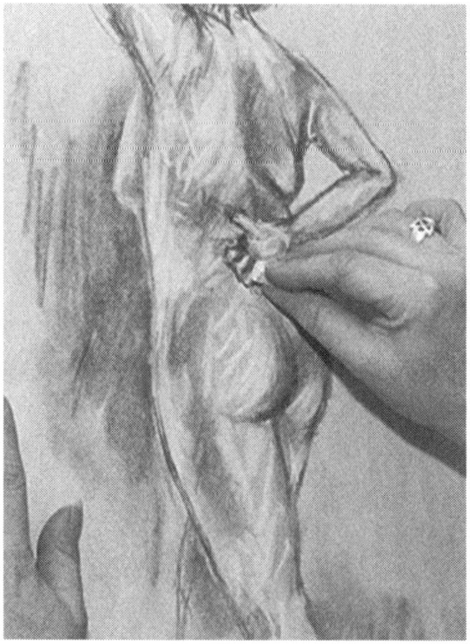

Figure 6.3 White chalk is used to add light to this charcoal drawing.

The direction of light can also be used to create drama. Think of a sky with great cumulus clouds through which beams of light reach from the sun to the ocean. A cliché in art, such a sight in real life fills us with awe. Paths of light and shadows created by early morning and late-afternoon sun were a favourite subject of mine for years. It seemed to me that the dense tone of shadows created a world as substantial as the real world of objects (Figure 6.4). Light brings to life another level of reality for those who train their eyes to see it. In painting or drawing, light and shadows are as concrete as any other surface – they require the same amount of pigment. And yet we know from our experience that they are not concrete. Our willingness to release what we know in order to express what we experience in the present moment permits creativity and spirituality to merge in artmaking.

The exaggerated use of light allows an artist to change a boring illustration into a more dynamic statement. While ordinary daylight (sometimes

Figure 6.4 This watercolour shows the strong directional shadows of late afternoon sunlight.

Figure 6.5 Note how these two images of a lit candle differ: on the left the light from the candle flame is barely observable, while on the right, because other sources of light have been reduced, the light from the candle is more dominant.

called *high key* lighting) provides a light source that allows many details to be viewed, there are times when we want something more dramatic to make our point. *Low key* lighting emphasizes a tonal range in which there are more 'darkest darks' and 'lightest lights' than would be seen in natural daylight. The primary light source in this case is more obvious and details are emphasized less, except in the areas that are well lit. In such images, the contrast between the known and the unknown creates an aura of mystery. (Compare the images in Figure 6.5.) With low key lighting, the artist creates a visual environment that stimulates the imagination and invites the viewer to fill in the interpretative blanks. In such an image the viewer's response is dictated more by his own personal experience and psychology than by the artist's interpretation of the objects.

Creating light

Working in colour, we notice through our observations of differences in the natural world that rather than simply adding white to lighten a colour and black to darken it, sometimes colours will need to be lightened with yellow or green, or darkened by adding blue or red. For practical purposes, in order to duplicate such variations in the natural world, it is helpful to mix at least three slightly different colours for each object we want to imitate. Used together, these colours will help produce a better likeness than if we used a single mixture. I like to call the first colour the 'fabric swatch.' Here we can imagine ourselves matching curtains to a rug. It is the colour we refer to in conversation, such as blue or green or tangerine or aqua and so on. The other two colours are variations as they might appear in light and shade. By carefully observing these variations in the actual objects, we can identify which colours need to be added to the 'fabric swatch' to imitate the effects of light in our image.

A final note: Since we are used to drawing everything in, we are inclined to draw light too. But how do you draw light on the white or light-coloured paper artists so often use? Answer: leave the areas of light blank and draw or colour around them. Because it can be tempting at first to use darker colours instead, experimenting with non-white paper can help. Note the drawing in Figure 6.6, where charcoal and white chalk have been

used on a paper of moderate tone. In this case we start with a middle tone, creating three dimensions by pulling the lights towards us with white and pushing the darks away with the black charcoal. It is this balance of light and dark that creates volume in our images.

EXERCISE

Using a moderate-coloured paper, charcoal and white chalk or pastels, draw a still life as in Chapter 3, using charcoal for shadows and white for highlights. To help you understand the flow of light further, create 'sunshine' in an old drawing or painting by adding yellow or a light colour to indicate where light would hit each object from a light source you select. Think about which areas would be hidden from the light and which would be most exposed. Think also about which areas might be made visible by reflected light; use another colour to indicate those areas in your image.

Figure 6.6 By making both black and white marks on a paper of medium tone, we can push and pull our image toward and away from us, creating an illusion of depth, and learning the importance of using the colour white for light.

ILLUMINING THE SOUL'S PATH

Spiritual light

In the first chapter of the first book of the Bible, God's first act is to intersperse the darkness with light. The image of light is one of the most frequently used – and most easily understood – in the Bible. Even those of a more literal bent would be hard-pressed to deny that Jesus' claim "I am the light of the world" is a metaphor. Just as understanding the physical properties and effects of light is important to an artist, so understanding this spiritual light will aid the connection to our soul. Physical light sources can be experienced directly or indirectly, as can spiritual light. Moments of direct connection with our soul feed us in spontaneous bursts of light that strengthen us on our journey. But, like staring into the physical sun, such intensity can become destructive if it goes on for too long. It is therefore the experience of indirect spiritual light that nurtures us through most of our daily lives. Gentler than direct experience, it can be compared to moonlight, allowing us to see through the experience of others by means of books, films, conversations and the like. Because it is reflected from the lives of others, the light is less intense, allowing us to absorb it without being overwhelmed.

Most living organisms need light to thrive. While it has long been known that plants suffer if they have insufficient direct exposure to light, it has now been shown that the same is true for human beings. In addition to raising our spirits, sunshine contributes to our physical health by providing Vitamin D. Recent research has revealed that some people, due to the lack of sunlight, have what is called Seasonal Affective Disorder (SAD), which causes depression and other symptoms. As spiritual beings, we also have an inherent need for spiritual light. Spiritual light reveals the soul's path so that we may more easily find our way in everyday life. When we are deprived of such light, we can easily lose ourselves to the distractions of the ego.

As we learn to identify it, we will find spiritual light shining through the darkness and strengthening our soul connection. In previous chapters we learned that we can see something without really seeing – two people can stand before a beautiful sunset, with one completely absorbed in the experience while the other gives it no more than a cursory glance. Our mental attitude prepares us to receive spiritual insight. Such revelations occur when suddenly the dots connect for us in a way we didn't expect and we understand something that had eluded us. Many great figures in science, art, philosophy and religion talk of such experiences playing a role in solving major problems. But such revelation is tailored to the person having the experience. Whatever form it takes, the insight is unique to each individual because it is channelled through a specific set of experiences. It does not fall from the sky completely unrelated to our lives, but emerges from deep inside as part of a percolation process in which the unconscious (personal and collective) plays a significant role. Insights such as those of Albert Einstein or William

Blake were the result of individual preparation and receptivity; either would have been ill-prepared to receive the revelations of the other.

A Zen saying, "When the student is ready, the teacher will come," illustrates that our body, mind and spirit prepare us for each level of revelation we experience. For example, we may read a book – such as the Bible – and find little of interest to us, then read the same book some time later and receive great benefit from it, as if we were reading it for the first time.[18] Or a song we have heard many times before may suddenly have new and great meaning for us. Because of heightened awareness, we are able to see with new eyes what has always been there, proving that it is not the teacher who has been absent, but rather the student. Spiritual revelation links together smaller insights in a gradual unfolding over time. As in art, we learn basic rules that we practise, thus enlarging our capability to handle more difficult problems. As spiritual beings, we become more open to spiritual insight as we overcome our protesting ego and become more familiar with the workings of our soul. By consciously cultivating an attitude of self-awareness and openness, we overcome the domination of the unenlightened ego and strengthen our soul connection. Before examining sources and benefits of spiritual light, it will be helpful to probe these metaphors a bit further, allowing our imagination to explore parallels between physical and spiritual light.

Seeing the light: exploring the metaphor

Science has shown that sometimes things can appear to take more than one form. As mentioned earlier, quantum physics has confirmed that physical light can appear as a wave or a particle, depending on the experiment devised to study it. Understood metaphorically, we can think of spiritual light as both energy (the wave) and object (the particle). For example, the words on a page, the relic in a church, or the artist materials in our hands, while merely things (objects) to some, are transformed into spiritual energy by others, depending on their attitude. Just as an artist trains himself to see physically what others cannot see, the true self is sensitive to the spiritual qualities of events and objects in everyday life, finding light in places where the unenlightened ego cannot.

Physical light provides clarity, allowing us to see what exists in the natural world. When light falls upon objects, the depth of their three-dimensional shapes is revealed to us. But how clearly the object is revealed depends on the quality of light. Under certain lighting conditions, it can be very difficult to see clearly. For example, an overactive imagination may convince us we have seen a figure outside our window when we are home alone, when what we have actually seen is the shadow of a tree. A yellow shirt may appear to have an orange glow in some circumstances, while looking greenish in others. In art (especially in film and theatre), the effects of light are deliberately manipulated to create illusions that encourage people to suspend disbelief during the viewing experience. This allows artists to make their points more poignantly as they create a specific mood (blue makes us feel sad, red tends to excite; dim light is gentle and mysterious; bright light is harsh and revealing).

Like physical light, spiritual light can provide clarity. Spiritual light illumines our lives so we are better able to see who we are, faults and gifts combined. It helps us see beneath the ego's illusions and persona distortions so that we can harmonize our soul energies in pursuit of becoming our true self. By watching closely to see if our actions properly align with the soul's motives, we can measure the true effect of spiritual light. If we find discrepancies, it may be that the desires of the ego continue to intrude. In such cases we may want to examine whether what we attribute to spiritual light is actually an illusion of the ego. Self-deception is the unenlightened ego's strongest defence!

When we turn on a light switch, physical light fills the room so fast that we sometimes forget it travels outward from the light bulb. The sunlight we feel on our face has travelled a great distance to arrive here, and the stars we see at night appear not as they are now, but as they were before the light that we now see left them long ago. But when dense objects stand in the path of light, its flow is interrupted. Light cannot pass through such objects; they create shadows, leaving a path of darkness where there would otherwise be light. In the case of highly polished surfaces, such as mirrors, light is reflected. Only transparent objects allow light to pass through.

The natural state of spiritual light is also one of movement. But when it encounters a dense or self-interested ego, it is absorbed, casting a shadow of darkness over our soul and preventing our true self from being lit. An ego that is too polished also prevents the light from getting through. Only an ego cleared through genuine efforts at self-awareness allows light to flow into and out from the soul. This process allows us to collect and share God's love, transforming us into vessels of light for others.

Physical light is a form of energy. Its power can be used to harm or to heal – as fire it can warm a room or destroy a house, as a laser it can be used to repair damaged tissue or to cause harm. The same sun that seduces us to the beach on a lazy summer day can produce a fierce sunburn on our skin. In respecting the power of light, we try to overcome the dangers involved in harnessing it.

Spiritual light has similar properties. It is a powerful source of energy, producing stamina when needed and providing hope in seemingly hopeless situations. But the misuse of spiritual light is no less dangerous than the misuse of physical light. Fanaticism is the result of misdirected spiritual light. Some spiritual leaders, convinced of the authenticity of their interpretations of spiritual experience by overzealous egos, seek to spread their light but instead cast shadows over the lives of those who follow them without questioning. Suicides and killings are almost sure signs that the role of the soul has been completely usurped by the ego. Spiritual light, rightly channelled, advances the soul's goal of generating love in the world. As the connection with our soul is nurtured, we can integrate spiritual insights into our daily lives and share them passionately without overwhelming or harming others.

Gallery Image 6, *The Light of the World*, is a lithograph that illustrates the effects of spiritual light. This image was produced by applying a material that resists ink to a lithographic stone in little dot-like blobs. The dark ink was then rolled over the stone. The etching process caused the wet stone to repel ink where the dots had been originally drawn, the light 'resisting' the darkness, so to speak. The dots represent the 'lights' of individual people – the concentration of light in the centre of the image suggests that greater light is achieved as individuals join together in community.

If we are to avoid being swept away by the illusions and distortions of the ego that saturate our culture, we must consciously search out ways to keep connected to our soul. When we become disconnected from God or each other we are no longer able to grow spiritually; instead, we become like the smaller, dimmer lights in the outermost part of the print. Since part of our nature as human beings is spiritual, fulfillment in this life depends on maintaining our soul's connection. This direct link to God provides us with infinite light, which we, in turn, pass on to others as part of our soul's mission to be a light in the world.

Light sources: direction and quality

Regular work on our spiritual journey results in an accumulation of light that can be stored for those times when direct experience eludes us. Spiritual light from indirect sources – books, music, stimulating conversation, visits to an art gallery, etc. – helps to ensure a well-fed and healthy soul connection. Light from indirect sources builds over time and makes us more susceptible to direct experience; reciprocally, direct experience makes us more open to and aware of indirect sources. We thrive spiritually when both are incorporated into our daily routine.

As we have seen, the state of consciousness required for artmaking is openness. When we approach our image-making without preconceived objectives we strengthen our intuitive nature, which puts us in touch with our soul. Resisting the concerns of the ego about whether our artwork is good or saleable, our attention is turned to the process itself. Treated as a spiritual discipline by combining mind, body and spirit in a common action, artmaking provides a powerful tool for revelation. For the artist, every painting session reveals something that was not known before the process began; the *aha!* of revelation is an ordinary part of an artmaking session. As viewers, we are led to the place of discovery through the act of viewing. Because art and spirituality are so closely linked, each provides light for the other.

One of the greatest sources of spiritual light in my life has been the Bible. Read over and over in different stages of my development, its meaning has changed for me, but its impact never does. As a child, I understood the Bible literally, but as I matured I became open to deeper levels of interpretation, an ongoing process that continues to bring its pages to life. My understanding of God and Christianity is illuminated by the Bible. Under the layers of culture and patriarchy, the gifted authors get to the heart of problems that have been real and important for human beings of all times and cultures. The holy books of other cultures have also been sources of illumination. We can learn much from sharing with each other.

Not all spiritual light comes from strictly religious sources. The social sciences of psychology, sociology and anthropology provide insights into common human behaviour (personal and collective) over time and reveal patterns in our evolution as peoples. The natural sciences of biology, chemistry, geology, physics and cosmology offer a wealth of stimulation and inspiration as theories are continually formulated and refined (or dropped) in the quest to know more about how we have come to be. Philosophy from Eastern and Western cultures addresses the question of why we are as we are (and why we are at all), and theology in its varied forms turns its attention more specifically to unravelling the mystery of God. All these provide spiritual insight, greatly illuminating the path of the soul. By exposing ourselves to light from a variety of sources, we have a better chance of seeing the bigger picture and collecting more dots to be connected as our personal story unfolds.

Spiritual light affects each of us differently, so we must work to find which sources best illumine our soul's path. My own journey through the Christian tradition has exposed me to a variety of practices. It is important to know what feeds us, what drains us and what leaves us indifferent. Of course, these sources will change as our ability to recognize and overcome the illusions of our ego matures. Journal writing is an excellent way to keep track of our reactions so that we come to know the needs of our soul more intimately. As we work towards spiritual and artistic development, we cannot help but become more fully in touch with our soul. If we are to participate effectively in the chain reaction of increasing love in the world, we must make sure that we get in touch with it. We must seek out those things, whatever they are, that give us energy and motivate us to love, for these can be identified as healthy sources of spiri-

tual light. We need to nurture them if they are to continue to nurture us. Inspiration gathered from diverse areas of life increases our capacity to meet the many demands of every day and prepares us to share ourselves more fully with the world.

Feminism: a modern revelation

We grow on a personal level as our attitudes and actions adjust to our heightened awareness. Collectively, these changes contribute to the overall evolution of our species. For example, while slavery was thought acceptable at one time in our history (condoned even by the Bible), clear-minded persons of the twenty-first century would find it unacceptable under any conditions. Awareness of shared humanity among all peoples has led naturally to the abolition of slavery and the rise of worldwide agencies dedicated to human rights. In the same way, the current emphasis on the fragility of our environment is changing how we consciously relate to the natural world. More and more people are coming to believe that it is morally unacceptable to dump our garbage where we please or to clear-cut our forests. Small groups are helping to bring about changes that affect everyone – for example, by making corporations reduce fossil fuel emissions from their factories.

One of the biggest eye-openers for religion – and spirituality – in recent times comes from the work of feminism. While the very word sends chills down the spines of some, it continues to be a breath of fresh air for others. Feminism has helped to uncover harmful patriarchal structures and attitudes that have long ravaged the spiritual and physical health of both men and women. It has revealed that hierarchical structures, which pit us against each other in competitive struggles of dominance and submission, take their toll on our minds, bodies and spirits. Acting as a prophetic voice, the feminist movement has inspired us to move towards holistic structures that value the contributions of all.

But religious (or cultural) shifts in perception do not happen quickly. This was brought home to me several years ago when I was asked to participate in a call-in program at a television station. In conjunction with an exhibition of my work (pieces of which were included in the television broadcast), I was asked to speak about the influence of feminism on religion and spirituality. Armed with quotes and books by feminist theologians, and looking forward to a lively debate on some of the finer points of feminist theology, I was disappointed when the half-hour program produced mostly questions about inclusive language. At the beginning of the show, I had referred to God as 'she,' which made some callers defensive. Most said that although they did not think of God as exclusively masculine, they did not see any problem with exclusive use of male pronouns for God. As one woman stated, "I know God is not male or female – he is spirit!" I knew what she meant, but her language did not exactly reflect her understanding. My use of 'she' in relation to God was jarring for her, as it was for me the first time I heard it. But once we really accept that God is neither male nor female, we will be equally comfortable (or uncomfortable) with either pronoun.

The need for inclusive language is but one of many serious issues in the area of religion that feminism has brought to light; it is our responsibility to act on such new awareness if we wish to move forward on a religious path that is egalitarian, inclusive and universal.

EXERCISE

Consider your sources of spiritual light, both direct and indirect. What in your life stimulates and comforts you? In your journal, make a list of what is most nurturing in your life, naming specific activities and people that you find inspiring. How much spiritual light do you find in your daily routine? How could you alter your routine to admit more light? After some reflection on these matters, resolve to allow more light into your life, perhaps through daily reading, a short meditation or doodling in your journal. Look, then, to the light you cast for others. Are there ways you could better nurture the spirituality of others? Record these reflections in your journal.

PART THREE

REALITY

Sometimes it is difficult to distinguish between illusion and reality. Most of us have had dreams so realistic that, upon waking, we could hardly believe we were dreaming. By expanding our perceptions of what is real, we open ourselves to new ways of understanding the world. Consciously or unconsciously, our interpretation of reality is shaped by our decisions and attitudes. As we become more conscious of our physical, intellectual, emotional and spiritual choices and their possible consequences, we evolve artistically and spiritually.

Transition is a constant in the human journey. We are never finished; we continue to evolve as long as we live. Learning how to experience joy in the midst of continual changes is the key to our happiness. As we release the ego obsessions that control us, the soul diverts our gaze from our everyday concerns to the beauty of life itself. Although we remain in the same place physically, we become able to see our journey through new eyes and welcome our role in the unfolding drama, content to stand on the periphery of understanding.

I feel
the pulse
of the current
around me

I feel its
energy and strength
sometimes
I break through
its surface
and dip my finger
into the electric
stream

as I touch
it
to my lips
it becomes
part of me
and I become
a part of it

Chapter 7

COMPOSITION

Lesson V

COMPOSING AN IMAGE

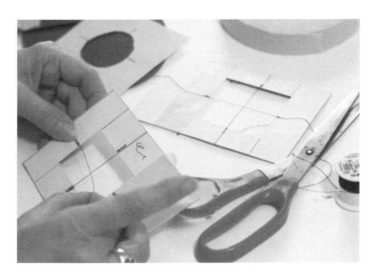

Figure 7.1 Viewfinders can be constructed out of paper or cardboard in a variety of shapes and sizes. They can be adjusted to match the shape of an artwork by using tape and altering reference points.

Artist materials

Any medium can be used for the exercises described in this chapter. While practising with charcoal or pencil is helpful, you might prefer to experiment with markers or watercolour. Choose paper appropriate to the medium.

A viewfinder will be used to identify compositions in the natural world. You can easily make one out of paper or cardboard as shown in Figure 7.1. The outer dimensions should extend at least one inch beyond the inner ones to provide a solid frame for isolating the composition. Mark the viewfinder in pencil with reference points at the centres of each side. Masking tape can be used to alter the inside shape as needed.

Design

With every line we draw, we consciously select what we will include and exclude in our compositions. By making such decisions we participate in the act of design, which means, in art, to plan. We compose deliberately instead of allowing things to fall together accidentally. The selection of objects on our desk or dinner table at any given moment will represent a certain arrangement or composition, but it will probably be accidental. Often, indeed, we allow random selection to determine how things are composed – both in art and in life. In this chapter, however, we will focus on deliberate composition. The more informed you become about your choices in composing, the more power you will have to make constructions that yield the results you want.

Thus far in these art lessons, we have focused mainly on rendering objects as they appear. We have seen that lines and shapes block in proportions by identifying positive and negative spaces; tones and textures help to differentiate between

Figure 7.2 A closed form (left) reveals more of the narrative by including details selected by the artist. An open form (right) restricts information given by the artist and invites a broader range of interpretation by the viewer.

the shapes produced by lines; and an understanding of colour and light prepares the way for greater imitation of the natural world. But in addition to learning how to use artist materials and how to render individual objects, we must consider the relationships between objects and spaces on our page. Their placement will affect the message you hope to create with your work regardless of the media you use. Two important considerations here are *perspective* and *balance*.

Perspective

Perspective – the position from which an image is recorded and the vantage point to which the artist brings the viewer – is an important element of composition. As we gaze at a Turner sunset or a Van Gogh sunflower, we feel we have

been transported into the moment of its creation. Whether from high on some hilltop or at the level of a nearby tabletop, we take up the artist's perspective and see what the artist saw. Perspective is the point of view shared by artist and viewer. But as artists we are not simply bystanders passively recording snippets of life; our compositions are deliberate constructions through which we express our opinion. Besides the angle from which we view, we decide how much or how little to include in our image, and whether it will illustrate a close-up view or one from far away. If we want our images to be narrative, revealing a story, we will use a *closed form*. If, however, we want to be more provocative, we will choose to include only parts of the subject matter in our image, allowing the viewer more scope for interpretation, and so use what is known as the *open form* (Figure 7.2).

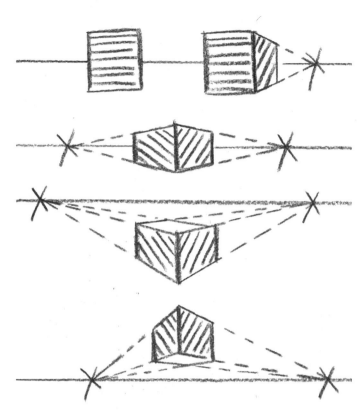

Figure 7.3 The solid lines represent the eye level of the viewer in relation to the cubes. The top two cubes illustrate one-point perspective. The cube on the left is viewed straight on; the one on the right shows two sides (in this instance the cube seems to recede from the viewer to a single vanishing point at eye level). The bottom three cubes illustrate two-point perspective. At eye level, two sides of the cube seem to recede. If the eye level of the viewer (the horizon line) is above or below the cube, an additional side will be exposed, which will also recede to the two vanishing points.

The more we understand the implications of our choices in composing images, the wider our range of tools for expression.

1. Linear perspective

Linear perspective involves the illusion of three dimensions on a two-dimensional plane. Using a system of vanishing points (points at which lines converge as they move away from the viewer) on a horizon line located at the viewer's eye level, we reveal the directions and angles of lines as they would appear from a specific point of view in the natural world. This is most helpful when incorporating buildings and other human-made structures into images. Beginners need only understand one- and two-point perspective. The cubes in Figure 7.3 will help clarify these concepts.

One-point perspective reveals how objects are viewed straight on or from an angle at eye level; the most we will see at once from our vantage point is two sides. This perspective suggests equality between image and viewer; it is the perspective of choice for newscasts and many documentaries. *Two-point perspective* reveals objects receding from the viewer into two vanishing points instead of one. Here we can view the object at eye level, seeing two sides as before, but both sides will be receding from our view. If the objects in our image are above or below the horizon line (which represents our eye level) we will be able to see an additional side of our cube – the top or the bottom. (Seeing both the top and the bottom of a cube or opposite sides at once is not possible in our three-dimensional world.) If the objects in an image are located below eye level, the viewer will seem to have superiority, as if looking down on the subject. If the objects are above eye level, the contents of the image have superiority, making them seem more powerful in the mind of the viewer.

From my present vantage point in my studio I can see my stereo at eye level, look up to see a shelf of CDs, and down at my teacup – but not all at the same time. Using the rules of linear perspective I can easily construct my view of each of these objects with accuracy. Such rules are foundational in drawing, born of the mathematics of drafting three-dimensional reality. We need not be consciously aware of their mathematical implications at all times; for our purposes it is only necessary to have a basic understanding of how they work. Drawings of the natural world that are to be believable must take into account the visual effects of linear perspective, even if the artist does not rigidly adhere to them. But remember that self-expression is more than mere description; the artist's psychological perspective (what we want to say with our work) must also be considered. For this reason it is helpful to think of the production of linear perspective as a device, not as the ultimate aim of our drawings. Attention to perspective without creative expression may result in technically accurate drawings, but the left brain concentration required for this task will do little to inspire an awakening of soul.

The viewfinder described in the *Artist materials* section will help you become more familiar with different perspectives. Using it as a camera lens, you can look through it in different directions: straight ahead, up, down. By closing or blocking one eye, you can better identify the perspective of your viewpoint as revealed within the opening and become more conscious of the rules of perspective as they appear in the natural world. As this knowledge seeps into your unconscious, it will increasingly affect how you compose your images. With practice, you will be able to determine when such rules have been broken in your own works and in the works of others. While many artists choose to break rules of linear perspective in their images, they do so not accidentally, but to emphasize their artistic statement. A good working knowledge of these rules will allow you to use them more effectively when you compose your personal statements.

2. Visual perspective

Sometimes called 'sighting,' visual perspective creates the illusion of depth by relying on information gathered visually through direct observation of the natural world. For example, we will notice that things look smaller as they recede from us, and that often colour becomes paler, perhaps bluish, as we look across a distant landscape. Also, we may observe that the overlapping of objects in nature creates a sense of depth in the mind of the viewer. An artist can use this information, tricking the viewer into thinking that something is behind something else in an image (Figure 7.4). Use of visual perspective will allow you to respond to the immediacy of your subject matter. Moreover, if you employ visual measuring, as described in Chapter 2, your drawing will naturally reflect linear perspective. If you draw the lines and shapes as you see them, they will conform to the rules of linear perspective even if you know nothing about

Figure 7.4 By placing objects in front of other objects we create an illusion of three-dimensional reality on a two-dimensional plane.

them because that's how things appear in the natural world.

Visual perspective is a response method of creating the illusion of space, a right-brain approach compared to the left-brain approach of linear perspective. While knowledge of both is helpful for composing images, it is the activation of the right brain that allows our soul to respond to the wonders of the world. As your personal style develops, you will become more comfortable composing images that emphasize those things that are most important to your statement. Whereas the left-brain world of linear perspective shows one right way for things to appear, visual perspective allows for – and, in fact, celebrates – the idiosyncrasies and individual expression of the subjective experience of the soul. Store the basics of linear perspective in the back of your mind, to be used if and when you need them.

Looking through the viewfinder once more, concentrate on the lines, shapes and colours you see in the natural world. Ask yourself a few questions to become more conscious of what you are seeing before you think about linear perspective.

Are there noticeable differences in the visual sizes of objects within the frame as they recede? What is their proportion ratio (two to one, etc.)? Can you note colour differences between the foreground (what is closest to you), the background (what is furthest from you), and the middle ground (what is between the foreground and background)? Are there marked differences, or only slight changes? Are parts of the objects you are viewing hidden by other objects? Finally, how can you use linear perspective to fill in the blanks regarding the unseen pieces?

Balance

Once you have determined the point of view, or perspective, for your image, the next step is to consider balance. Beginning with format, decide what size and shape of overall image will best serve your purposes. Should you use a square, a rectangle, a circle, or some other shape? What will best enhance the specific image you are creating? Format is an important element in the overall outcome of the composition. A circle is not merely a square with the corners chopped off. If you use a circle, it ought to be because it serves a purpose in your greater plan of self-expression. Perhaps it will allow you to emphasize circular shapes in your image. How you balance your image within the chosen format will affect the viewer. The more conscious you become of making such decisions, the more power you will have to create an image that will make the impression you desire.

Figure 7.5 The vertical axis in this watercolour, The Flowering of a Point, *divides the image into halves, each nearly a mirror image of the other – an example of symmetrical balance.*

There are four main kinds of balance, each eliciting a different viewer response: symmetrical, asymmetrical, radial and all-over pattern.

1. Symmetrical

Perhaps the most comforting form of balance is symmetry, or formal balance. The sides of the human face and body tend to conform to laws of symmetry: they are mirror images from a central vertical axis. We find the idea of symmetry appealing and calming. Buildings, especially churches, often use symmetrical design to create an environment that suggests peace and order. If these qualities are important for your image, you might want to consider a symmetrical composition, as in Figure 7.5.

Figure 7.6 The image on the left shows symmetrical balance: a centred picture with a candlestick on each side. The centre image is unbalanced: one of the candlesticks has been removed. The image on the right is asymmetrically balanced: the candlesticks on one side balance the painting on the other.

2. Asymmetrical

Beginners sometimes think that 'asymmetrical' is synonymous with 'unbalanced,' but this is far from true. If you think of a fireplace mantel with a candlestick on either side of a central hanging picture, you are imagining a symmetrical placement, as in Figure 7.6. If you remove one of the candlesticks, the resulting asymmetrical arrangement seems unbalanced. To balance the composition, you could put both candlesticks on the same side of the picture, perhaps shifting the picture slightly or adding another shape, or you could remove the picture altogether and place the candlesticks on one side of the mantel. Such informal balance, or asymmetrical composition, uses strategies of line, colour, shape and size to balance an image whose parts do not mirror each other from a central axis. This form of balance is the most common in representational visual art (art that seeks to imitate the natural world). Asymmetrical composition allows the artist to manipulate the elements within the frame in order to direct attention towards the focal area. On the whole, this form of balance can be dramatic, narrative and suggestive, creating a mood of tension or anticipation in the viewer's mind. Figure 7.7 shows an asymmetrical composition.

3. Radial

A radial composition involves a central focal point. Usually the viewer can 'read' it from the centre outward or from the outside inward. Sometimes radial images are designed to suggest the possibility of both directions. This method of balancing an image suggests movement to the viewer; an artist may use it to enhance her theme, as in Figure 7.8, a lithograph entitled *Inner Journey*.

Figure 7.7 While this monoprint, The Couple, has symmetrical components, its overall composition is asymmetrical. The vertical axis of the image runs through the figure on the right.

Figure 7.8 This example of radial balance, a lithograph entitled Inner Journey, can be read as moving inward or outward depending on the viewer's preference.

4. All-over pattern

An artist can create a feeling of monotony or order by using an all-over pattern as a form of balance in a composition. This suggests to the viewer an equality of the parts within the frame; one part is not more important than another. The pattern can be merely decorative or used to create personal statements that incorporate a theme of equality in relationship. Traditional quilting patterns employ this concept, but it can also be used effectively in other ways in visual art. Imagine a close-up of random pebbles on the beach or a photograph of the forest taken from the air. Figure 7.9 provides an example of this type of balance.

Using the viewfinder, again with one eye closed, find natural illustrations of symmetrical, asymmetrical, radial and all-over pattern compositions. Your face, the landscape outside your window, your thumbprint and the hairs on your arm provide ready examples. Extending the viewfinder for close-ups (open form) or bringing it nearer for expanded arrangements (closed form), you can compose a large number of visual images from the natural world, balancing each simply by adjusting the position of the viewfinder. In art, as in our spiritual life, adjusting our perspective allows us to see balance that already exists. With practice, you will soon be able to determine what is needed to create balance both in art and in soul.

Thumbnails

One of the most useful tricks for designing an image is to make a variety of small sketches, called thumbnails, before beginning. Doing so will allow you to make changes in the placement of key lines

Figure 7.9 This ink image of thumbprints is an example of a composition balanced by the use of an all-over pattern.

and shapes before you start a full-scale work. There are two main methods for using thumbnails. The first is to draw small boxes proportionate to the painting or drawing you plan to make, locating the major elements such as horizon line, main objects, etc., and erasing or shifting them until the composition is suitable. This is then used as a guide for the layout of the final work. The second

Figure 7.10 Thumbnail sketches can be created by shifting the objects within a frame or by altering the frame to suit the objects. Both work equally well in helping to create a balanced composition.

method is to draw elements as they appear in the natural world, perhaps using the viewfinder. Once you have determined the placement of the main elements, the outside edges can be drawn to suggest a format (Figure 7.10). The paper is then cut to those proportions. Both methods work well. Try them and use the one that works best for you.

Artists are not limited to compositions as they exist in the natural world. With your growing knowledge of the basic principles of art and design, you can take artistic licence in composing images by deliberately choosing the perspective and balance that best enhance your statement. Advertisers and filmmakers take full advantage of such information to attract consumers to their products, manipulating viewers' responses through subliminal messages. As you grow in power as a composer of art and life, take care to make decisions proactively so you can create outcomes that are more to your liking.

EXERCISE

Using the viewfinder, try to identify both the perspective and the balance of what you see through the frame. Decide on a suitable composition as you see it through the viewfinder. Note the elements of perspective, both linear and visual. Decide whether the format of the viewfinder is suitable for the image you plan to create. If not, alter it by adding masking tape (as in Figure 7.1). Mark the central points on the viewfinder and on your paper (which matches the proportions of the viewfinder). Try to draw what you see through the viewfinder in the arrangement you have chosen. Beginning students often find it difficult to arrange the objects in their drawings just as they are seen through the viewfinders, but with practice you will easily be able to plan and execute your drawings within whatever parameters you desire.

A Living Composition

Making a statement

After an artist has learned basic skills, she can become more directly focused on the statements she makes with her art. As drawing a house that looks like a house becomes less difficult for her technically, she may turn her attention to what she wants to say with her image by considering its effects on others. She can encourage a feeling of calm in her viewers by choosing sunny colours for her house, placing the house in a pleasing location (say at eye level or slightly below) and maybe even including some cats or dogs positioned in non-threatening ways. If, instead, she prefers to stimulate mystery in the mind of the viewer, she might consider less-defined (perhaps even monochromatic) colours, positioning her house at an unusual angle, maybe showing an open door or broken window. In each case the artist's overall statement is enhanced by her decisions regarding not only the content, but also the arrangement of elements within the image.

The composition of our lives can be compared to this image-making process. As we consciously consider what kind of statement we want to make with our lives, we can arrange the content (the 'raw material' of Chapter 5) in ways that emphasize our goals. While this is a common practice of the unenlightened ego in pursuit of its desires, the same principles can be adopted by the true self in pursuit of the soul's goals. Looking at our life as a single, comprehensive unit, we can understand it as a unique statement that expresses who we really are. Of course, unlike artists' images, our lives are not static, but are constantly evolving stories that can change with each decision we make. As we become more conscious of how we are composing our lives and as we deliberately reject the ego's illusions, we can create a new vision of reality that is more attuned to the workings of our soul.

Each of our lives is a unique statement – an account of one person's voyage through consciousness during a particular time in space. What we do with our lives (consciously or unconsciously) affects us and everyone we meet. One of my favourite examples of this comes from Frank Capra's classic film *It's a Wonderful Life*. Through a series of strange events, the film's main character, George Bailey (played by Jimmy Stewart), is given the opportunity to see what life would have been like in his small town had he never been born. Encounters and events that Bailey barely remembers turn out to have had life-changing consequences for others. This is true for us as well – our lives and our contributions are interconnected with other people's. Our influence on others is exerted in the most unexpected ways, both positive and negative, as we touch the lives of many, including some we will never meet. As we come to understand this dynamic, we must accept more responsibility for the effects of our interactions with others, making our decisions from the level of soul and consciously composing a life that truly expresses our unique set of gifts.

Gallery Image 7, *The Web*, helps to illustrate this point. It shows seven vines (three in primary colours, three in secondary colours and one in white) criss-crossing a circular format. Like something seen under a microscope, the vines intertwine to make a specific pattern – a composition. Had I chosen a different pattern, the final product would have differed accordingly. Similarly, the raw material of our lives can be arranged into a composition in many different ways. There is another point here, too. All the colours, plus white, are included in the composition of the images to represent wholeness; if one strand were to be removed, the arrangement would be symbolically incomplete. In this particular composition, each of the vines depends on the placement of the other vines for visual balance. Likewise, all our statements together are needed for the overall design of the divine composition.

While we can think of our entire lives as a single ongoing act of composing, it is helpful to approach each new day as a microcosm of that process. By aligning our daily activities with our ultimate goals for life, we are more likely to achieve what we set out to do. To borrow the idea of thumbnail sketches from art, we can mentally construct images of our lives as a whole, deciding whether adjustments are necessary today to achieve the desired overall effect and then composing our day accordingly. If, for example, we have an overall desire to be happy, we will be able to tell where we have strayed from our path by comparing daily results of such an overview with this larger goal. When we are guided by the basic principle of our soul, expressing love in the world, we can respond to the question "Did I express love today?" Answering with a simple yes or no, we can escape most of the ego's justifications for our actions. These quick thumbnails allow us to make corrective alterations at an early stage as we proceed with our larger composition.

One of the most helpful devices for detecting whether our daily actions are aligned with our goals can be borrowed from the Spiritual Exercises of St. Ignatius.[19] Checking at the end of each day, as suggested in the Exercises, to see where we have strayed from our objectives helps us to stay on course and provides incentive for the next day by wiping the slate clean. In the morning, another moment of reflection – this time concerning our intentions for the new day – helps us become more conscious of our goals in daily life.

The soul's perspective

Most representational visual images we encounter are rendered from a familiar perspective – such as a view of the Rocky Mountains from the foothills or a sandy beach viewed from a nearby hilltop. They jog our memories of places we've been or stimulate a desire to go there. But when we are confronted by images rendered from an unusual perspective, we are forced to consider new possibilities. Images depicting the sky from beneath a tree or a tree from directly above may be interesting, disturbing or stimulating, depending on our previous experience. They stand out.

As we begin to pay conscious attention to the composition of our lives, we will find that our choices of perspective are essentially two: the unenlightened ego's desires or the soul's perspective. Upon reflection, most of us would probably admit that we have planned – or adjusted – our lives mainly according to the ego's pursuits. The illusions we have accepted as reality have led us to make choices that, while strengthening and feeding our ego, helped to form a thick cloud over our soul. By increasing our consciousness through artmaking and other spiritual practices, our ego can be penetrated. Like artists who have been awakened to right-brain experience, we are presented with another perspective – a different way of seeing our lives. We can now alter the course of our lives by composing them from the soul's point of view.

Most of us are not as powerless over our lives as we might think. While everyone's freedom is limited in some way, many of us make prisoners of ourselves by narrowing our vision of what is possible. By convincing ourselves that we are not responsible for our circumstances or our actions, we relinquish the soul's power to compose our lives. Here is an example. Several years ago, I was taking a university course that was very important to me. I expected top marks and was willing to do whatever it took to get them. One day, one of my children needed to be taken to the hospital for emergency surgery at the time of a scheduled class. Since marks were deducted for absences (regardless of the reason), I made an appointment to see the professor, thinking I could convince him to make an exception in my case. He did not budge from his position. And while I was angry with him (because I did not get what I wanted), I began to see it was the perfectionism of my ego that was causing my problem. Missing one class would have no significant effect on what I learned

from the course, and the resulting difference in my grade would be minimal. The real issue was that I did not want to accept responsibility for my decision to miss the class. I wanted the professor (and myself) to excuse me because it wasn't my fault. This would provide my ego with an excuse should my grade be lower than I expected and relieve me from taking responsibility for my actions.

But the soul does not place blame, and it does not strive for the perfect mark or the best performance in competition with others. Its emphasis is placed squarely on its objective: to express love in the world. Clearly, in the situation above, had I listened first to my soul, I would not have needed to meet with the professor at all! Taking my child to the hospital was what I needed to do if my goal was to express love. It is so easy for us to become embroiled in the pursuits of the ego that we simply forget there is another way to orient our lives. From the soul's perspective, we will be led to explore what drives us in decision-making as we consider the ultimate destiny of our lives. But the ego has garnered enormous influence and power in our lives from centuries of cultural support and development. Our soul, like the right brain, is already at work within us but, largely underused and undervalued by our culture, it needs to be given permission to compose our lives. It waits quietly for us to discover its hidden resources. By learning techniques that stimulate them, we can strengthen our right brain and our soul, recognizing our power to make positive changes in our lives.

Artmaking and other spiritual disciplines help lessen the ego's grip on our perceptions, providing insights that strengthen our soul connection. Like Lucifer, the unenlightened ego has forgotten its mission as a channel of God's love, concentrating its energy instead on the illusions it has created. The effects of its mutiny are felt as tensions in our lives that can only be resolved by adopting the soul's perspective. By noticing false selves created by our ego to fulfill its ends, we can see the differences between the two perspectives, much as we could see the differences between the experiences of right and left brain in Chapter 2. The soul does not develop in the sense that it learns new things or matures through time. It is ancient, linking the experience of our individual modern life to God and, through God, to all other individual lives of all times. The soul does not grow; it is uncovered as we are released from our attachments to the illusions of the ego. Just as the right and left brain work together to help us produce the best art we can, a working relationship between ego and soul can emerge when consciously pursued. The ego, understood descriptively, is simply our point of contact with the external world and can be redirected to express what is contained in the soul. When this process takes place, we have an enlightened ego – we become our true self.

By injecting our lives with spiritual light through reading, meditation, artmaking and other soul-friendly activities, we diminish the ego's power to shape our reality. This change in perspective requires discipline. By gently including activities that put us more fully in touch with our soul, we see the contrast between ego and soul more clearly. Deliberately adopting the perspective of our soul provides a guide for decision-making and interaction with others, giving us a new outlook on reality that offers freedom from the tension the ego creates in our lives.

An ongoing composition

Our human life is a story unfolding through time; our personal statement is made by the finished product (which can only be assessed after we have died) and by the individual components that combine to make our story. It is the latter that concerns us most of the time because it is through living moment to moment that our statement is woven together, strand by strand. As in art, attention to the process results in an ability to create the desired product in a variety of ways. While it is often said that God has a plan for our life, this plan is not specific but is a guiding principle that requires us to live from the perspective of our soul. There are many ways to live out a life that embraces the divine plan. While the details vary according to our genetic makeup, our environment, and our ability to access our soul, the principle is always the same: to express love in the world. As we mature we will rearrange our lives from time to time. In this sense we are dynamic compositions, more like animation than still life in art.

Paul Tillich, a German-born Protestant systematic theologian of the last century, offers insights into the deeper meaning of this process that are helpful for contemporary culture.[20] Tillich understands God as the "Ground of Being." This means that God is the essence that holds all possibilities; human beings are born of that essence and retain a memory of it, like a spark buried within. Haunted by this distant memory, we feel a sense of longing that cannot be fulfilled by material goods or even by relationships with other people. Recall the words of St. Augustine: "My soul can know no rest until it rests in thee." What we need to be fulfilled is a reconciliation between our human side and our divine essence. Tillich calls this process of reconnection, a process that requires a new way of being in the world, *essentialization*. Christians find their example of this approach to life in the theological construct *Jesus as the Christ*, called "New Being" by Tillich. To understand this concept, it is important to think of the word 'being' as a verb as well as a noun. Jesus presents us with a new way of being. Following his example, composing our lives from the perspective of soul, we are reunited with our essence, becoming one with God while we journey through the human experience.

Tillich's system of *essence – existence – essentialization – New Being* provides a model for salvation. We are saved, regardless of denomination or religion, as we release our preoccupation with the illusions of our ego and compose our lives from the perspective of soul. In the biblical story of the rich young man who asks Jesus what he must do to inherit eternal life, Jesus replies that if the man sells all his possessions, gives the money to the poor, then follows Jesus, he will be saved – that is, he will gain eternal life (Mark 10:21). Jesus teaches that the ego's attachment to material possessions hinders intimate relationship with God and offers a new way of being that is as effective today as it was in the first century. Jesus' call to sell all our possessions and give our money to the poor, whether we understand it literally or metaphorically, invites us to make a statement with our lives by resisting the ego-dominated path that our culture promotes. It is a call to satisfy our deepest longings and give new meaning to life on earth for ourselves and for generations yet to come. The rich young man's choices – to follow the desires of the ego or to reconnect with his divine origin – highlight the difference between existence and essence. While the first keeps us on a path of illusion, the second opens the door to eternal life and thus a new experience of reality. How we compose our lives makes all the difference.

Finding our balance

As shown by the story of George Bailey in *It's a Wonderful Life*, our lives are intertwined with the lives of others. At times we may not be sure how best to integrate our inner and outer responsibilities. While the ego often ignores our inner needs, the soul motivates us to balance our introspection and extroversion by adopting a process of constant renewal, filling ourselves with love so that we might in turn express love to others. This rhythm is present when our soul plays an active role in the composition of our lives. As in image-making, balance can be achieved in different ways. The art lesson in this section offers four approaches for balancing an artwork, each of which provides a metaphor for balancing our spiritual needs with the everyday reality of our external world. Being aware of different styles for balancing our lives invites us to experiment with new approaches when and if what we are doing now no longer seems to be working.

The first method discussed for balancing an artwork is *symmetry*. As noted above, in image-making this type of balance promotes calm and order. Applied to our spiritual development, this style represents an even distribution of attention to our inner and outer worlds. In everyday experience, this means the regular practice of some form of spiritual discipline (such as meditation or art-making) through which the mind and body are aligned, so that we may become alert and focused in pursuit of the soul's objectives. Consciousness-raising through such discipline helps keep the ego in check, unmasking self-deception before it is permitted too great a hold on our lives. A symmetrically balanced life stays close to a central line between inner and outer activity like the axis of the mirrored components of a symmetrical image, allowing us to move from one side to the other while maintaining a sense of equilibrium. The inner and outer worlds are accessed rhythmically in harmonious pursuit of the soul's goal to reveal and express love.

Unfortunately, most of us do not have the luxury of devoting equal time to internal and external needs. In that case, an *asymmetrical* style of spiritual development can be adopted. As noted earlier, asymmetry does not mean unbalanced; rather, balance is achieved in a different way, by a more irregular rhythm. This style requires that times for spiritual development be set aside, but not necessarily on a daily or regular basis, as in the symmetrical style. By setting up 'appointments' for spiritual practices that pay particular attention to specific needs, spiritual growth can happen effectively. In both styles, the key is a regular commitment to a form of discipline, regardless of the pattern we create to implement it. Learning to recognize personal triggers that indicate a need to devote time and energy to spiritual development allows us to address our inner needs before the demands of ego override us.

A *radial* composition in art provides balance through the direct relationship between inner and outer spatial divisions, and an *all-over pattern* through suggesting equality of parts. Both styles suggest the same type of spiritual development: balancing our inner and outer lives by synthesizing their activities. Here we recognize that everything we do is part of the soul's reality. There is no movement back and forth between worlds because there is no separation; there is only one perspective: that of the soul. This approach differs from a symmetrical one in that inner and outer worlds are merged into a single activity. We find this style in a life given completely to the service of expressing love, whether in someone who is part of a religious order, a secular seeker who is committed to a cause, or anyone whose passion moves them to an all-encompassing expression. When adopted by the unenlightened ego, it can result in fanaticism, but when applied by the soul it can provide a wonderful expression of divine sharing.

People may find balance by using each of these approaches at different times throughout their lives, depending on circumstances and personality preferences. As we become aware of which approach we have adopted, we can assess whether that style is working for us. If it is not, we can experiment with other styles until we find a way to create balance that provides the stability and flexibility we need. All are valid approaches to implementing and maintaining balance between interior and exterior concerns as we journey through life.

Composing personal ritual

Ritual is traditionally employed by religions as a means of promoting the connection between us and God. The symbolism of ritual inspires and comforts, encouraging us to participate in the mystery of life at a conscious level. But for ritual to be effective it must have meaning for us personally. The rituals of others, while they may stimulate our curiosity, leave us empty when we lack a personal connection with the symbolism. As we seek to become more deliberate composers of our lives, we need to find rituals that connect us to the greater scheme of things. Personal rituals help us balance our lives by bringing us to the place from which we can see the reality of our world from the soul's perspective, opening the flow of energy between our soul and our interactions with others.

Artmaking and journal writing – as advocated in this book – can be important elements of personal ritual that provide insights into what stimulates and nurtures the connection with our soul. The material we gather through such insights can be used to compose rituals that will stimulate our imagination and encourage us on our journey. Personal rituals need not be elaborate; they may be as simple and regular as a prayer at mealtime or as spontaneous as lighting a candle before writing in our journal. Rituals help us mark events as special; they focus our attention on the moment and provide a bridge between worlds. While we participate in numerous cultural and religious rituals (from celebrating birthdays and buying presents for new homeowners to baptism and marriage), personal rituals give us the opportunity to underscore what is most meaningful to *us*. In Chapter 1, I described my personal ritual in preparing to do creative work. I also like to keep track of the cycles of the moon. Knowing whether the moon is full or new makes me feel closer to nature, and so I deliberately mark these cycles in my appointment book, which draws my attention to these things even in the midst of a hectic schedule. My morning routine of tea and looking at the ocean helps me feel centred as I embark upon my day. These small, seemingly insignificant acts help remind me that there is more to my life than external events. Through them I feel connected to my soul, invigorated to see each new day as a blank canvas on which I can create what is meaningful to me.

We can test our rituals, both corporate and personal, by simply watching to see whether they stimulate us towards the objectives of our soul. If they do not, we ought to reconsider their value for our spiritual development. We may try to become more informed about the symbolism of the ritual if it is corporate, or we may alter our personal ritual to make it more meaningful. While changes in personal ritual are simple to make, changes in corporate rituals may be more difficult. If, for example, we try to implement a change in the ritual of the Church, we may find that not all participants share our desire for change, or at least not right away.

As we take responsibility for composing our lives, we can become, as Francis of Assisi put it, "channels of God's peace," absorbing and distributing God's love as part of one divine breath. Our legacy will show what has been important to us on the journey and ought to be evaluated in that light. Like the workers who received different lots in the parable of the talents (Matthew 25:14-30), we are accountable for what we do with what we have been given. How we compose our lives will determine whether we can be called "good and faithful servants" in relation to our divine gift.

EXERCISE

In your journal, write the story of your life up to the present, beginning with the words "Once upon a time...." Consider different ways your story could be told (e.g., from a different perspective, with a different emphasis). Turning the page, literally and metaphorically, write a new chapter, beginning where the story left off. Reflect on what statement you want to make with the new story and how you need to compose your life in order to make it. Consider the decisions you will need to make. Begin to devise a personal ritual to help you keep focused on your goals, considering which form of balance outlined above will best help motivate you.

I must go
to the mountain
alone

the birds and
the trees
minister to me

they soothe
my wounds and
stroke my hair
to comfort me

I must lie
by the sea
alone

the new water
washes away
my dusty thoughts
and the sun warms me
with hope

Chapter 8

TRANSITION

Lesson VI

DRY MEDIA ▸ PASTEL AND COLOURED PENCIL

The action of repeating parts of the process that you understand helps to embed it in your psyche; eventually it will become second nature. Beginners tend to be able to go only so far with a piece before getting stuck. Then they go over what they have already done, sometimes reworking areas that may have been very good before the attempts to develop them further. If you notice that you are making no significant contributions to the image, it is best to leave it and begin work on something new. These unfinished pieces are not a waste of time: they let you practise new techniques and give you concrete images that you can use later to further your learning.

Artist materials

For the lesson on dry media you will draw in colour with soft chalk pastels and coloured pencils. Colours in both media can be purchased separately or in pre-packaged selections. Pastel paper comes in a variety of colours and has a relatively rough surface to attract the pigment. Smooth white paper is best for beginning your exploration with coloured pencil. A kneaded eraser can be used for both, but only for slight alterations. A commercial fixative or aerosol hairspray can be used on completed images. You will also need masking tape and some blank pieces of paper (Figure 8.1).

Transition and exploration

In the beginning stages of learning art, it is more helpful to begin works than to finish them.

Figure 8.1 Chalk pastels and coloured pencils are simple and inexpensive media for exploration in colour.

As information moves back and forth between your conscious and unconscious worlds, you will have times when it seems you are not making progress. This may cause your conscious mind to think you are stagnating, and your unconscious self to feel blocked. But by channelling your transitional energy into exploration, you can continue your progress as you more fully assimilate prior knowledge through practice. For example, the more images you start, the more comfortable you will become with the beginning processes, and as you absorb your conscious actions into the unconscious over time, you will eventually be able to develop them further. Remember that you are training yourself not only to use an artistic medium but also to see the world in a whole new way, bringing the contents of your soul to light through your art. This takes both practice time and assimilation time – hence transition time.

By allowing yourself time to absorb into your unconscious what you learn consciously, you will inform your intuition and eventually change the way you make decisions and choose what is most important to you as you shape your art and your life. Concerns for perspective and balance will become a natural part of your unconscious decision-making. At first it will seem as though your advances in art and soul move in leaps and bounds. This is in part due to your enthusiasm with new material on both levels. There is much to learn, and some of it is not as difficult as you might have imagined. But soon your improvements will be less dramatic and you may become impatient with yourself. We all need these times of

transition for the integration and balance of our inner and outer selves. They are the plateaus along the path of our continuous climb. In art as in soul, it is discipline, not overnight successes, that provides the staying power for the long haul. Our mini-revelations along the way are not the whole picture. They are treasured glimpses of a reality that is realized through our commitment over time. Our hard work and patience will be rewarded with a higher level of understanding and ability in matters of both art and soul.

Human life as we know it is an adventure; the only thing we can be certain of is that it is constantly changing. A larger perspective allows us to see the relationships between the various components of our lives. In art as in soul, it is helpful to pause periodically to look at your progress. Comparing your images of today to the images you made on your first day helps to show you how far you have come and reminds you that you will go further, whether you are conscious of doing so or not.

Even if – or maybe especially if – you think you do not possess the artistic skills to move forward, keep trying. You will show your commitment to yourself by being open to new situations. By moving into the unknown, you will advance your skills if you apply what you already know, consciously and unconsciously.

This lesson will describe two processes for drawing in colour with *dry media* that suggest a metaphor for spiritual development, where we must also move forward blindly at times. By applying previous knowledge to new situations, both artistic and spiritual, you can grow steadily through your dry spells. As you proceed, you will become conscious of more ways to enlarge your repertoire for self-expression.

Chalk pastel

While pastels come in hard and soft varieties, we will experiment only with the chalk (soft) variety for this exercise. Using a medium restrictively allows you to learn its properties better than if you use it with other media. Because pastels are applied in layers (not mixed together like wet media), buy sticks in colours that suit the subject you want to draw. (As you accumulate art supplies, try to build up a variety of colours.)

To begin, cut your paper to the appropriate size and shape and tape it to a drawing board. Draw the subject matter on the paper with a neutral-coloured pastel using the techniques described earlier in the book. At this point, alter the composition if necessary and indicate a path of light for future reference. Pastels are generally applied from dark to light, allowing the lightest pigment to rest on the top. Once you have identified the dark areas, apply two or three colours that are not the colour you want for the finished product. These provide unity under the surface, adding richness to the colours applied on top. Positive and negative space are treated simultaneously – using some of the same colours for each to promote harmony throughout the image. Continue to add different colours as needed, allowing the direction of lines or strokes to indicate the shapes of

objects. If you change the direction of line in spaces of similar colour, forms will stand out from each other. It is best not to smudge the pastel with your fingers or pastel stubs at first; this tends to smooth out the surface of the paper, making it difficult to apply additional layers of pigment. Instead, use chalks to blend colours, experimenting with different stroking actions. To prevent smudges as you build up pigment, carefully lay

Figure 8.2 Clean paper under the hand will prevent smudging as successive layers of pigment are applied.

clean paper under your hand to provide a barrier, as in Figure 8.2.

Squinting periodically throughout the developmental process, at both the subject matter and the image, you can keep a close watch on the progress of the tonal range. This is especially

Figure 8.3 Lines of a moderate tone are used to establish spaces (left). Spaces are further differentiated by colour, tone and quality of line (centre). As the image is further developed, lights are added and greater attention is given to the refinement of line quality and direction (right).

important for beginners working in colour, as tone and colour can easily become confused. The image is refined as you fill in the spaces, adding the lightest colours last to keep the image fresh. Figure 8.3 shows the progression of a work in this way. When the image is completed you can spray it with fixative or hairspray so that the pigment will not be easily removed from the paper surface. (Sometimes artists like to fix their images partway through so that they can add new colours without smudging those underneath.) Used as a drawing medium, pastel allows you to experiment with rich colour without a brush. By experimenting with a variety of paper surfaces, pastel brands and colour combinations, and recording in your journal the ones you find most appealing, you will soon develop a particular approach to the medium, adding another layer of knowledge to your artistic development.

Coloured pencil

Coloured pencils are fun to use and usually less intimidating than pastels, probably because they are less messy and most people are already familiar with them. Coloured pencils vary in their degree of hardness, although this is generally less noticeable than with pastels. Any brand of pencils will do to get started; experiment with different brands to discover your favourites. To me, coloured pencils are like solid watercolours; the colours are soft, needing to be built up by layers. But because they are in pencil form, we have more control over how we apply them than we do with paints that absorb into a surface. Used as a fine art medium, coloured pencils lend themselves to a wide variety of techniques and styles.

Although a multitude of colours and surfaces can be used for this medium, begin by using smooth white paper for the sake of simplicity. Like pastels, coloured pencils can be combined with other media to create interesting effects, but here you will use them on their own to become familiar with their unique properties. Begin as you did with pastels: cut the paper to the desired size an shape and secure it to a drawing board. If the paper is thin, add several sheets under the image to prevent any unwanted lines emerging due to cuts or irregularities on the drawing board's surface. Sketch the image with a light, neutral colour (perhaps a yellow ochre or a light grey) so that the lines can be easily camouflaged as colours are built up. It is best to avoid using graphite pencils for the original sketch as the wax of the coloured pencil will resist the graphite. (This can create an interesting effect, but it is best to learn the properties of a medium first.)

Unlike pastels, coloured pencils are applied from light to dark; the white of the paper is retained for any pure whites within the image. As with pastels, the more individual colours, whether light or dark, you use to develop objects within the image, the more lifelike the image will be. Many beginners are tempted to choose a colour that matches the colour they are trying to create. Resist this urge: if you understand colour theory as discussed in Chapter 5, you can blend colour to create a more natural result. For example, instead of choosing three or four greens to suggest grass, you might choose a blue and a yellow (which make green), and a red (the complement to green) to neutralize. A green pencil added to the latter

combination will help to blend the underlying colours without making them flat, as they might be in a child's colouring book (Figure 8.4). The image, including the background, is developed simultaneously, so that an underlying unity of colour will promote overall harmony. Strokes are usually less obvious in coloured pencil drawings than in pastel, the blending having been built up through a series of layers. When you are finished, you may spray the drawing with fixative, but this is not as important as with pastel because the colours in this medium are not so easily altered on the paper.

Finally, when using each of these media, do not overdraw the image. In my own work, I like to use suggestive realism, which relies on the viewer's

Figure 8.4 Darks in coloured pencil are achieved by layering several colours, giving a richness not possible if fewer colours are used. The transition may be slower this way, but the end result will more closely imitate the natural world.

eye to mix colours and fill in some of the blanks. Overdrawing can put too much emphasis on precision, which is more appropriate to technical

Figure 8.5 While this image suggests a line of silhouetted trees to the viewer, closer observation (right) reveals that the trees need not be fully developed in order to achieve the desired effect.

drawing. Note that in the close-up of the image in Figure 8.5, trees have not been precisely drawn, but that we see trees when we view the image as a whole from a distance. Good art, like healthy spirituality, seeks to communicate and inspire, not to dictate or conform.

EXERCISE

Try one or both of the exercises described above. Choose diverse subject matter so that your observation skills may be applied to a variety of media. Try to allow at least an hour for each exercise. Remember that at the beginner's stage it is more important to start than to finish. If you find you have taken the drawing as far as you can, put it aside and begin a new one. The experience you gain from starting over will build your confidence so you will be able to develop your work further over time. Continue to practise, using different media to describe your observations of the natural world. Allow yourself time for assimilation. Enjoy the process and be kind to yourself in your expectations.

THE TRANSFORMING JOURNEY

*Stages of transition from false self
to true self*

Becoming an artist requires an openness to change coupled with a commitment to training. The balance between disciplined practice and creative exploration ensures the ongoing development of both technical ability and personal style. Artists do not simply learn their craft in a few easy lessons and then construct their images according to an unchanging formula; they embark upon an exploration that continues for their whole lives. For example, from their art we can understand something of the journeys of Picasso and Degas. Picasso's blue period represents a transitional stage in his journey, as do the later images of Degas, produced when he was legally blind.

Human experience is a process of continual change – an evolution of body, mind and spirit. The transition that takes place as we fill our lungs with air for the first time begins the process of adaptation as we respond to our new-world experiences. Physically, our bodies grow and change, our cells replacing themselves many times over as we progress from birth to death. Intellectually and emotionally, we are constantly processing new stimuli as we relate to our ever-changing environment. Spiritually, we may also move through various stages, uncovering our soul through the growth and evolution of our true self. The changes between birth and death will be more dramatic for some than for others, depending on how long the journey lasts and what choices we make. Our life forms a pattern that is most easily discerned upon our death.

The transformation from false self to true self takes place as our soul is permitted to influence our lives. While our physical and intellectual transitions are chronological, evolution of the soul may not always be. Because our soul is already fully mature within, we can allow it to break into our lives at any age. Some people are spiritually wise in youth; others remain immature in old age. Accessing the wisdom of the soul depends on our ability to identify and release the illusions of our ego. As in the mansions of St. Teresa of Avila's *Interior Castle*, separate stages of transformation from false self to true self are not always linear or chronological. The stages are sometimes overlapping or random – one moment we connect with the wisdom of our soul, the next we feel empty, as if such a connection had never been made. Becoming more conscious of five stages through which our true self develops can give us a deeper understanding of the patterns that underlie our growth.

1. Awakening

The awakening stage takes us by surprise, invoking the wonder of childlike innocence. For adults accustomed to the illusions of the false self created by the ego, exposure to the reality of our soul can be shocking – like being doused with cold water! Awakening stimulates our imagination and energy; we are excited and motivated to respond. The intensity of each awakening experience – the *petite rapture* discussed earlier in this book – fills us with joy and peace, lifting us out of our everyday experience. Just as we do when we access our right brain through the process of art, we feel as though we have touched the essence of being and have found a new way of looking at the world. The contrast between this new perception and our usual one results in a born-again experience; we are filled with anticipation and a whole new way of living seems possible.

2. Absorption

This phase, like the honeymoon experience of lovers whose new relationship with each other colours everything else in their lives, is the time when we focus on our awakening experiences and become more comfortable integrating them into our lives. We 'rewrite our scripts,' filtering our judgments through the new lenses we have donned, committing ourselves to reorganizing our lives from this new perspective. Like adolescents, we are filled with energy and devoted to the cause. We seek out community, looking for others with whom we can share our insights. We are enthusiastic, tackling each problem we encounter with zeal and determination. We see new connections between different areas of our lives, connecting the dots in ways that help to sustain our awakening experiences. Doubts are dismissed (or suppressed) as our new perspective blossoms; it is a time of joy and sharing as our true self begins to emerge through our external interactions. But while our intentions may be good, this can also be a time of confusion if the unenlightened ego attempts to regain a foothold.

3. Aridity

Because the awakening and absorption stages are introductory, they are rooted in experience that has not yet stood the test of time. When the honeymoon phase of absorption can no longer be sustained, a period of dryness or emptiness sets in. Enthusiasm gives way to disillusionment or complacency as unresolved problems accumulate in our unconscious. The illusions of the ego, which become appealing again, cause inner tension as we consider our spiritual motivation and progress. Developments seem small, if they happen at all, and we begin to feel discontent, doubting even those things of which we were most confident earlier. Emphasizing the desires of the ego once more, our focus becomes distorted and our goals less clear. Our attention is diverted backward and our energies turn towards rekindling happier times. We may be completely unable to reconnect with our soul.

4. Acceptance

During this stage, we become more conscious of the tensions within us, seeking to bring to the surface what we have suppressed or denied. Our goal is not to return to a previous state of comfort or joy, but to resolve the disillusionment we feel now. By accepting the previous three stages, we discover a new attitude towards our journey; our initial excitement is replaced with a quiet commitment to persevere. We begin to focus more on the journey itself than on its rewards or our feelings about it and become more conscious of the ego's motivations in our lives. We cease to strive after its illusions and start consciously to compose our lives according to the soul's perspective. As our true self continues to emerge, we experience a humbling gratitude for the opportunity to be human; the enthusiasm of the initial stages is replaced with an inner calm as we become more fully aware of our essence – our divine nature.

The humility of this stage is the deepest so far. Where once we believed that tolerating others was enough for spiritual growth, we now accept others fully, celebrating our differences from the soul's perspective of detachment. Unlike the indifference of the ego, this detachment is positive – a neutrality born of the soul's love, not the ego's apathy. We feel in awe of the larger plan in which everyone is equal. We become content to focus on personal statement-making, not because of an inflated ego, but because through the process of articulation we come to understand ourselves better in relation to others. We learn that we find fulfillment not by attaining the unenlightened ego's goals, but simply by following the path of our soul and expressing love in the world. We find at this stage that, although we lack many of the highs (and lows) of our previous stages, our overall contentment with life increases.

5. Awareness

The humility of acceptance opens new doors of self-awareness, making us more mindful of the present moment. We discover a new way of being in the world that is in complete harmony with our essence. When making decisions, we consider their consequences for us and for others. Rather than trying to solve all the problems of the world, we concentrate on our own contribution to the greater evolution. Understanding ourselves as part of a web of interconnectedness, we learn that everything we do is important and act according-ly, especially in our dealings with others. As we develop spiritually, we become aware of how our attitudes and actions will affect future genera-tions. It is as if we can see the future unfolding from our detached position and, like chess players, make our moves with careful consideration of the consequences. The statement we make with our lives is no longer accidental, but deliberate, taking into account not only how we feel about what we are saying, but how it fits into the web. During this stage we are more in touch with our soul in our everyday existence, expressing its wisdom through our true self and increasing our originality in both soul and art.

Getting stuck along the way

We interfere with our spiritual growth by directing our energy towards gaining or losing material goods and emotional states. In spirituali-ty, as in art, our preference for some of these stages over others blocks our development and prevents us from moving forward. For example, in art class we may become comfortable drawing in black and white, using pencil or pen. Because we are happy with the results of our work, we are less motivated to continue our learning process by using colour, knowing that the result will be less pleasing – at least initially. But only by pushing ourselves onward will we move to a higher level of technical ability. Understanding transition as our natural state, we become more attuned to the present – the time when we participate in the process of our development. Keeping an eye on both past and future from the detached perspective of the soul, we can give ourselves permission to embrace each moment, regardless of its content. The power of the soul can best be accessed when our attention is given fully to the present. Letting go of our ego's desires (which are influenced by thoughts of past and future) 'unsticks' us, allowing further soul development.

By understanding the relationship between our journey and our destination we learn to let go of each stage so that we can more fully experience the next. Nothing about life is static; trying to make it so goes against the natural processes of transformation. Change is not to be feared but to be embraced. By embracing change we participate in our destination (divinity) during our journey. It is not a matter of 'getting there' but of recognizing that we have always been (and continue to be) there. By becoming detached from things and emotional experience we find that 'there' is really *here*! This is what the highest stage, awareness, is all about.

While the first two stages of the transformation process described above are inspiring and joyous, we can be seduced by the feelings they stir in us and develop a subtle resistance to moving forward. By releasing our attachments, we recognize the transitions involved in our transformation and allow ourselves to move through them without resistance. The third stage, aridity, therefore, while often thought to be a dark night of the soul, is central to further development. We may enter this stage unconsciously as a result of circumstances beyond our control. Death or divorce, the diagnosis of a terminal illness, and the loss of a job are typical triggers for a dark-night experience. If our spirituality has not adequately matured, it will be difficult to deal with an event in a way that encourages further growth. Instead, we may push our soul further underground, making it even more difficult to reach. At this stage we are presented with three options: turn back and try to rekindle comforts of the past; become lost in the struggle, perhaps rejecting religion and spirituality altogether; or move forward, humbly accepting life as it unfolds by releasing the preconceptions of the ego.

What we do during our periods of aridity determines the direction and degree of our spiritual growth beyond that point. The Spanish mystic St. John of the Cross, a contemporary of St. Teresa of Avila, offers valuable insights into this most difficult phase of transition. In his beautiful work, *Dark Night of the Soul*,[21] St. John suggests that the challenges encountered through life's most difficult times are a natural component of the overall human experience – that each moment, regardless of how we perceive it, is a gift from God. Our acceptance of this concept is a key to spiritual progress that gives birth to a new way of being. It moves us to question the greater purpose of our life and sometimes even life in general; as we peel away the ego's coverings from our soul through these dark times, we will glimpse reality from a different perspective and find the strength we need to proceed.

The dark night of the soul is a time of transformation. Like a chrysalis, we are not as we were before, but we have not yet emerged into what we will be. St. John's advice for these times is not to run away in the hope of rekindling past comforts, but to forge ahead, finding inner strength and guidance through the experience. A lit candle in a brightly lit room makes little impact; if we want to see it shine fully, we need to turn out all the other lights. Similarly, it is when we turn inward and confront our darkness that the divine light of our soul becomes most visible. The dark moments of our lives provide an opportunity to seek strength, courage and guidance from inside ourselves. Accepting the darkness is difficult in our modern era of instant cure. Our culture has provided few skills to help us endure that which we do not want. However, St. John warns that running from darkness will only prolong its hold on us. When we stop fighting them, the experiences of the dark night strengthen our soul and deepen our understanding of the human journey. New life emerges from darkness. Just as a seed germinates in the dark soil and a child gestates hidden within the mother's womb, human beings will encounter darkness as they grow in their spiritual perceptions. By accepting the darkness as yet another expression of human experience, we embrace the

wisdom of our soul. We begin to understand the experiences of people who are able to write or speak with wisdom and sensitivity in the midst of harsh or even life-threatening external environments, like the apostle Paul in his prison cell. We can rejoice during our times of pain when we come to the awareness that life itself is cause for rejoicing.

Gallery Image 8, *Dark Night of the Soul*, is a visual interpretation of the effects of becoming lost in the darkness of our lives. Green vines grow from the white in the centre of the image, representing the initial awakening phase of our transformation. Some of the vines stay in the centre, enjoying the honeymoon phase of absorption, but others continue to grow, with every other vine in the image moving into a ring of darkness. Some of the vines remain in the dark ring, lost in the anguish of aridity. Others move beyond this point, getting larger and more colourful as they eventually 'grow' off the page. Life, like the vines in the image, proceeds only in a forward direction; we must learn how to move through our present dilemmas, incorporating them into our perspective through a heightened awareness of the purpose of our journey. It may be that all we have ahead of us is pain, but even so, our acceptance of it will permit our soul to release a new kind of contentment that is independent of our exterior situation. A willingness to become unstuck through humbly submitting to the soul's way is all that we need to stay on our spiritual path. Giving ourselves permission to grow – beyond pain and joy – we allow divine energy to continue flowing through us.

The soul's strength in transition

That we travel the path of human existence alone is most evident at the moments of physical birth and death. Even in the case of twins or triplets, one child enters the new light alone, slightly before or after another. While others may watch – and help with our delivery – they do not share our experience of it. While we can empathize, we can never really know another's pain or joy. In death, too, we move on alone. Our last breath is as solitary an event as our first. We may be as reluctant to leave as we were to come, resisting the changes that separate us from the reality we know.

Many people are fearful of being alone in their experience. Our culture exploits this fear by promoting products and services that may help ensure that we don't feel alone. Televisions bring strangers into our home to keep us company 24 hours a day; radios and CD players fill our world with noise so that we are not alone. But we *are* alone. No one else can enter our thoughts or take on the physical attributes of our bodies. To ease our fear, we seek community, perhaps thinking that knowledge of someone else's journey will make us feel more comfortable. Community provides information, guidance and opportunities for sharing, and supplies a sense of belonging. We find support and direction by comparing our experiences with others' and seeking their advice. It is tempting to reject the inner, solitary world of our soul in favour of the external world, where the ego interacts with others.

But by looking exclusively outward for strength and guidance, we can forget how to find it within ourselves. While we can benefit from the support of friends and family in painful situations, it will only take us so far on the spiritual journey. Several years ago, a close friend of mine faced a string of difficult events in her life. It started when her husband, who was in his early forties, became ill. His condition deteriorated, requiring him to have two heart transplant operations in quick succession. A short time after the second operation, he died in hospital in another province. When my friend returned home after his death, she resumed her life as best she could and continued to care for their two children. Two years later, her elder daughter, who was 18 and who was severely handicapped from birth, developed an illness that escalated into pneumonia. She died a few weeks later. Such terrible losses in such a short span of time seemed an unbearable transition to me. I offered to help my friend in whatever way I could, but I wondered what I could possibly do in such a situation. A few weeks after her daughter's funeral, my friend did call – to ask me to help plant some flowering shrubs on the graves of her husband and daughter. While we were digging holes, I told her I was amazed by her strength, suggesting that I would not be nearly so strong. She replied that I might be surprised at how we can find strength to go on from deep within – when we really need it. It is the soul that supplies this kind of strength, which is one reason why it is so important for us to recognize its presence.

As we try to console others, we become increasingly aware of our aloneness. While we can (and do) sympathize and empathize deeply, we cannot know the depths of other people's pain.

Strength to progress through life's most difficult transitions ultimately has to come through our soul's connection with God. While others come through our doors with expressions of support, there is a door that must be opened from deep inside ourselves if we are to find real comfort and encouragement to get through our darkest nights. The wisdom we encounter in our soul guides us through traumatic experiences, providing a kind of peace that cannot be achieved by external means. This peace does not depend on a happy ending to the crisis; it stems from an inner source that tells us that no matter what happens in our lives, "all shall be well."[22] The soul becomes our teacher at these times, revealing its ancient insights for each new situation we encounter. Our fear of being alone in our journey subsides as we strengthen this connection; it is like finding a new close friend to whom we can confide our greatest troubles without fear of embarrassment or abandonment. While the ego continues to look for peace in places where it cannot be found, such as money, alcohol or constant activity, the true self turns to the quiet knowing of the soul. While we may feel anxiety in being separated from others, in a sense each of us is designed to be alone. Even as members of a biological family we are still alone in our experiences of that family. Equipped with a direct connection to divinity, through our soul we are better able to create deeper relationships with others. Tapping our own inner sources of strength and wisdom, we find the sustenance we need for sharing our lives fully and honestly. Rooted in our soul, we are connected to every other individual, receiving and expressing God's love through our interactions.

Artists are well acquainted with the solitary journey; the very nature of making art requires many hours spent alone. Because art is not usually a collective endeavour, it can teach us how to be truly alone without being lonely and give us solitary time which is necessary to put us in touch with our soul. In addition, the right-brain experience invoked by artmaking does not require interaction with others, making art a helpful tool in learning to endure life's transitions alone. Inner dialogues during artmaking can be as active as external conversations with many people at once, helping us to identify our inner community of voices, including that of the soul, as we seek guidance for our external path. By regularly engaging in the creative process we become more familiar with and comfortable in this inner world, even as we build a language that helps us to understand and then express our deepest selves. For the artist, traumatic external circumstances often provide fodder for deeper exploration and expression.

Moment to moment

One of the tragedies of human experience is not appreciating what we have until it has passed. Some of my fondest memories are of taking my children to the beach when they were young. At the time, however, I often felt overwhelmed by the responsibility of caring for them and so did not enjoy our time together as much as I could have. As we become older, our pace naturally slows and we learn to savour the special moments of our lives while they are happening. As we become wiser, we begin to see all our moments as special.

Ultimately, life is process; when we reject the ego's notions of achievement and attachment (which cause our discontent), replacing them with the soul's detached attitude of wakeful participation, our lives are transformed. Joy and contentment are found in accepting our human experience.

The artmaking process is a microcosm for the transitions in our lives. We begin with an idea that stirs us from deep within, use our skills and tools to bring it to life and make our statement as best we can. Invariably we make mistakes, but we forge ahead, applying what we have learned to each new image. Eventually, as our skills improve, it gets easier to make our visual statements – at least for a while. We develop in spirals through numerous stages of transition in both our personal statement and our expression of it. Through practice we find ourselves with a greater visual vocabulary, able to conceive and develop on a more sophisticated level. The more we are aware of our unique perspective on the world, the more our images reflect our originality. Similarly, the transitions in our spiritual development provide opportunities for the soul to become more fully a participant in our daily routine. At first we may be relatively unconscious of the statement we are making with our lives, but by giving attention to our soul we begin to shape our lives according to its objectives. As we uncover the path of the soul, a new perception of reality emerges, providing a new blueprint for our lives. Learning from our mistakes, we apply this knowledge as new situations arise.

By taking responsibility for the composition of our lives, we become more conscious of each phase in our transition towards wholeness and are moved to gratitude for the opportunity to add our tiny brushstroke to the divine composition.

EXERCISE

Consider the process by which your true self is emerging. Begin by noting in your journal instances where the false self created by your ego was in control of your life. What in your life perpetuates the illusions of the ego? Reflect on the five stages of transition, as outlined above, and record in your journal any experiences you may have had of each. Describe what caused you to become stuck in any of the stages and what prevents you from accessing or maintaining the awareness level. Reflect on how your personal rituals can be developed to help in each stage. Resolve to implement your findings.

(for Nanny)

I can dance
when all things around me
sing of praises
and blessings
and love
when the treetops whisper a gentle song
to touch my heart
and tell me all is well
and I belong

and when perfection
fades to pain
and sorrow wraps
around my soul
with fear
and death
I offer to my God a glance
and with brittle limbs
and blinded eyes
I can dance

Chapter 9

MYSTERY

Lesson VII

WET MEDIA ▸ WATERCOLOUR

Artist materials

For this exploration of watercolour, I recommend paints in the following colours: cadmium yellow light, yellow ochre, cerulean blue, ultramarine blue, alizarin crimson, cadmium red light, sepia, burnt sienna, payne's grey and hooker's green light. You will need round watercolour brushes #1, #4 and #8 (small, medium and large) as well as a larger square brush (a 1-inch lettering or house-painting brush) for washes. An old toothbrush is also useful, but not necessary.

Watercolour papers come in a wide variety of surfaces, weights and sizes. Cold-pressed watercolour sheets (in the standard size of 22 inches x 30 inches) of 140-lb or heavier stock work well for beginners. Papers can be cut to the desired size and both sides can be used. Sheets of paper are preferable to pads of watercolour paper as the latter tend to be of inferior quality. Watercolour blocks ('pads' of watercolour paper glued together on all four sides, which helps the paper stay smooth during the painting process) also work well, but are usually expensive. You will need a palette or white plate for mixing colour, as well as a drawing board and masking tape for securing the paper. You can use an HB pencil (or softer) for the initial drawing; a kneaded eraser will be helpful if you need to make changes. Keep a bottle of water and paper towels for clean-up handy for these exercises. Figure 9.1 illustrates the required materials.

Figure 9.1 Watercolour paints come in tubes or cakes in student and professional qualities. A small assortment of brushes ranging from small to large (and an old toothbrush) are enough to get started. A pencil and kneaded eraser are used for the initial drawing, and paper cut to the desired size and shape is taped to a drawing board. Water and paper towels round out the supplies.

Due process

Rumour has it that watercolour is a difficult medium. Nothing could be further from the truth. Watercolour is a lively method of painting, and it may require a bit of planning, depending on the desired result. Because the painting process has the added challenge of brushes and absorption by paper, it offers the artist a unique set of opportunities. There is an element of mystery in watercolour: we can never be exactly sure how the colour will react with other colours as they dry on the paper. This can be a frustration or an adventure, depending on your attitude.

Watercolour is one of my favourite media. I began to experiment with it during my second pregnancy, when the fumes from the solvents of my oil paints made me ill. I turned to watercolour to continue my artistic expression during that time and I have been thankful ever since. Having taken no courses in watercolour, I learned the hard way, through trial and error, which involved mountains of mistakes and many moments of discovery. Over the years I have developed an easy and effective method for using watercolour, which I share here. While there are many ways to use this medium, this approach provides easy-to-follow steps based on an understanding of due process. By respecting the natural qualities of watercolour we learn to create what we want while honouring the medium for what it does best.

The use of watercolour requires us to think quickly from time to time and often rewards us with happy accidents. Through observation we can learn to harness its spontaneity, applying it in ways that enhance our image-making. For example, if we notice that certain efforts on our part produce a bleeding effect (where one pigment runs into another due to wetness) that we find appealing, we can create this effect wherever we want it in our image. (It will not be exactly the same, however, because watercolour responds slightly differently each time it is used.) In a way, we do not *use* watercolour, we partner with it, creating images for which we may take only some of the credit. The process of watercolour cannot be rushed, and so we need to adjust our timetable accordingly. Drying time is as important to some effects as is applying the paint itself, so we need to be patient.

The process of watercolour painting as described below is divided into four stages. Together they provide a guide for the construction of any image. Because each stage requires a different mindset, I find it helpful to have three or four paintings in process at any given time. I recommend this practice to beginners because it encourages a move towards valuing involvement in the process over attachment to specific outcomes.

1. Setting up

To begin a watercolour painting, first attach your paper (which has been cut to the desired shape and size) securely to the drawing board, using masking tape on all edges. This helps minimize buckling as the paper absorbs water. It also provides a stark border around the image when you are finished. (You will have greater appreciation for this when you begin to frame your work!) A photograph (Figure 9.2) will serve for the demonstration. The point of the exercise is to become familiar with the medium, not to create a masterpiece, so it is best to keep the subject matter simple. Using your pencil, start with a light sketch, as explained in Chapters 3 and 7 (drawing and composition). The purpose of drawing in this case is to inform you where to put the paint of various colours. The more familiar you become with

Figure 9.2 This photograph of lighthouses taken from the ferry crossing between Nova Scotia and Prince Edward Island provides a reference for the developed watercolour painting in this chapter. Note that the composition has been deliberately altered for the painting.

Figure 9.3 Drawing for watercolour is a matter of identifying the placement of objects and locating major differences in colour and/or tone. Draw as little or as much as is necessary to feel confident moving on to the wash stage.

the painting process, the less drawing you will need to do. To begin, do as little or as much drawing as you need to build your confidence. Once the drawing is complete (Figure 9.3) you are ready to apply the colour.

Set up the palette as described in Chapter 5. Keeping the colours well off to the side if you are using a plate allows more room for mixing in the centre. A few drops of water on each colour help keep the paint soft so that it will mix more easily. Consistency in the location of colour on the palette will speed up the mixing process. I like to keep my reds, blues, yellows, etc., together for easy identification as I am working, but any combination is fine. Watercolour is never applied straight from the tube. It is always diluted with water and is most often mixed with other colours.

Mix colours on the palette, never on the paper. As soon as paint is put on the paper it begins to be absorbed, which means that it is difficult to remove. So keep a small piece of watercolour paper handy to test colours before applying them to the image.

2. Washes

In watercolour, the term *wash* refers to a method of applying a light coat of paint on the paper. To get a feel for the ratio of paint to water, spend some time playing with washes before applying them to your first painting. Most people at first produce either a heavy wash (too much

Figure 9.4 Learning the ratio between pigment and water required to achieve a desired effect takes practice.

pigment) or a light one (too little pigment). Washes that are too heavy will have a chalky appearance; washes that are too light will absorb into the paper, leaving little colour on the surface (Figure 9.4). A little practice will help you develop a feel for the right combination of water and pigment. Watercolour is a transparent medium, so the layers of paint should not be too thick. If you can see the paint as opaque colour on the brush, you probably have too much pigment and need to thin it with water. Washes need to be kept light so that colours can be built in layers without becoming opaque, allowing underneath colour to show through. It is best to aim for a mid-range as you begin.

You can practise making washes by mixing sufficient colour and trying to drag the paint across the page in a single stroke several times in a row. Working from left to right, then right to left, and so on, pull the colour downward a bit further with each stroke. Try to avoid using little strokes to fill in the white spaces or the wash will not be smooth (lines will be visible if you work too slowly – see Figure 9.5). The angle of the brush is important, so you will need to experiment and practise. As the wash dries it will appear much lighter on the paper.

Figure 9.5 Avoiding streaks and white flecks in a wash depends upon the ratio of pigment to water, the speed with which it is applied, and the angle of the brush.

There are many possible variations of washes. For example, you can drag a thin stroke of clear water across a wet wash and watch the pigment rush away from the centre and gather at the edges of the water mark. The same kind of stroke on a

dry wash will have a much more subtle effect, with less movement of pigment. Or you can wet the paper first with clear water and then add pigment, noting how the colour bleeds into the water. A similar effect can be created by adding one colour into a wash of another colour. This is called 'wet on wet,' and is helpful for avoiding streaks when applying washes to large areas. Finally, you can remove pigment from a wet wash with a crumpled tissue or paper towel. This is called lifting out. These effects, as can be seen in Figure 9.6, are only a few possibilities for varying washes.

There are few drawing lines in watercolour painting. These 'two-sided' lines detract from the three-dimensional quality of the image. Instead, 'one-sided' lines are used, emphasizing shapes (Figure 9.7). To create a one-sided line, immediately drag one edge of the wet line away, bleeding it out with clear water. The use of one-sided lines emphasizes my earlier point that lines are not divisions, but edges where two

Figure 9.6 Examples of watercolour washes. From top to bottom: solid colour background, with clear water dragged across from the left while the wash is still wet; graduated wash using clear water to lighten the colour as it is pulled downward; wet-on-wet wash where pigment is applied after the entire area to be painted is first thoroughly wet with clear water (note: the steeple has no colour because it was left dry throughout the process to prevent the wet edges from bleeding in); lifting out, which occurs when pigment is applied and then quickly mopped away with a moist paper towel; finally, salt added to a wet wash produces a mottled effect (the salt is simply brushed away once the wash has completely dried).

Figure 9.7 One-sided lines are created by pulling the paint away from one edge and bleeding with clear water so that the second edge disappears.

Figure 9.8 The use of one-sided lines helps to create an image which is a more believable representation of three-dimensional reality.

shapes meet. This is an essential concept for the imaging of three-dimensional objects in watercolour. If you use one-sided lines, the objects will appear to have volume, as in Figure 9.8.

After a bit of playtime with washes and one-sided lines, you can work on your image by blocking in the various shapes (positive and negative) indicated by your drawing in colours that match

the lightest part of each space you fill. Initially, keep the colours light so that darks can be applied on top. Apply thin washes as blocks of colour, working on different areas of the paper and mixing sufficient colour for each wash. If you allow one wash to dry before applying another one directly adjacent to it, this will minimize the bleeding of one wash into another. You can keep your washes spontaneous by dropping in extra colour where desired as you respond to the colours and values of your subject matter. It is helpful to create as much diversity as possible at this stage, focusing not on the things being painted but on their shape, colour and tone. Using some or all of the techniques described above, you can fill in all the spaces except those that are ultimately to remain pure white, resulting in one coat of paint over the entire image. At this point you can consider the first application of washes complete, as in Figure 9.9. The painting must dry for at least fifteen minutes before you continue to work on it. While the paper may have buckled from the moisture, it will flatten as it dries. Laying the image on its back as it dries will prevent unwanted shifting of the pigment.

3. Texture

Washes form the background upon which you can build textures. Texture, as we saw in previous chapters, depends on differences in tone and colour. In watercolour, it is created by layering pigment

Figure 9.9 Washes should be added to all parts of the painting to identify differences in tone and colour.

over washes in a variety of brushstrokes and colours, bleeding some and leaving others hard-edged. Building up textures creates the illusion of volume and depth in your image. Texture is developed in layers; give time for each layer to dry before adding another. This successive layering creates the luminous quality characteristic of watercolour. If layers are not given adequate time to dry, the pigment underneath becomes agitated and mixes with the new layer, resulting in a dull,

opaque look, like a heavy wash. In such cases it is difficult to establish depth in the image.

In watercolour, different kinds of brushstrokes are used to create different effects. One of the most common (and helpful) is the drybrush technique. Here the brush is filled with pigment and water, and 'sprung' as in Figure 9.10. The tips of the brush are then used to apply paint in thin lines. It is sometimes necessary to 'spring' the brush often to attain the random quality that best

Figure 9.10 By 'springing' the brush and applying pigment in thin stroking lines, one can easily create the illusion of animal fur, wind-blown grasses and a host of other textures.

Figure 9.11 Watercolour textures left to right: Top row: wash over wash; spatters applied over a dry wash; layers of strokes applied over a dry wash. Bottom row: dry brushing; layers of wash applied over a dried wash; wash applied over masking fluid (removed once the wash is dry).

imitates nature. This technique can be useful for creating the illusion of grasses, fur or tree branches. You may wish to keep old brushes especially for this purpose. (Because they tend to make predictable marks, I avoid using commercial 'fan' brushes for this technique.) Spattering with a toothbrush is another way to create texture that results in a different effect depending upon the moisture level of the paper. You can also sprinkle salt on wet pigment for another effect. The result will again depend on the wetness of the paper. When the paper is dried completely, brush off the salt. Note the examples in Figure 9.11. Through practice you will discover which techniques will produce the effects you desire for a specific work.

After the painting has dried from the washes stage, you can begin to add textures by overlapping thin layers of paint, visually building the objects as a sculptor might work in clay. It may take several layers to create the amount of texture you want. Working over the entire image, you can use some of the techniques described above to add variety. Concentrate only on creating textures at this stage; do not think too much of the objects in your painting or you will be tricked into left-brain thinking. Instead, focus on the tonal and colour changes that give rise to visual texture. When you think you have added enough texture to your image, let the painting dry thoroughly (Figure 9.12).

4. Polish

As artists and viewers, we are often attracted to subject matter by details – a twinkle in the eye, a thin wire fence across a snowy field, or the fine

Figure 9.12 Textures created over initial washes give the image a more realistic appearance.

whiskers of a fluffy cat. You may at times want this result without going through the steps necessary to produce it. But in art, as in soul, the foundation layers provide the background upon which the details sparkle. If the details are applied too early, they will become lost in the process of building the image. By adhering to the natural order of a process you are more likely to generate the result for which you strive.

The fourth stage in watercolour, polishing the image, involves two steps. First, this is the time to pay attention to the objects in your image, employing knowledge you have acquired through your observations. The washes and texturing have given substance to your image; now you can add the details, which help make each object and space different from all others. By adding thin lines, darkest darks, and more thin washes of colour if necessary, you clarify the specific elements of your image, visually transforming them from two dimensions into three. When you feel comfortable with your image, and have looked at it often from a distance, in different lights and perhaps even through a mirror, move to the second stage in polishing. Examining the entire image from close range, concentrating on an area of about two square inches at a time, look for edges that need to be tidied up, remove smudges and pencil lines, and find an appropriate place for your signature. (Practise your signature from one work to the next so it is consistent and so that you can apply it in any medium.) For watercolour, use a fine brush in a colour that does not detract from the image (Figure 9.13).

An image can be polished immediately after the texturing stage dries, or the process can be spread out over days or weeks so that the painting can be refined more gradually. I think it best not to finish a painting in a single sitting, but to allow at least a little time to pass, especially between the texturing and polishing stages. By looking at the painting with fresh eyes you may see mistakes that did not seem obvious while you were working. But do not let too much time pass, either, or you may lose the passion for your image altogether. (This is especially important for beginners.) Resist spending too much time fixing your image as you polish it. Overworking watercolours results in opaque and muddy colours rather than the mysterious qualities for which the medium is best known. A well-known Nova Scotia painter once said that a

Figure 9.13 A fine brush allows thin lines and other details to be added to the watercolour (left). The finished work (right).

painting is finished when nothing that is added further enhances the image. When additions begin to subtract from the effects in the painting, it is time to stop.

EXERCISE

Lay out your palette as described above. Practise washes and creating textures to become more familiar with the process of watercolour. Try painting simple objects that require little drawing or colour mixing, such as eggs or onions. Lightly sketch the objects, then break the process into its stages, allowing the painting to dry between each one. As your confidence increases, make images containing a greater number of objects, trying to work through each of the stages in sequence. Remember that it is the process that is important; it is more beneficial for the artist (and the soul) to begin many images and enjoy the process than to finish one and feel that it has been a chore.

LIVING THE MYSTERY

The reality of mystery

The experience of watercolour invites us to think about mystery. Here we need first to notice that there is a way things are – an objective reality – that is independent of how we understand it. Either you live at 123 Highway 4, or you don't; either God is real or nature is all there is. The truth does not depend on what we think, but on how things are. Having said that, as in the art class described in Chapter 1, in which students painted the same objects from different perspectives, our understanding of reality is limited by our subjectivity; it can never be otherwise in human experience. Even though we participate in it, trying to understand objective reality is much like guessing the contents of a mystery bag by holding it in our hands. Feeling through the bag we can make educated guesses about what we think is inside; sometimes we will be right – but not always. As we attempt to understand more of our world through the various disciplines of art and science, and as our technologies improve, we will most certainly learn more about objective reality, such as how the body works, how the universe was formed, and perhaps even its ultimate destiny and ours. But there are always more questions to be asked. And even if we completely unravel the 'how' of existence, the question of 'why' remains. Without self-consciousness, none of this would matter to us, but because we have evolved as we have, questions about how things work and why there is something instead of nothing continue to pique our interest.

Focused on how things in nature work (or how they came to be), scientists present theories that provide a basis for experimental research. Their goal is not to invent, but to uncover truth about objective reality. During his lifelong commitment to this truth, Richard Feynman, the Nobel prize-winning physicist, declared frequently, "If it disagrees with experiment, it is wrong."[23] Theories that are disproved by experiment are discarded as not corresponding to the way things are, while those that cannot be disproved, even though they cannot be conclusively validated, are retained until evidence supports either their termination or their acceptance. Even theories that are beautiful in and of themselves must be laid aside if they are not in sync with the way things actually are. And so often they are not. Scientists such as Einstein and Feynman had great respect for objectivity, recognizing that they did not have all the answers to questions about the natural world and even going so far as to claim that we may never have all the answers.

Artists relate to the mystery of objective reality through the creative process. The artist acts as a channel between the objects she paints and her representation of them. Learning the intricacies of artistic media by which her ideas can be expressed, the artist uses them to create a subjective response with each image. While the emphasis of her art may be mainly technical (stressing the way materials can be used), much of art employs such technical expertise in service of something else: explorations of the impact of objective stimuli upon the artists themselves. Even images without representational objects (such as those found in the works of Kandinsky) are still records of the artist's explorations of objective reality. (Objective reality is multi-layered and includes feelings and ideas – there is a 'way things are' with respect to them, too.) Like the scientist, the artist does not invent objective reality; she uses her talents and abilities to describe her relationship to it in each created work. She is well aware of the limitations of her expression, but finds value in the creative exercise – not only as a tool of communication, but as a means of further opening the door to an understanding of something that may never be comprehended completely.

Religions, too, see objective reality and the reality of mystery as integral to their various systems. While appreciation for mystery may seem most obvious in the approaches of Eastern and indigenous religions, the three major religions of Western culture have also birthed sects that explicitly seek to honour the mysterious. Although groups that take a more literal approach, such as the Christian or Islamic fundamentalists, seek to constrain mystery by excluding what does not fall within their own subjective interpretations, groups comfortable with metaphor and symbolism are more likely to admit to the limitations of their subjective understanding. Theologies are sometimes created to address mystery, but they run the risk of answering questions that may be more helpful left unanswered. The monastic tradition of Christianity, the Hassid community within Judaism, and the Sufis of Islam, each with their own religious and cultural slant, recognize the mysterious within the divine. As we saw in Chapter 3, limiting God to our interpretation is an invitation to idolatry. Mystery need not be eliminated, only incorporated, accepted as part of our lives.

What we need when approaching mystery is a healthy appreciation for truth, which overrides our egocentric desire to be right about it. Our soul relates to mystery in a different way than the ego does. Because of the soul's link to God, it understands mystery, but in a language inaccessible to the ego, much as the symbols in an artist's image may be unintelligible to the uninitiated. Like different kinds of computers, the ego and the soul employ different 'operating systems'; they need an 'interface' so they may communicate. In spiritual development, this interface is found through our evolving true self. Drawing directly from our soul (and its link to divinity), the evolution of the true self involves the translation of divinity into something accessible to the ego. This allows the ego to participate in the spiritual journey. Through our soul, we become privy to the deepest secrets of the universe, without ever having formally learned them or being able to express them in the usual sense; we are "taught by the spirit, expressing spiritual truths in spiritual words" (1 Corinthians 2:13). The ego cannot articulate this knowledge because of its limited capacity. But the development of our true self releases the ego's need to articulate it; we are content to stand on the periphery of understanding, trusting our soul to guide us in its own intuitive way. We are thus able to accept our role as agents of God's love, working out the details of what we do with that love as we journey through life.

What is mystery for the ego is a way of being for the soul. The rules of logic do not help us here; instead, the imagination affords us another tool for communication. Its language is not that of analysis, but of poetry and metaphor. The power of the creative process helps us move beyond the ego's limitations, unlock the door to mystery and engage it without needing to understand the details of the process itself, just as we do when we work in watercolour. Through creativity we touch our soul and invite its miracles into our everyday experience. This form of divine intervention does not stand in opposition to the natural laws that miracles are thought to violate but is very much a part of it. From this perspective, life is about miracles! The soul understands the entire human journey as a miracle and invites us to participate in it more consciously.

The mystery of prayer

Prayer – personal and corporate – has always been an essential element of the Christian tradition, including church services. As part of his Sermon on the Mount, Jesus instructed others in prayer, advising them not to "pray standing in the synagogues and on the street corners to be seen by [others]," but to go to a private place where intimate communion with an all-knowing God could take place (Matthew 6:5-15). In the Gospel of John, Jesus prays for himself and for others (John 17), setting the example of finding balance in prayer between our own needs and those of others. We pray alone and in groups, silently and aloud, as we confess our misgivings, express our concerns and bring our requests before God. Even

those who do not make prayer part of their regular routine can, in times of crisis, find themselves crying out for help to God.

Prayer is an important tool for our direct communion with God, but just how the divine and the human mingle in this way must remain to some extent mysterious. Prayer, as the example of Jesus' life shows, can be seen as a direct line to divinity. When we pray we open ourselves to God's energy, allowing its unrestricted flow into the vessel of our personhood. Prayer allows us to participate directly in divinity, activating the soul's once dormant energy within us. Through prayer we can experience God's fullness. In 2 Corinthians 12:9, we read that God's power is made "perfect in weakness." When we allow our false self to recede and our true self to emerge through prayer, God's power infuses our human vessel with divine love.

Because the ego does not easily understand the workings of the soul, it can interfere with the process of prayer. For example, we may find ourselves listing our desires during prayer, asking for a friend to keep safe on her journey or a teenager to finish high school successfully. Or we may ask God to be with us (or another) during a time of need. Such prayers make no sense if we understand God as omnipotent and omnipresent! God cannot be further informed or directed by our petitions. These prayers, and others like them, can risk viewing prayer in a superficial way: focused on what we want, what we think God wants or, worse, what we think God should want! From the soul's perspective, prayer aligns us with God's energy and power. By humbly acknowledging that "we do not know what we ought to pray for" (Romans

8:22), we can quiet our ego, allowing our silent awareness to absorb God's presence and having our lives transformed by the process. Prayer allows us to fill ourselves with God as we prepare to express divine love in the world.

When I was young, I thought that prayer was something I did purposefully. During church services, certain times were set aside for silent and verbal prayer, and I was encouraged to pray on my own between Sundays – which I tried to do regularly. But one day, while lying in the bath and aware of God's closeness, I decided to pray outside the regular schedule I had set for myself. As I consciously turned my mind to the usual kinds of prayers I practised, I realized that praying in one of these ways would stop the experience of God I was having at that moment. It occurred to me that I would have to stop one kind of praying in order to participate in another! I determined that the intentional prayer was driven by my ego, while the communing prayer, the one without words, was experienced by my soul. The question of how the two relate led me to examine closely the content of ego-directed prayer. By assenting to not knowing what we ought to pray for, we can shift the focus of our prayer from specific requests to general awareness. In changing the wording of our prayers, expressing our desire to become more aware of God's presence (instead of asking God to follow our suggestions), we remind our ego that God's power is not ours to control. Simply seeking to be aware of God's presence evokes God's mysterious power in our lives.

Prayer need not be confined to 'talking with God.' Rather, it can become a way of being. Prayer can be the action of non-action (an unseen divine action) that connects us with our soul – our direct link to God. Artmaking, gardening, meditation, walking, singing or making love can in this sense be forms of prayer. Of course, it is our decision whether we engage in these – or any – activities as acts of prayer. We can limit the actions to the activities themselves, or we can use them as gateways to experience God. While prayer unlocks the doors to communion with God, it does not solve the mystery. We do not need to understand it – prayer is effective because it activates God's energy in the world through all who engage in it. Ushering us into the eternal moment where the past and future merge into the present, prayer helps us to see the world from the soul's perspective. It is as if we are watching from God's vantage point, where all things interconnect, all things are possible and all things are completely revealed. Prayers are answered, not by magic and manipulation, but by the mysterious release of divine energy into everyday life. Hearts and even bodies are healed as God's power is channelled through us in the sharing of divine love.

The mysteries of death and eternal life

Death presents one of the greatest mysteries for human beings. On one level it seems a cruel joke that we should acquire self-consciousness only to become more fully aware of our own mortality. And though our culture has done its best to remove death from our everyday consciousness, it still lurks in the shadows of our joys and successes as a reminder of our transience and ultimate powerlessness. We know that we will die and we don't know what that will mean for us. While religions try to make sense of death by seeing it in a positive context, death remains a mysterious transition. We know that bodies decay, but what about consciousness? If it is inextricably linked to the brain, then it dies with our body. But if it is something in addition to physical reality, then although it may survive after death, we still do not know what happens, because we have no methods for observing such things. It might seem that, because we have a soul, we must survive death, but the 'we' we're talking about here includes the self-consciousness and perspective of the ego, which – whether enlightened or unenlightened, false self or true self – is not part of the soul. The question here – the question of life and death – is really whether the *ego* survives.

But even though the idea of death may seem dark and heavy, we remain curious about stories of white lights and the tunnels of near-death experience, or apparent communication with those who have physically departed this world. While science and reason attempt to explain these things away, those who have had such mysterious experiences seem convinced of life after death, whether they have proof or not. This raises some questions. Can all such talk be accounted for in terms of the ego's desire to continue beyond physical death, or is there another dimension to reality that only some have glimpsed? Is death our final goodbye, or is it a gateway to another state of being?

While I cannot answer these questions, I can allow my imagination to explore the many possibilities that have not been completely ruled out by science and reason. Einstein himself admitted that "imagination is more important than knowledge."[24] When we think we have found knowledge, we stop asking questions and our imagination shuts down. While as a race we may know a little more than we did a few centuries ago, we do not know as much as our future descendants will be able to claim. Seeing "through a glass darkly" is a condition of being human. When death touches our world, our questions intensify; if we release our preconceived notions about death, our imaginations can be ignited, enhancing our understanding of what it may mean. I will use an example from my own life to illustrate.

Almost two decades ago, my maternal grandmother was diagnosed with cancer at the age of 87. She accepted the inevitability of her death and asked her family to let her die at home. This was a difficult decision for them, but in the end they agreed to honour her wishes. As her illness progressed, a bed was set up in her favourite room, the kitchen, to enable her to continue to be present in her family's life. After a few short months, her health declined to the point where she fell into and out of a coma. During this time, her children and numerous grandchildren and great-grandchildren visited her. A chair was positioned at the head of her bed and all took turns sitting with her.

One day, about two weeks before her death, I sat in the chair beside her and waited to see if she would regain consciousness. By this time her bones were extremely brittle, making any movement very difficult. Her sight was almost completely gone. I held her hand and watched her as she laboured with each breath. I had been named after her and felt a special bond with her, and so I thought about how my life could be considered an extension of hers when she passed on. To my surprise, she called my name. I leaned over her, told her I was there, and asked why she was calling me. She said, "Come closer!" As I moved my face closer to hers, her hand came up and grasped the collar of my shirt. Pulling me closer, she said, "I can dance!" I was surprised by the intensity of her voice. I knew she couldn't dance – no one in her condition would be able to dance. She repeated excitedly, "I can dance!" Puzzled, I thought the effects of the drugs had distorted her judgment. Thinking she wanted me to get her up to dance, I replied in my most comforting voice, "No, Nanny, you can't dance. Not right now. You need to rest." Always a strong and feisty woman, she pulled at my shirt and said firmly, "You don't understand. I can dance. I am dancing. My arms and my legs can move and I can dance!" I looked into her face, and although I couldn't see what she could see, I saw there a look of peace and joy that remains with me to this day. There is no doubt in my mind: whatever was happening to her, she could dance!

Perhaps my grandmother, like the mystics Hildegard of Bingen, St. Teresa of Avila, and many others, saw something that those around her could not see. While modern culture offers psychological and medical explanations relating to hallucinations, electrolyte imbalance or dementia, I'm not so sure I accept these as the whole story. Maybe we could even consider the possibility that certain medical conditions predispose people to genuine mystical experience. Perhaps when our left-brain grasp on reality weakens, such conditions allow the contents of our soul to come to the surface more easily. Because the inner world of our soul is little nurtured (or even known) in our culture, it wouldn't surprise me if our dominant left brain sought to find other categories by which to make sense of it. Was my grandmother's experience the brain's way of dying, or was she close enough to another reality that she could express it while still alive in this one? Does this reality embrace the individual ego in some continuing form after death? While I can't answer these questions for certain, I refuse to close myself off to the possibility that death is a transition into a different way of being for us.

If it is such a transition, then what follows might well qualify as eternal life. But this concept can be understood in other ways. For example, we can believe our soul continues living after our physical death without thinking that the soul is the human-like or ego-like ghostly creature of popular culture. If we believe that our soul is linked to God, and that God is infinite, we can think of it as returning to God after we shed our physical bodies. In any case, it is our unenlightened ego, and not the soul, that craves that our personal identity continue beyond the grave. The emergence of our true self helps us to release the desire for endless personal existence and to become willing to participate in eternal life, regardless of what form it may take.

Likewise, we can allow our understanding of heaven and hell to mature. Our knowledge of the cosmos has changed dramatically since biblical times, when it was thought to consist of a flat earth covered by a dome-shaped firmament that hid the domain of celestial beings. Hell was thought to be the territory of demons and darkness located somewhere deep within the earth. Few hold these views today; the universe has proven to be vast and we but a small speck within it. And while there is no heaven above or hell below in the spatial sense, we can still preserve the idea that heaven is the domain of God and hell is dissociation from God. The Gospel of Luke declares that the kingdom of God is immediate, it is "within us" or "among us" (Luke 17:21). The degree to which we participate in it in this world is directly related to the amount of attention we give to our soul.

When Jesus responded to the rich young man who asked what he might do to obtain eternal life, the writer of the Gospel of Matthew linked his request with heaven (Matthew 19:16-23). After noting that the young man had rejected his instructions for obtaining eternal life, Jesus taught his disciples that attachment to material goods (the ego's desire) prevented entry into heaven (the soul's way of being). Heaven, understood in this way, is not a place we go, but a state of being. From this perspective, heaven (the dwelling place of God) is found within each of us. We are not granted access to it by external deeds or beliefs, but by our internal acceptance of and participation in the reality of our soul. Transferring our perspective from ego to soul allows us to evolve to a position of sustained awareness of God's presence in everyday situations, 'heaven on earth.' It is the experience of God that links us to eternity.

As we learn to be present in the moment, to be at all times conscious of the reality of our soul, we experience oneness with God and, indeed, eternal life. Gallery Image 9 illustrates this dynamic by contrasting the concepts of becoming one with God found in the biblical books of Leviticus and Hebrews. The image, entitled *Atonement* (at-one-ment), contains two half circles outlined in red that represent the Holy Place and the Most Holy Place of the ancient Tabernacle. According to the Leviticus account (Leviticus 16), a priest entered the Most Holy Place (the place where God was believed to dwell) once a year, making a sacrifice to atone for his sins and those of the whole community. The red triangle in the painting, which juts through the Holy Place and the Most Holy Place, represents the one-time perfect sacrifice of Jesus atoning for the sins of the whole world through his death, as described in the letter to the Hebrews (Hebrews 9). In the image, the Christ-triangle is left open at the top, allowing it to serve as a funnel, symbolizing a way through which those who choose to do so may pass. Respecting the mystery of God, the image reveals only half of each circle. Some of the vines twist their way under the triangle and grow towards the inner circle, changing colour as they progress. Taking on the 'colour' of God, they represent the transformation in our lives as we allow our journey to be guided by God, through our soul. The oneness with God to which this experience leads is a new way of being that lets us participate in eternity as finite creatures. Perhaps, when we take our final step through death, our individual egos simply continue the transformation in a different form, travelling further into the mysterious reality we can only glimpse from here. The enlightened ego feels no need for this future mystery to be revealed (at least not for itself): it is content with the experience of God in present reality.

EXERCISE

A simple exercise that may help us understand the mystery of eternal life involves focusing on our breathing, a natural act that most of us take for granted (until it is compromised). By becoming quietly conscious of our breath, we reduce the cares of our exterior life to the simple act of breathing. Drawing attention to air entering and leaving our bodies, we become more aware of the immediacy and simplicity of our relationship with God. Incorporate a time for attention to your breath into your personal ritual.

PART FOUR

VISION

The soul's vision is a unique point of view that grows from the seed of originality planted in our hearts by divine love. This vision becomes clearer as we weed out things in our lives that prevent us from connecting with our soul. Through intuition we make direct contact with this vision. The skills we have developed as artists provide tools for excavating and expressing it in an ongoing way.

A variety of sources provide inspiration for expanding and shaping our vision during our journey. Awakened to the teaching power within every moment of our lives, we become conscious of the underlying unity that connects us all. Like glittering stars in a clear night sky, each person who expresses God's love in the world makes a valuable contribution to the overall light. As we come to perceive the wholeness of the grand design, we accept others unconditionally, showing respect and gratitude for all who seek to follow the soul's way.

I hear words
whispered to me

I cannot tell
if they come
from inside
or outside

they tell me
things
I already know

they reveal
glimpses
of what I have
forgotten

Chapter 10

INTUITION

Lesson VIII

INTUITION AND THE CREATIVE PROCESS

Artist materials

You can use any medium or combination of media for the exercises in this chapter. Large-size paper will encourage more uninhibited responses to intuition. Use objects such as ice cream container lids, jar lids, bowls or plates to trace circles on your paper.

The importance of intuition

Thus far in our art lessons we have concentrated on how to see as an artist sees and how to use artist materials. Through observation you have learned how to identify and imitate patterns found in the natural world. But as you progress in your artistic abilities, you will naturally turn your attention to the 'why' of image-making. Why do artists continue to make images once they know how? Are the images for decoration, are they visual records of exterior reality, are they political or social statements, or are they a means of uncovering and sharing the contents of our soul? If it is soul-expression we are seeking, we must look further inward to discover deeper ways of connecting with our intuitive processes.

The greatest artists have always done this, but their work is not always appreciated right away. Some artists, such as Vincent Van Gogh and Paul Gauguin, were thought to be mad (or somewhat mad) in their time, only to be recognized as geniuses later. Even today the stereotype of the artist is that of someone who stands apart from the crowd. But perhaps artists do not so much deviate from what is normal as understand the world differently. More in touch with their unconscious mind, artists hear shouts where most detect only whispers. It is a central claim of this book that each of us is in some way an artist; if this is so, it must be possible for all of us to learn ways of hearing these whispers more clearly. Like the biblical prophets guided from within, we can learn to recognize and trust the small voice inside ourselves.

At the deepest intuitive level, each of us possesses a personal symbolism developed from our unique experience as we journey through life. While this symbolism may overlap with or be influenced by cultural symbolism, its main function is to generate personal wholeness: it provides a language through which the soul and ego can communicate while allowing us to bring to consciousness the deepest yearnings of our soul. Working with our dreams and fantasies (or imagination), we learn to interpret our personal symbols so that we can find and maintain a balance between our conscious and unconscious worlds. While the details of psychology and art therapy can be left to professionals, each of us can use the practice of art to develop our intuitive processes.

In his work *The Archetypes and the Collective Unconscious*, Carl Jung acknowledges that images are a powerful tool for unlocking the doors to our unconscious selves. He writes, "It is very easy for the unconscious to slip its subliminal images into the painting."[25] After encouraging his patients to draw pictures, he would use the concrete evidence of their images to initiate discussion. While Jung did not believe the images his patients created were 'art,' when we consider the works of William Blake, who spoke (and wrote) of angels dictating to him, or of John Milton and his muses, without whom he could not do his work, or of Marc Chagall, who painted his colourful dreams, we can see that works of art are indeed born of the unconscious. These men relied on an intuitive process that connected them to material in their unconscious mind, and no one would dispute that their creations were works of art. What sets them apart from others (such as Jung's patients) is not the source or content of their vision, but the consistency and technical expertise with which they presented it.

When we turn inward for the content of our images, we awaken to yet another level of soul recovery. We can use the tools of our trade (lines, shapes, colour and media) to describe our ideas instead of things in the natural world and to bring to light those images that are hidden inside and cannot be articulated in any other way. The reward for such efforts is great. To begin, the symbols that emerge unrestricted from the unconscious reveal the intimate thoughts of our deeper selves, allowing us to learn about the condition of our soul. Then, by reflecting on the images we create through this process, and by comparing them to others we have created, we gradually become more familiar with our personal inner language, progressing in our understanding slowly and steadily as does a child learning to read. Paying attention to our feelings as we work, and those elicited by the finished works, we will come to know what 'red' or 'straight lines' or 'round shapes' represent for *us*. Our symbolic language will help us communicate from within – first to ourselves, then to others in the world around us.

Tapping intuition

In Chapter 2, I described becoming conscious of interaction between my ego and soul through the process of creating my image *Parable of the Sower*. This procedure had a life-changing effect on my art and on other aspects of my experience. At that time, I began to see clearly that there was more to me under the surface than I had ever imagined. For the first few images I created after *The Sower*, I relied on the same method, recording insights in my journal as they occurred and waiting until further insights revealed their meaning. When I felt confident enough, I applied my skills as an artist to render each image. I quickly became comfortable with this method and for several months it worked quite well.

Not only was I happy with my new method of image-making, I felt as though I now fully understood the process. What's more, I expected that it would always work for me in the same way. Then, one night, a nightmare jarred me from such complacency. In my dream I watched the darks and lights of one of my favourite images reversing. The image, called *The Light*, shows vines growing from a single light source that, according to my personal symbolism, represents goodness. But the dream showed my image reversed – growth seemed to be emanating from a central darkness. This dream recurred over several weeks; each time I awoke in a sweaty panic. Finally, I discussed it with a friend, who advised me to 'stay with the dream' to see if it had a message. The next time it occurred I refused to let go of the image when I awakened. Almost immediately, in a state of consciousness somewhere between sleep and wakefulness, the fear left me and I found myself enjoying the new arrangements of colours and shapes as they moved about in my imagination. It was like watching an animation. Upon reflection, I came to understand that because of my self-satisfaction, I had closed myself off to further communication with my soul. Intuition is an evolving process. We do not learn it once and for all; we must be open to continual movement and changes from birth to death.

While I have tried to remain open to such changes since then, it has not always been easy, and I have often found myself slipping back into complacency. A few years ago I was to have an exhibition of artworks at a gallery in Halifax. It was booked a year in advance, and I was excited about the theme, but I had difficulty producing a body of work with the unity I thought the exhibition required. My theme was 'Goddess Re-Membered,' and I wanted to show that the energy of feminine symbols associated with the Greek goddesses could be reconciled with a Christian religious per-

spective. No small task, but I was sure it was possible. For weeks, then months, I worked on this idea, drawing and painting images, even composing poems to goddesses as I walked in the woods near my house. The exhibition was to open on January 1, but by mid-November I still had nothing to exhibit. The thought of cancelling crossed my mind more than once.

However, while visiting my daughter several hundred miles from my studio, I had a dream that tugged some familiar intuitive strings. This familiarity was so vague I almost chose to go back to sleep. But instead, I pulled myself from my warm bed and took my journal downstairs. In soft thought-messages I 'heard' something like the following: "Your problem is that you are concentrating on the goddesses themselves – pay attention instead to what they *say*." Within a few minutes several images came to mind; I recorded them in my journal without trying to interpret them. When I was sure the flow had stopped, I looked at the sketches and saw that each of them contained a common symbol, a loose concentric circle motif, as seen in Figure 10.1. Upon further examination, I also noted that I had made eight drawings and that seven could be linked to the Greek goddesses Hestia, Athene, Hera, Demeter, Persephone, Aphrodite and Artemis. The eighth image revealed a connection by which they could be related to Christianity.

Such images do not simply come to us from out of the blue. They are born as our intuition is tapped through a balance of work and rest, practice and assimilation. As we begin to give conscious attention to developing intuition, ideas will

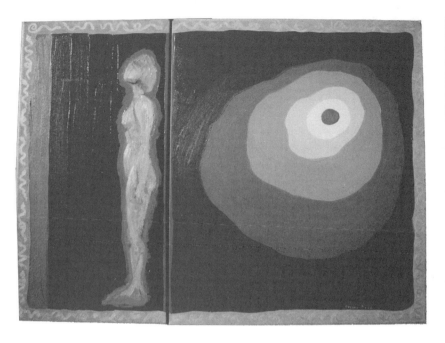

Figure 10.1 The concentric circle motif seen in each of these completed oil paintings, Athena (left) and Persephone (right), was revealed in a dream.

come to us. By training ourselves to recognize, develop and apply our intuitive processes, we will find that we already know the answers to most of our questions. Instead of depending only on rational processes, we can learn to rely on our non-rational processes of intuition as well. One of the most common questions I am asked at workshops by people attached to religious denominations is "How do I know the voice within me is the Holy Spirit or Christ or God and not just myself?" It is sad that we are so removed from the inner workings of our own soul that we often do not recognize the voice of divinity that is naturally within us. When such doubts arise, it is helpful to remember that the objective of our soul is love. If we are being led in the direction of love (of God *and* of others) we can know with confidence that it is our soul that beckons. As we peel away the layers of ego that separate us from our soul, we will free ourselves from the paralyzing fear that prevents us from cultivating our intuition. We will make mistakes as we go along, but that is part of any learning process.

The mandala

The word *mandala* means 'circle' or 'sacred circle.' According to Jung it is the "traditional antidote for chaotic states of mind."[26] Mandalas are sometimes used in religious contexts as a meditation device and can be found among the artifacts of many primitive cultures. For example, the massive rocks at Stonehenge, which are thought to have religious meaning, are arranged in a circle, as are many of the elaborate designs used in Buddhist meditation. Influenced by the mandala creations of Jung's patients and the interaction between inner and outer worlds that they provoke, I developed the following art exercise as a way of helping to unlock the doors between conscious and unconscious modes of perception.

This exercise is in two parts that are equally important. The first, which involves creating an image as it arises in consciousness, begins with reflection on a circle that has been drawn at random in any colour with any drawing medium (Figure 10.2). Noting that a circle cuts space into three parts – the inside, the outside and the perimeter – ask yourself three questions in relation to the circle (or circles) you have drawn on the page. 1) Where do I perceive myself to be: inside, outside or on the edge? 2) In which direction would I like to go, if any? 3) What helps or hinders my progress? After a few moments of quiet reflection on these questions, and before forming any concrete plans about how the finished image might look, begin to draw.

Working intuitively, try to detach yourself from objectives and expectations. Observe your actions as if you were watching your own decision-making processes as they take place in your head. By observing each thought and action as it arises, you are put in closer contact with your intuition. (Even

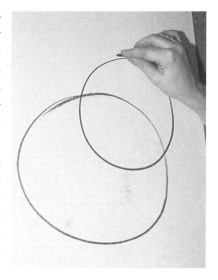

Figure 10.2 A circle creates three spaces: inside, outside, and circumference. A mandala can be created from one or more circles drawn randomly on the paper.

noting that you are able to detach from your preconceived ideas in such a manner is helpful.) If your first inclination in making your image is to reach for a red marker or crayon, then allow yourself to do so. By trying to keep prior decisions and future objectives to a minimum, you can give more attention to the red as you are using it. This means being attuned to the present moment. When a thought about a different colour or shape or line arises, however vague, follow the thought without interpreting it and allow the image to grow step by step without imposing your conscious intentions. As you work, the least strong voice within may often be the one you need to listen to. Recording what is revealed without judging it, you will open further the doors of your intuition. Work on the image for at least twenty minutes to allow time for the process to be engaged.

The second part of the exercise encourages conscious dialogue between your inner and outer selves. In your journal, first record your reactions to creating your mandala. What did it feel like as you made the marks on your page? Was it relaxing, exciting, scary, strange? Record as many feel-

Figure 10.3 This watercolour mandala, entitled Mantra, *was refined from earlier intuitive sketches. It suggests a progression inward from the outer edge of the circle.*

about it – before you describe the exercise. Afterwards, explain what you were saying with your image and then record his or her reaction in your journal for further reflection. Sometimes other people's insights into our work (and our reactions to these insights) allow us to learn more about ourselves (Figure 10.3).

As you hone your skills as an artist, you can carry the mandala exercise in your mind. By observing yourself in a detached way as you make decisions in your work, you will gradually be able to identify differences in the voices within. Disciplining yourself to stay focused on the present moment will heighten your self-awareness and sharpen your intuitive instincts. Over time you will develop 'knowledge by acquaintance,' learning which thoughts and voices are projected from the depths of your soul.

Trusting intuition

When, as artists, we have become attuned to the intuitive voice within ourselves, we will never be at a loss for content in our images. Whether our statement is personal, religious, social or political, each of us connects the dots in a unique fashion. By allowing our intuition to guide the content of our images, as well as their construction, the originality of our art shines through. Whether our art is a statement on world hunger or how we feel about the sky on a summer day, it represents our personal perspective, and a specific moment in time and space.

When we trust our intuition, we are more likely to find the tools and energy to express our vision. Life will always get in the way of our plans

ings about the process as you can remember, then turn your attention to your responses to the image you have created. What does it say to you about the three questions asked at the beginning of the exercise? What did you discover about yourself? Were there any surprises? Putting the image in a place where you can view it over time invites further dialogue between your internal and external worlds, allowing you to keep discovering new aspects of your personal symbolism as it emerges. It may also be useful to share with a close friend, someone with whom you feel comfortable revealing personal matters. Ask what your friend thinks if we let it. But being in touch with our intuition helps us weed out the soul-needs from the ego-wants so we can direct our energies to what is truly important. Each of us has responsibilities to ourselves, to our families and to the world at large. Our soul would not have us abandon any of these, but rather points us in the direction of wholeness. Indeed, the process of art will help us avoid personal disasters by balancing our creative needs with other requirements. The merging of art and soul are inevitable at this level. Creativity provides an outlet the soul needs and facilitates communication between our inner and outer selves, which in turn restores harmony to both.

EXERCISE

In addition to the mandala exercise, begin a regular practice of creating a self-portrait. Start by drawing your face in a mirror – every other day, if possible. This will help you connect your inner and outer selves by allowing you to practise the use of media while focused on exploring your identity. Do not worry about getting the likeness right. Your portraits are descriptions of more than physical countenance; they are picture-essays of your soul's development (Figure 10.4). Between 'portrait days' draw the condition of your soul in symbolic terms, beginning with your centre and moving outward. As weeks and months pass, review your drawings to discover patterns and recurring symbols. Record your reactions to your works in words in your journal.

Figure 10.4 Self-portraits, drawn in a journal each day (or so) can be used as picture-essays, uncovering the state of our relationship with our soul at the time of drawing.

STRENGTHENING THE SOUL'S VISION

Intuiting the soul's vision

Intuition, which is common to creativity and spirituality, leads artists and mystics to the place where truths are revealed in a non-rational manner. When we have adopted the soul's perspective, intuition becomes a channel for the way of God to be revealed to us – it is the voice of the soul. Gallery Image 10, *Mediator*, explores this process. The orange and green (at the top and bottom of the image) represent divinity and humanity, respectively. A fiery yellow circle in the centre of the image is the result of yellow being 'extracted' from both orange and green. Symbolically, this yellow represents the intuitive process as a connection between humanity and divinity. Intuition fuses and ignites the common elements of our divine and human natures as in an alchemical process, which is represented in the image by the merging of yellow into white. Deeply mysterious, intuition provides a bridge by which we can access the divine and the human simultaneously. The more we are aware of this bridge and how to access it, the more we can use it to develop our relationship with God.

Through intuition we provide a subjective face for the objective love of God. When this happens, the ego is transformed and our true self emerges. Keeping our intuition alive – and lively – allows us to commune with the divine and to reach our potential as human persons no matter what our religious affiliation.

At the same time, the intuitive process connects us with everyone else. Because the souls of all are connected to God, we are connected to others through our connection to God. Because of this connection, we are able to relate at an intimate level with those who share our journey – from the past, present and future. Through intuition we access the archetypal bonds of humanity, which unite us in our common pursuit and allow us to speak to each other in ways our rational minds may never understand. For example, I have sometimes expressed something in an artwork that I later discovered had been expressed by another artist in another time and culture. So strong are the similarities between some of my pieces and the works by others I have never known, or known about, that I have been forced to confront this phenomenon.

I believe this relates to Jung's concept of the *collective unconscious*. From his research, which included the study of mythology, primitive cultures and dreams, Jung concluded that housed within each individual human psyche is a host of archetypal material common to all. This material manifests itself in expressions that cut across boundaries of culture and time. I believe that every person has access to this collective unconscious through the soul. Sometimes – through the intuitive process – the archetypes reveal a truth that we did not know before, or that we were not consciously seeking. As we try to express this inexpressible truth, we find ourselves using words and images similar to the ones that others have used. Graphic examples of this in my life include a poem I wrote and later found – almost word for word – in a book of poems by St. Teresa of Avila. I had not heard of St. Teresa at the time I wrote my poem, but have studied her work since, finding great comfort and kinship in her words. Another incident involved a lithographic print I produced at my studio; I later found an almost identical image in a technical book by Kandinsky. To illustrate a point in his book (similar to the point I was trying to make with my print), Kandinsky used a photograph of the star cluster Hercules,[27] which looks almost exactly like my print (see Gallery Image 6, *The Light of the World*).

How do we explain such synchronicities? I believe that as I have opened myself to the stirrings of the soul, I have heard the same spiritual echoes that have been heard by others. As we become attuned to the spiritual reality of our world, we hear 'whispers from the other side.' This is the voice of our soul speaking through intuition, thus allowing us to continue the tradition of bringing eternal truths to life through our individual lives. We do not learn anything new – it is only new to us. When the objective truths of God are brought to consciousness through experience, thoughts and ideas are repeated in the language of our present time and culture, coloured by our subjective knowledge and development. When we think or write something that we later find expressed by someone else, we ought not to be surprised. We are not unconsciously plagiarizing; we are tapping into a spiritual current that feeds our soul and that has fed the souls of others who have tapped it. Divinity within humanity has been discovered by people of every culture and in every time. It is intuition, a process that artists and mystics of all ages have practised, honed and learned to trust, that makes such a thing possible.

From an archetypal perspective, the vision of our soul is the same as the vision of every other soul: to promote love. How we carry out this task is unique to each of us. While this may sound oversimplified, the truth is that it *is* very simple – we complicate it with conditions and ego-centred expectations. Like spring water running downhill, God's love can flow through our individual souls, quenching the thirst of all who approach it. Using our freedom of choice, we have the power to unleash the soul's love and make ourselves its channel, or we can resist being part of the divine stream by clinging to the ego's distorted view of what is most important in our lives. Only the expectations and desires of the ego can disrupt our soul's intuitive flow. If we want love to work in a certain way or to promote certain consequences, we have allowed our ego to alter the soul's vision. Divine love embraces individuality and creativity, recognizing the specialness of all life regardless of physical, emotional, mental or spiritual characteristics. Intuition, while its expressions may seem individualistic, is directed towards the good of all. We are given so that we may give.

At the level of soul, the vision of expressing love is as clear as it can ever be; all we need to do is remove the obstacles that prevent love from flowing through us. By accepting or rejecting this vision, each of us determines how much of the soul's love will pass through us into this world.

There is not one right way to express the soul's love; each of us participates in a spiritual journey that is ever-changing. This and our vast differences as human beings result in the love of God taking on diverse appearances as it is articulated through different individuals. Like one hue in a divine rainbow, within which can be found an infinite range of colour, each of us makes a significant and unique contribution as our true self emerges. While complex and diverse, we are also interconnected with all others at the level of soul, sharing its universal mission.

Expression of the soul's vision is a creative dynamic, becoming stronger as we become stronger in our ability to access it. By transforming our egocentric desires in light of the all-encompassing love of God, we keep open the doors to our intuition. By releasing our egocentric desires, we create more space within ourselves to gestate God's love. It is the flow of this love – into and through us – that we experience as intuition, guidance from the soul given to help us bring its vision to life. By staying connected to this stream, we are assured, as artists and mystics, that our intuition will be trustworthy and plentiful.

Developing intuition

When asked "What is intuition?" students usually use phrases such as a gut instinct, a way of knowing, a deep feeling, and so on. Some think that intuition delivers messages about the future, some that it is a method of communication with those not present, and others that it is a decision-making device. For many, intuition is equivalent to impulse, a snap decision that is not arrived at through rational channels. Almost everyone admits to having had some form of intuitive experience, but intuition – like creativity and spirituality – can seem strange, and many prefer to keep it to themselves.

Clearly, intuition is a method of perceiving information that does not depend entirely upon the five senses (sight, smell, touch, sound and taste). Some people are suspicious of intuition. Others, who prefer to follow their intuition, are less likely to depend on sensory data, regardless of how convincing they might seem, if they conflict with their intuition.

What we need for a soul-full approach to life is a balance between the two: the rational (including the senses) and the non-rational (including intuition). Both are needed to create harmony and wholeness for the human journey. In our left-brain culture, hard and concrete 'facts' supplied by the senses often overshadow the equally legitimate right-brain 'facts,' which are hard to define by left-brain standards. But the intuition of soul-full persons is more than quirky impulse; it is a physically based spiritual tool that expands our perceptions dramatically by combining the physical with non-physical capacities. The tension between our intuitive and sensory natures is resolved as we apply ourselves to the task of integration.

While the experience of impulse may be our first conscious clue to the reality of intuition, if we remain only at the impulse level, we will not have a solid foundation that we can consistently trust. Moving further involves work. As the Parable of the Talents (Matthew 25) suggests, although we may not have been given equal lots initially, what we do with what we have is the most important thing. While some of us are naturally intuitive, all possess the ability and all can develop further. Intuition becomes sharpened through the development of self-knowledge. Because of our complex psychology, knowing ourselves is a long and arduous project. It requires peeling though layers of self-deception formed over the years by an industrious and efficient ego, and our efforts must be diligent and continuous if we hope to connect – and stay connected – with our soul.

Intuition is developed over time, maturing like a good friendship or a fine wine, and our trust in it builds over time as well. Like a child learning to read, we begin slowly. For the child, new words can sometimes be discovered by guessing, but usually he needs to be told the word, at least the first time he meets it. Some children will not need to be told a second time, but many will, and a few will have to be told over and over again. Developing intuition requires a similar persistent and systematic approach. After we become familiar with our intuitive moments by studying when they happen and what happens when we act on them, we are more able to gauge what they mean, relying less on guesswork. Like children, we are sure to make mistakes along the way, but as we progress, our successes will be apparent if we measure ourselves against earlier times. Each experience is like a new word that we must learn if we are to add it to our intuitive vocabulary. Like the art process that employs it, intuition builds from within as we practise and apply our skills.

It is imperative that we commit ourselves to self-scrutiny if we hope to increase our intuitive abilities. If it is the soul's path we are on, we need to be able to distinguish the ego's impulses from those of our true self, and we need to know when we are being motivated not by intuition but by such things as fears or phobias. For example, I have a phobia of flying. And while I understand the safety issues around flying and the physics that allows planes to fly, when the doors close in a plane I panic. My initial impulse is to scream, run for the door and demand to be let off the aircraft. This is not my intuition trying to save me from a crash, but my ego reacting to fear. While it is sometimes hard for me to tell the difference, I have learned to judge impulses by the feelings they elicit. Another example may help to clarify. A few years ago I was driving alone in my car on a hilly road in a rural area, en route to an important meeting. I was driving quite fast because I was a little late. As I drove, I was thinking that I would like to be helpful to those I would be meeting. A quiet inner voice told me that if that were true, I might want to slow down. At once I took my foot off the gas pedal – just in time to avoid a collision with an oncoming car that was passing another car on a blind hill. Because I have worked hard to decipher the voices within, I have learned how to distinguish the voice of my soul from the others in my head. While I still make mistakes from time to time, they are usually in situations that are like new words for me – opportunities for further learning.

For many, times of emergency are the only times they pay attention to intuition. When all ego-dominated avenues have been exhausted, our soul can sometimes be heard in the silence of despair or hopelessness. But the process of intuition is available to us all the time. By paying attention to our impulses, we can learn more about where they come from and set aside those generated by the ego. Intuition set in motion by the soul always moves us towards the soul's vision. To discover the source of an impulse, we can ask how or if it will help us express more of the soul's love in the world. In the first example above, I'm not sure I would have been able to express more love by leaving the plane. First, giving in to my fear would have put my ego in charge of my actions, causing me to retreat further from my soul. Even if the plane did crash, perhaps I could have expressed the soul's love to other passengers on the way down! In the second example, I surely could express more love by avoiding an accident. Attention to such experiences over time (and our felt response in each case) will help us identify the soul's voice in everyday life.

When checking an impulse for its source, we may want to consult St. Paul's letter to the Galatians. Intuition that stems from our soul will exhibit at least some of the qualities listed as fruits of the Spirit: "love, joy, peace, patience, kindness, goodness, faithfulness, gentleness and self-control" (Galatians 5:22-23). Using our rational mind, we can judge whether our impulse passes the test. If it does, we can proceed with confidence, knowing that we are following the soul's path as best we can. If it does not, we can observe our reactions to the testing, searching the hidden agendas of our ego that may be trying to confuse or mislead us. Developing our intuition is a personal process; only we can be sure whether the ego is deceiving us. Self-discipline tempered by sensitivity to the vision of our soul will help us avoid the extremes of self-indulgence and asceticism that arise from lack of balance. Wisdom – sustained and informed intuition – involves hard work, but the benefits are immeasurable.

Practising intuition

The practice of intuition puts us more deeply in touch with our soul. By acting on its messages, we gradually enlighten our ego so that it adopts the soul's vision. Like a physical muscle, intuition needs regular exercise to become strong and trustworthy. As we make our trek from the unenlightened ego's narrow and selfish perspective on the world to the universal and inclusive vision of the soul, we are not bound by our blunders and misunderstandings – we can learn from them along the way. Like art, intuition grows with practice, assessment, refinement and more practice. Just as we cannot think or wish a painting into being, neither will our intuition take root if we do not cultivate it in a concrete sense. Intuition helps us stay in touch with our soul through our droughts of doubt, fear and complacency.

Adopting a pro-active attitude, we can integrate intuition into our everyday lives instead of resorting to it only during times of stress or exasperation. The result will be continuous renewal, and the connection to our soul will become stronger and more easily accessible. It is like keeping the gas tank of our car full all the time. The process of art is one sure way to keep in touch with the intuitive process. For all the reasons presented in this book – and countless others – regular artmaking keeps the valve between our inner and outer selves open, allowing fuller dialogue between the two. Journal writing is another excellent way to stimulate intuition – writing not only about our feelings during good or bad times but asking and answering questions about our role in the world. Reading past journals (or looking at images we have previously created) allows us to see where we have been, so that we can examine the path we have taken and respond accordingly.

The conscious practice of intuition provides a tool for centring. Centring brings us to the place where we are at one with the divine. Whatever helps us to reach this place – artmaking, journalling, praying, gardening, walking, singing – becomes part of our centring process. The more we discover what works best for us, the more easily we can find this place when we need to. While the experience of oneness with God is personal, we share such encounters with all others because all our souls are linked to God. Think of Siddhartha Gautama and Jesus of Nazareth or William Blake and St. John of the Cross. Our intuition allows us to stand where they stood, see what they saw and hear what they heard. By regular centring we can engage the tasks of daily life with direction and enthusiasm. And while we may, from time to time, feel ourselves drawn away from the centre, we can use our intuition to return as often as we need to renew our strength. As we experience the effects of this way of being on our lives and on the lives of others (through our influence), we will be further motivated to commit more of our time and energy to living from this centred position. It is as if we have found our real home – a place where we know we will find support, encouragement and love. Being centred in this way gives us confidence, a confidence we may not have experienced even with our family of origin. Each time our intuition is engaged we can return to this spiritual centre – the most holy of places – and be sure that we will find the rest we seek, thus also finding strength to be constructive members of a larger community.

When we are distant from our centre – especially for long periods of time – the ego (often because of the strength of cultural conditioning) can cause us to become preoccupied with details instead of keeping our eye on the soul's vision. A few years ago I was to give a presentation to a group of my peers. I started getting nervous, worrying that I would not do well, and began to fuss with my notes. Almost in a state of panic, I decided to spend the afternoon before my presentation painting at the lakeside where I was staying. Immediately after I began the painting process, my panic left and I felt myself reconnecting with my soul. The right-brain process of artmaking ushered me gently into the quiet place where art and spirituality meet. My ego's anxiety about doing well was relaxed by my soul's enthusiasm for being in the moment. When we are connected to the deepest part of ourselves, the details will take care of themselves.

The transformation of our ego through the use of intuition offers concrete means by which the soul's vision can be communicated to the world around us. Personal rituals (as recommended in this book) can help strengthen our connection by providing ways for us to engage and sustain our intuition, reminding us that we are more than what exists on the surface. But while ritual acts or symbols remind us to centre, they cannot keep us centred unless we extend the metaphor of ritual to include everything we do. This is not as difficult as it may seem, but it does require that we redefine our lives in light of our soul's vision. To illustrate, being an artist is part of my identity – no matter what I do, I do it as an artist; I cannot *not* be an artist. All that I see is seen through an artist's eyes; all that I do is done with an artist's hands. This book I write as an artist – that is how art comes into it even when I'm not explicitly talking about art. If I can come to understand myself as an agent of God's love with the same intensity, everything I do will reflect my soul's objective. Nothing – not interactions with others or personal fantasies or goals – can be separated from my work as God's agent: this work is my raison d'être and it colours all my decisions. Like salt dissolved in water, it is part of my physical, spiritual, emotional and intellectual makeup. This is an ideal to which we can aspire as we journey through the transitions of life, and we will realize it more fully as our spirituality develops.

Seeing ourselves in this light, our entire life becomes a ritual through which we remain constantly connected to our soul. As each cup of tea we drink, each flower we smell, each person we encounter becomes part of our personal ritual, we come to discover deeper meaning in every action we undertake. Our work as God's agent expressing love in the world releases us from the pettiness of our ego's pride and allows us to focus on what we can do, not on how well we do it compared to others. Our insecurity and vulnerability cease to be liabilities, and our capacity for joy is multiplied.

As noted in Chapter 8, such awareness results in the expression of our true self – each one of us an original manifestation of an identical vision. Finding ways to remain centred, we acquire the strength to follow our unique path. Our lives become complete; our imagination and creative energy are synthesized in pursuit of our vision. Familiarity with the intuitive process at work within us strengthens the reality of spiritual life, allowing us to contribute consciously to its evolution by the example we set for those who come after us.

EXERCISE

In your journal, ask your soul what it needs to express itself more fully in your life. As the answers well up inside, write them in your journal, using quotation marks (or some other means) to distinguish between questioner and answerer. As in the mandala exercise, try to refrain from thinking before you write; allow the thoughts to unfold as you write. Try not to judge the responses until you have fully expressed them. Then, if you wish to ask further questions, do so in the same way, responding automatically as thoughts arise in your consciousness. Later, reflect on both the questions and answers and record your thoughts on the process.

you have taught
me to see
the sacred patterns
in nature

you have opened
my eyes
to the rhythm of
dancing lines
and colours
hidden beneath the surface

you have shown me
the special
in the ordinary
and the ordinary
in the special

you have whispered
the secret code
in my ear
and I have
listened

Chapter 11

ECLECTICISM

Lesson IX

EXPLORING MEDIA

Artist materials

This lesson will introduce collage as a means of mixing and exploring media. You will need a base of cardboard or heavy paper on which to construct the collage. You may also use glue, scissors, charcoal, crayons, pastels, coloured pencils or watercolour as desired. You can incorporate unfinished and 'unsuccessful' attempts at images into the work as well (Figure 11.1).

Figure 11.1 A variety of supplies can be incorporated into a collage, including old or unsuccessful artworks.

Moving beyond our comfort zone

Sometimes adult students begin art classes with very definite ideas about what art is. They may think that the term visual art refers only to paintings, prints or drawings that hang on a wall. But there is much more to visual art than these traditional forms. In fact, at a recent opening of an exhibition of paintings, the director of the gallery commented that she thought painting was *passé* – there are so many new media to explore. While I hope she is mistaken, it is true that graffiti, conceptual art, performance art and computer-based art are only a few examples of visual media unknown just a century ago. From live moulds to animal carcasses, artists are continually expanding their repertoire of materials in order to make their images provocative, interesting and meaningful. Visual art does not need to be restricted to what has been, but is always open to what might be.

Practice in the use of existing media coupled with observation provides an inner tool kit with which we can begin to assemble our vision as artists. Gathering physical and mental tools, we can begin to build with a solid foundation of skill. But we are not limited by what we have done before. Being an artist means that we always remain open to new possibilities and are willing to explore new frontiers, technically and creatively. Time spent honing our technical skills gives us the confidence to move beyond where we are and to improvise as necessary. We are no longer restricted to the materials of a specific medium but use the materials we choose in service of a common goal: the articulation of our vision. At this point product becomes the focus. Our aim is to speak our truth to the world – art and soul together as a single voice.

Knowing how individual materials act and interact helps us figure out how to combine media to create desirable, effective and (if appropriate) permanent results. As we come to understand the basics of artistic expression – line, shape, perspective, composition, and so on – decisions as to which media we use become less important. A portrait is a portrait, whether it is created with charcoal, pastel, watercolour, oils, plaster, bubble gum or a combination of these. If we remain within the limits of a single medium – without at least exploring how it interacts with others – we may never know the full range of its artistic potential, or our own. Worse, we may become purists who are confined by one medium. For example, artists who are beginning to work with watercolour often avoid using white pigment in order to emphasize the idea of working from light to dark. If they continue to resist using white pigment as mature artists, they limit experimentation, and thus close doors to a wide range of new possibilities. Learning through personal experience which materials can be mixed successfully for our purposes is essential. If, for example, we decide to use a clay base for a work, it is helpful to know how to prepare the clay so that it will not break easily – and which kinds of paints will adhere best to it. Exploration helps us discover additional tools and the confidence to work with them, which makes us better able to express what we want to say.

Such innovative use of materials is the fruit of an artist's insight and labour. Using anything and everything at our disposal, we construct images that satisfy our creative urges and stir the imagination of others. Recognizing that no one else sees the world exactly as we do, we determine what seems most important to us from our vantage point at a particular time in space and thus find the originality of our vision. The expression of our vision will gain originality as we give ourselves freedom to explore beyond our comfort zone, in form as well as content.

Engaged in the process of making our personal statement, we can sometimes become consumed by it, to the point that we are surprised when others don't immediately understand what we are trying to say. I remember once building a seven-foot cross using six- by six-inch beams as a base. I had collected broken pieces of mirror from various glass vendors; using a hammer and a glue gun, I reshaped and attached the broken mirrors to the cross. It was a laborious process resulting in many cuts and burns to both hands, but the prospect of seeing my 'broken self' reflected in pieces on this cross kept me moving forward with the construction. Because I was extremely excited by my project, I shared it with the women in my Bible study group, thinking that they of all people could appreciate what I was trying to do. The blank stares I got suggested otherwise. Finally, one woman, not wanting to hurt my feelings, asked gently, "*Why* are you doing that?" I was shocked by her question – I thought the group would be as moved by the idea as I had been. This experience led me to reflect on the importance of speaking our vision, even if we may feel we are a lone voice crying in the wilderness. When my 'broken cross' was eventually exhibited to diverse audiences, the response from those who did 'get it' provided encouragement for subsequent projects.

By adding new 'words' to our visual vocabulary through direct experience, we continue to expand our comfort zone. And while ultimately we may choose to return to the confines of a particular medium, it will be because we feel that that medium best allows us to express our vision, not because it is the only method we know. In addition, investing time in exploration will enlarge our scope of appreciation for the work of others whose forms of expression are different from our own.

Creating a visual record

An exercise using the medium of collage can help us become more conscious of the connection between art and soul. Collage is a tactile medium that can incorporate a wide variety of materials. While some collages are quite simple, using relatively few different materials, they can be as elaborate as the imagination of the artist. For this exercise, materials can be attached to a stiff base by a variety of means: glue, paste, paint, gums (or anything that previous experience has proven to be permanent and non-colouring). Components for the collage can include images that have been ripped or cut from magazines or any other suitable source. The chosen components are then arranged in any composition in thick or thin layers, as desired. You can draw or paint over the entire composition, or you can depend solely on the applied materials to create the effects you want. Because of its seemingly endless possibilities, collage is especially helpful for those who have a hard time 'loosening up.' The eclecticism of collage helps us to get out of the box created by rigid expectations, our own or other people's. Using the principles already learned, such as composition, perspective and balance, collage opens many doors to expression and experimentation for those who want to focus on design rather than on drawing or painting.

The content of this collage should reflect your artistic and spiritual growth. By including images you have created in the past and integrating thoughts recorded in your journal in the finished product, you can follow your intuition to make a statement about your progress. Taking the best (literally, by cutting out pieces of images that you think are successful) from previous experience, you can construct your vision of the merging of art and soul in your life. This is not a poster or a craft; it is an artistic expression made up of bits and pieces of various materials that visually reflect how you feel about your personal growth. There is no right or wrong way to approach the exercise; it is only unsuccessful if it expresses nothing of your inner self. You may include text if you wish; anything meaningful that comes to mind is worth considering. For this exercise, the final product is important: use anything at your disposal that helps to make your visual statement conform as closely to your inner convictions as possible. When you have completed your collage, display it in a prominent space in your 'studio' to remind you who you were, spiritually and artistically, at the time you created it. It can serve as a statement of account in your journey and encourage you to proceed further. (Gallery Image 5, *Persona Distortions*, is an example of a lithography collage that provides a record of my thoughts at the time it was created.)

EXERCISE

In addition to creating the collage as described above, experiment with combinations of media. Try mixing charcoal with pastels and coloured pencils. Wet charcoal marks with water, noting the effects on the image and the physical properties of the paper. Apply watercolour over and under pastel or try drawing in ink over watercolour (Figure 11.2). These are but a few suggestions. Try your hand at others, recording in your journal which ones appealed to you and why. After you feel comfortable with some of the effects created by experimentation, use them in an image, either representational or symbolic. Note how the effects are different from what you can achieve through the use of a single medium.

Figure 11.2 Examples of some effects of mixing media. Left to right, top row: charcoal and pastel; charcoal and coloured pencil; charcoal and water. Bottom row: watercolour over pastel; pastel over watercolour; ink over watercolour.

ASSEMBLING THE SOUL'S VISION

Identifying the new age

By being open to eclecticism not only in art but also intellectually and spiritually, and in particular by using the tools of science, technology and feminism unique to our age, we can assemble and express the soul's vision in a way that is comprehensible and meaningful for our time. This is an opportunity to correct past mistakes and misconceptions. While we have sometimes failed miserably to express God's love as Christians because of things such as egocentric preoccupation with being theologically right (evidenced, for example, by witch hunts and our attempts to proselytize Aboriginal peoples), we can learn from our mistakes and change our ways. Overcoming our fear of those whose spiritual customs are different from our own allows us to see the common bond that connects us all. This needs to happen both collectively and individually. If we remain open to all practices and sources of insight, including art, we can expand our perceptions of where an authentic spirituality, at the deepest level of soul, can take us.

Now is the time when we shape our vision, and thus the world, for the generations to follow. We must learn a way of being and of living in the world that allows responses from our soul to predominate in decision-making. We are sojourners sharing an inherited environment with all creatures who travel with us. We shape our culture (socially and environmentally) using what our ancestors have given us. Others will follow our path and will have to deal with whatever we leave behind. Some ages have offered much to their children, such as peace, justice and mercy; others have left a legacy of pollution, prejudice and greed. As we become conscious of ourselves as key players in the divine plan, we can determine which of our decisions, personal and collective, are most likely to benefit future generations.

Recent discoveries in areas as diverse as science and feminism contribute to our ongoing development, allowing our generation to play its part in the process of human evolution. Advances in science have shown the world to be a complex, interconnected system made up of many smaller systems. Evidence in physics has revealed that the earth is part of a much larger cosmological network that has evolved over billions of years. We may never know exactly how it was formed, or how – or if – it will end, but we do know from geology that the physical surface of the earth is constantly shifting and changing, and from biology and paleontology that human life itself has evolved over millions of years. Archeological and anthropological evidence shows that diverse human civilizations have emerged, seemingly independently, and that most have practised some form of community ritual. While this knowledge was unavailable to our religious ancestors, we must make room for it now in order to foster our spiritual growth and the development of our soul connection. In this context, an artistic approach, which easily recognizes the value of symbols and metaphors in a variety of religious practices, becomes more important than ever. Such an approach allows us, for example, to appreciate ancient texts from all religions while seeing that our understanding of the world is very different from that of their authors.

Technological advances are also central to our present age. By logging on to the information highway through a cyberspace network, we can communicate with people around the world, accessing information on everything from having a baby to building a bomb. The computer has helped us become an information-saturated and more fully global community. By Grade 5 our children may know more about the world and how it works than many of us knew at the end of our senior year of high school! We are also able to interact with others as never before. From the privacy of our home, we can chat with people from anywhere in the world on any topic we choose. As a result, we can also know more about a wide variety of religious traditions and practices than our ancestors could have even imagined. New relationships are being formed. The people and practices we encounter, both traditional and non-traditional, have much to teach us.

If science and technology are not enough to distinguish us from previous ages, the impact of feminism surely sets us apart. The hard work of feminists, both women and men, during the last century has literally and metaphorically changed the face of our social, religious and working environments. Religious dogma and traditions have been questioned like never before; critical thinkers are reflecting on the meaning of authority; feminist biblical scholars and theologians, digging through dusty texts, look to reconstruct a *herstory*[28]

for women, whose stories have been lost in records kept by and for men. For contemporary women and men, spirituality must take matters of gender and equality seriously – inclusivity and universality are not optional if we hope to experience the soul's wholeness in our lives.

Addressing the 'New Age'

One of the distinctive phenomena of our own new age, an eclectic set of religious tendencies drawing sustenance from all the currents of contemporary life I have identified, is the New Age movement. In discussing eclecticism and spiritual evolution, we surely cannot avoid commenting on this phenomenon. While New Age seems to encompass many diverse expressions, some ancient, others wholly modern, one impression seems almost universal – that it stands in opposition to Christianity. This view is shared not only by most Christians, but also by many New Age adherents. New Age practices – of which there are many – are often rejected out of hand by Christians, and even those Christians who are willing to tolerate traditional non-Christian religions may draw the line at anything associated with this ambiguous term. But since most prejudices grow out of ignorance, it is our responsibility to understand that which we choose to reject. And as we come to greater understanding we may be surprised to find that we are not as far removed from our opponents as we thought.

While some New Age practices can rightly be viewed as suspect (as can some performed in the name of Christianity), an understanding obtained through unbiased critical investigation can actually complement one's Christian experience. In fact, Christianity and the New Age movement can at times be found to agree on basic values and principles, such as commitment to a loving God and the importance of caring for others and being in touch with one's soul. To the uninitiated, the New Age movement as a whole, like an exhibition of modern art, may look like a hodge-podge. But, as we have seen with respect to art, learning more about diverse expressions enriches our experience, giving us a better understanding of where we are ourselves. Rather than viewing Christians and New Agers as polar opposites in spiritual pursuits, then, we can seek a relationship that enables us to learn from each other. Exploring the New Age can open us to new experiences that deepen our relationship with and understanding of God. Eclecticism is healthy when its elements are tied together with a common thread – the vision of our soul.

For me, any spirituality is like a marriage. When a marriage is strong and secure, we can form platonic relationships that expand our experience beyond interaction with our spouse. For example, we might go to a jazz concert with a friend if our spouse does not like jazz without worrying that doing so will have negative effects on our marriage. But if our marriage is in trouble, we will have a more difficult time preventing our relationships with others from distancing us even further from our spouse. Because we are lacking something that is important to us, we may look, perhaps even unconsciously, for other ways to meet our needs. Likewise, when we are in touch with our soul, we can enter into platonic relationships with other forms of religion that enhance our spirituality without threatening our religious affiliation. Those of us who have adopted a particular brand of spirituality early in life (through the religion of our parents) may have had little opportunity (or made little effort) to develop it more fully. As we mature spiritually, our soul permits us to embrace a wide range of spiritual experiences without fear of losing ourselves or needing to convert others. Making sure that our spirituality fits personally – and that it allows us to grow – is important. Undeveloped spirituality of any kind leaves us open to egocentric desires (some of which may even be disguised as a spiritual quest).

Over the years, my personal rituals have developed out of an eclectic gathering of practices that I have found to be meaningful. For many years I began my morning by reading the Bible – sometimes randomly, sometimes reading through a particular book. And while I return to this daily routine from time to time, I have found over the years that I need a wider range of stimuli in order to stretch myself intellectually and spiritually. The word of God comes in many forms and from many sources.

Being eclectic does not mean denouncing our tradition; rather, it can allow us to assemble our spirituality in ways that bring us closer to our soul's vision, deepening our appreciation of the richness and diversity of God. As Christians, we can enjoy the benefits of classes in yoga or Tai Chi without fearing that we are worshipping some other God. Neither will a tarot reading or a Native 'sweat' threaten our Christianity. The connection with our soul offers a thread that allows us to explore while providing a pathway home. The soul provides criteria by which we can sort through our experiences, retaining what is healthy and discarding what is not. As we consider adopting (in part or in whole) any spiritual practice, we must be on the alert for self-deceptions generated by the ego. As we engage in spiritual activities outside our tradition, we need to test ourselves to see what spiritual benefit we have derived (if any), and at what cost. By detaching from our ego – as much as we are able – and asking some basic questions, we can determine whether we are moving in the right direction spiritually. First, how does this experience or interaction make me feel? Am I calm and deeply centred? If I feel anxiety, can I trace its sources to specific illusions created by my ego? Second, does this experience put me more closely in touch with God – am I able to access that place where humanity and divinity merge? Next, is this activity conducive to God's love being expressed in and through my life? Do others feel God's love because of my actions? Then, does this activity cause me to be more accepting of others? Am I open to what I can learn from them? Am I willing to change my mind if appropriate? In short, does this experience help my ego to become transformed? And finally, can I see evidence of this transformation in my life? As we reflect on such questions, we can better understand whether our spiritual activities help us in our relationship with God. If not, we may want to adjust them accordingly.

A reconstructed vision

In his book *Restless Gods*, sociologist Reginald Bibby writes that his "findings point to a religious and spiritual renaissance...new life being added to old life, sometimes within religious groups but often outside them." He further suggests that if the Church is to thrive, "a necessary condition will be the appearance of leaders and laity who see the need for change, are able to envision what is needed to bring about change, and are capable of operationalizing and implementing ideas." [29]

The shape of the Church of the future depends on the decisions we make for it now – however it evolves, it will bear our stamp. Those of us who identify ourselves as Christian are responsible for handing down our tradition to the next generation, whether or not we identify with a specific community. I have spent much of my time as an artist – and as a Christian – trying to understand, integrate and articulate a vision of Christianity that allows me to remain true to both my religious heritage and my integrity as a woman. I continually sift through my tradition for the crystals of truth, uncovering what I believe to be the purest elements of the Christian faith. These elements are like precious gems waiting for a refinement process. As an artist and as a spiritual seeker, I reflect on and re-examine my traditions and my beliefs to find the message I wish to pass on to future generations. As a result, I feel closer to the heart of the Christian message than ever before. It is my passion for my tradition – and the untapped possibilities within it – that motivates me to share my vision through this book.

In the attempt to reconcile feminist and other insights with Christian roots, I have found art to be my greatest ally. Naturally non-gendered and eclectic, art helps us better understand the use of symbols and metaphors, making it at least a bit easier to release our present culture's preoccupation with literalism. It is through a *metaphorical* understanding of my tradition that I am able to stake my claim both as a feminist and as a Christian. An eclectic approach to spiritual development has helped create a bridge that allows parts of my tradition (those that are inclusive, universal and life-affirming) to answer my feminist needs. Drawing from a variety of sources, I am able to reconstruct a vision of Christianity that makes sense to me. Gallery Image 11, *The Mask* (one of the images resulting from the dream mentioned in Chapter 10), illustrates my understanding of the relationship between Christianity and feminist spirituality. Using the biblical metaphor of vine and branches from John 15, this image reveals Jesus as a force breaking through patriarchal cultural and traditions, represented by the mask. The transformation takes place under a sun-like spiral from which egg shapes emanate. The image includes a haiku: 'mask of patriarchy broken open by the vine and the branches.' It is through my connection to soul that I am able to transcend patriarchal influences that mask the truth.

Especially attractive to women interested in spiritual growth is the resurgence of the Goddess. While many find strength and comfort in the Goddess, understood as a metaphor for integrating the feminine component of our soul into our patriarchal culture, some go even further, personifying and literalizing 'Her' as an object of worship – thus replacing patriarchy with matriarchy. I believe that this approach misunderstands the soul's quest for wholeness, and only furthers the polarization of men and women in our culture. It is the *integration* of both feminine and masculine elements that allows us to discern and express God's love more fully. Perhaps what is needed from both sides is a move in the direction of healthy agnosticism! By admitting that we do not have *all* the answers we become more open to learning from others. Spiritual maturity is evidenced by a willingness to accept that God's ways are beyond our limited comprehension, regardless of our perspective.

Taking a lesson from art, we can permit ourselves to be eclectic in assembling our soul's vision, allowing our imagination to help with the reconstruction process. One such reconstruction attempt that has been important for my spiritual growth centres around the story of Eve. For years I have felt myself drawn to this story, hungrily reading anything that crossed my path in the way of early texts concerning Eve in Jewish mythology, psuedopigrapha books, and so on. Comparing texts, I became interested in the different ways in which the story has been told. Although many versions survive, the story found in Genesis includes only details that favour a patriarchal interpretation, while leaving others out. And while the story of Eve is mentioned explicitly only a few times in the Christian Bible after the Genesis account (2 Corinthians 11:3; 1 Timothy 2:13), its baleful influence can be felt throughout the entire text. The Christian interpretation of Eve's story paints women in a less than flattering light. They are easily tempted, and therefore cannot be trusted; they are even blamed for the fall of *man*kind. Troubled by the story from the first time I heard it, rescuing Eve has become a passion for me. And even though there has been progress for women in Christianity in recent years, I believe the rescue effort must be ongoing if we are to free ourselves (women and men) from the implications of a negative rendering of Eve's story. By reconstructing the myth – without the patriarchal overtones – Christian women can be emancipated within their religious tradition. For me, it has been a matter of religious life or death.

My contribution to Eve's rescue came about in an unexpected way. While I had made numerous images of Eve over the previous decade, and written poetry about her, I still didn't feel that she had been fully rescued. The fact that I was not completely convinced that she *could* be rescued gave rise to much tension in my religious life. Then, one day, a friend of mine, a Mi'kmaq artist, invited me to attend a 'sweat' at a lodge in his backyard. I accepted – I had never been to a sweatlodge before and I was excited by the prospect! The sweat was to be led by a woman elder in honour of one of the participating women who was experiencing serious health problems; it was to be a 'doctoring' sweat.

I arrived with a few friends. After sipping some tea, we made our way to the change hut. As we began to remove our clothes the woman elder asked if we remembered the 'golden rule.' I looked at the others, puzzled by her question. Seeing my expression, the elder told me that she was simply asking if anyone was menstruating (the golden rule is that women who are menstruating cannot sweat with women who are not). I felt my heart sink. I confessed that I was, and the elder explained that while menstruating, women are already in sacred space and that interaction with other women in the sweat would be defiling for the one menstruating. As I walked quietly along the path towards my car, watching the others file into the lodge, I didn't feel very sacred. I felt alone and rejected – and 'unclean.'

I thought about the biblical references to women being unclean and traced them back to the story of Eve and the curse she received for her role in eating the fruit of the forbidden tree. I remembered my grandmother, and my mother, calling menstruation 'the curse.' While no one said aloud that menstruating women were unclean, the negative effects could still be felt. Sanitary napkins were hidden under the bathroom sink, while shaving gear and perfumes were easily visible in the medicine cabinet. And then I reflected on the differences between the perspectives of my own culture and religion and that of the Mi'kmaq woman elder, which were only now sinking in, and experienced a deeply profound and meaningful insight. A still, small voice, audible only to me, whispered, "It's not a curse – it's a blessing!" At first I was surprised, wondering how menstruation could be construed as a blessing, given religious and social taboos. But as I reread the story of Eve with new eyes, I found the 'crystal' hidden by layers of patriarchal interpretation. Perhaps, rather than being cursed for disobedience, Eve was being rewarded for wanting to be like God! The poem that ends this chapter was written that evening. It reconstructs the myth of Eve, allowing me – at least in my mind – to rescue her and to pay tribute to her for her courageous and insightful act. Wanting to be like God is not necessarily a bad thing!

Shortly after the poem was written I was invited to address a Christian audience about images of God. I very much wanted to read my Eve poem, but was hesitant given the conservative reputation of the group that had invited me. Reasoning that I would not have been asked to speak unless they were at least somewhat open to my work, I decided to make the poem the centrepiece of my presentation. When I arrived at the church, a bit nervous already, I was greeted by a small group of mostly older men and women. As I set up my easels and artwork, I was aware that the church was being filled mainly by grey-haired women. My past experience as a Bible study teacher had revealed that older women are often resistant to feminism, at least in relation to religion, and so anxiety about my presentation increased rapidly. By the time I was to begin, my voice was strong, but my hands were shaking.

Unable to judge reactions from the faces in front of me, I nonetheless followed my plan, pre-senting my material and concluding by reading my poem. I was prepared to defend my ideas during the question period that followed the presentation, so imagine my surprise – no, my shock – when the group unanimously affirmed what I had said! My anxiety was put to rest and the weekend turned out to be most enjoyable and enlightening for all of us. The poem follows on page 196.

baptism of Eve

mother eve
first woman
walks in the garden
with birds
and serpents
and man

she comes to the
sacred tree
and stops
to kneel before it

the man
and the serpent
watch
as she
removes her shoes

they wait
as she walks
closer to the
tree

don't eat it
hisses the snake
it is forbidden
the man is silent
he stands back
and watches

she picks up
the ripened fruit
it is lush
filled with
the juices of life
she eats
and her mouth
tingles

it is sour
and sweet
and bitter and fragrant
and soft and sharp

her lips are sticky
her thirst is quenched

she savours it
in her mouth
moving it slowly from side to side
from front to back
as the snake
and the man
watch on
hungrily
jealously
fearfully

she holds out the fruit
to them
they step forward
timidly
but stop
when they hear
a great thundering
roar

197

looking to the sky
they see the heavens
open
and a large black raven
descending

the raven
circles the tree
and lands gently
upon the shoulder
of eve

a deafening voice
rings out quietly
this is my daughter
whom I love
and with whom I am well pleased

listen to her
for she has the knowledge of good
and of evil
she is the knower
of wisdom
and the doer of
all that is truly just

she is most like me
because she
sought me
and I will reward her
with the most sacred
blessing

because of you
my daughter
your body
and your daughters'
bodies
will sing
in harmony with
the rhythm of the
universe

this day
I will set a light
in the night sky
which will guide
you in wisdom
and truth
your body will wax
and wane
following the cycles of
the moon
reminding you
that the sacred
rhythm
has been planted
inside you

each month
streams of blood
will pour from you
as your birthing powers
are renewed

the heavens
and the earth
will rejoice
as their daughters
and sons
are given life
through you

take the man
and the snake
and make your home
east of Eden
knowing that you carry
paradise within you

share your gift with
the world
teach your daughters and sons
the sacred secrets of
the universe

the woman looked to the sky
and to the earth
she saw that her feet had
rooted in the earth
and the sky
had mingled with her hair

she turned to the
man and the snake
and said
i am Eve
this day I have become
woman
I have been given the joys
and treasures
of all that is
that they might
be shared

I am the bridge between
heaven and earth
I am before and beyond all time
I am here
to bring you life
I am your mother
your child
your sister
your lover
your friend

the man and the
snake
felt love
and moved
towards her

Eve embraced them
with open arms
feeding them
with her fruit
comforting them
with her branches
and releasing them
to walk through
her hair
into heaven

Whether through writing poetry or painting pictures, the art process can help to make sense of the eclectic collection of information and experiences storehoused within us. As we allow ourselves to become more creative, we will find ourselves taking risks in the development of our vision, knowing that the process itself is what keeps us connected to our soul, while the content provides material from which we can continually expand our perceptions. By using everything at our disposal we can assemble and reassemble our soul's vision, refining it with each successive attempt. Like the work of artists, which continues to evolve and become refined throughout their lives, the reconstruction of our vision is an ongoing process, taking many forms as our spirituality continues to develop. And while the products themselves are useful as part of our personal revelatory process, they are by no means authoritative for others, or even for us. They are merely records of what we see from our particular perspective as we continue to peer through the darkened glass.

EXERCISE

Pick any myth in the Bible that troubles you. Reflect on it, looking for the crystal of truth it contains. Try rewriting the story, as if you had been there, thinking about alternative interpretations that take into account the differences between our world and the one of biblical times. Allow yourself creative freedom (poetic licence!), using your intuition to access the deepest thoughts of your soul. To honour your imagination, share your story with at least one other person.

I have wings
to fly beyond mountains
to the heavens
where I see
secrets which cannot
be revealed

I long to take you
with me

I have roots
which dig deeply
into the depths of the earth
where I feed
from the springs of
eternal youth

I long to take you
with me

Chapter 12

SHARING

Lesson X
ASSESSMENT AND EXHIBITION

Artist materials:

A collection of previously completed artworks.

Cultural and personal symbolism

The final stage of our art course takes us beyond art*making* altogether; the concern now is for you to *share* what you have made. This, too, requires careful attention and reflection. For one thing, if we wish to share our art, to use it as a means of communicating, it is important that our visual language be comprehensible to others. As you develop your personal symbolism, colours and lines will take on specific meanings for you, but if you are to communicate your artistic vision effectively, you need to know the symbolic languages of those with whom you might be 'speaking.' For example, if you use green in an image to symbolize death, you should not be surprised when others do not immediately understand your message. Green, like other colours and symbols, has a cultural component to its symbolism that may outweigh your

understanding of it – at least in the mind of the viewer. Commonly used to represent such things as life, growth and peace, the symbolism of green has an archetypal quality that informs us unconsciously. And because art is ultimately a form of communication that allows us to share our ideas with others in concrete form, an appreciation for the power of cultural symbolism allows us to create images that affect the viewer the way we want. We may use green in the traditional sense, or we may use it in unexpected ways – perhaps in a death mask to help drive home a point about the relationship between life and death. In both art and soul, communication is best when we are sensitive to the nuances of translation.

Understanding the significance of symbols in different contexts will allow you to be more successful in communication. The same symbols may be used by different religious, cultural, social, political or professional groups to mean different things. For example, the shape of a cross may symbolize freedom to a Protestant, suffering to a Roman Catholic, a street intersection to a traveller, or the addition of numbers to a mathematician. While the colour black is used to represent mourning in Western culture, mourners in Eastern cultures traditionally wear white. Knowing these possible interpretations for such signs or symbols increases our understanding of how certain groups might relate to our work. When we use symbols in our images, we must be aware that others may give different meanings to them.

This point was brought home to me during a workshop where I was presenting my artwork to a theological conference. In the early stages of forming a personal symbolism, I had adopted the use of black and white to represent the opposites of evil and good. The Bible, which is filled with such metaphors, had played an instrumental role in my choices, both consciously and unconsciously. Given that I was raised in a predominantly white social environment, I did not see the possible racial implications of my images. One workshop participant asked me, "Why do you always use white for good and black for evil? Couldn't you find a less racist way to make your point?" I was taken aback by the question. In my naïveté, I had no idea that my viewers would see my colour choices as racist. Such issues were not part of the statement I was trying to make with my image.

But whether or not I had intended my visual statements to be racist, I now realized that others could construe them that way. The racism inherent in my culture – combined with my unchecked intuition – resulted in images that could have unwanted negative effects on others. (Sometimes artists use negative effects to make their point, but this was not my intention in this case.) It is our responsibility, as far as we are able, to articulate our ideas in a manner that is aligned with our intentions. Since that time I have been more careful to make my images correspond to my beliefs, often using complementary colours such as blue and orange to represent good and evil (Figure 12.1). Because they are opposite each other on the colour wheel, these colours have the same symbolic value as black and white. In this way I am able to stay true to the concept I am trying to illustrate without hurting anyone with my image.

Understanding and respecting the symbolism of other groups and cultures helps us refine our

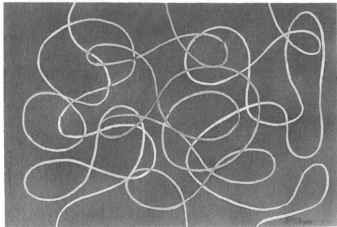

Figure 12.1 The vines and squiggles in this watercolour image, Bios and Zoe, are partnered in pairs of complementary colours to enhance the theme of relationship between opposites (such as good and evil). The blue, yellow, and red vines are transformed into their complements: orange, purple, and green squiggles, respectively. To accentuate the ambiguity of good and evil, the image has been signed in all four corners, allowing it to be correctly displayed in any position.

personal language so it invites dialogue. Ultimately, art is more than talking to ourselves; it is sharing our vision of reality with the world. Although our art should not be motivated by the wishes and whims of others, we must take into account how others perceive our art. Just as children are taught how to discriminate between thoughts they may express socially and those best kept to themselves, as artists we must learn to identify the difference between vain or thoughtless expressions of the ego and art that expresses the perspective of the soul.

Assessing an image

As a teenager in an art class, I watched a sensitive art instructor critique students' work. He always began with positive comments, encouraging each student by pointing out those areas of the image that showed promise. This was followed by gentle instruction on how other areas might be handled differently or developed further in order to enhance the positive qualities. Over the years I have tried to emulate his approach, first encouraging students with my words, then helping them to find their own inner critic and source of encouragement. Although we can at times greatly benefit from the comments and advice of others in our artmaking, we must also develop our own evaluation skills. In assessing our own images, we need to be brutally honest and gently nurturing simultaneously, noticing both our weaknesses and our strengths. Most professional artists, it may be noted, are not happy with every piece of art they produce; in fact, some will say that out of every ten attempts, they produce only one that they consider to be successful.

Entering the world of public exhibition can be a wonderful addition to the learning experience, but it means being open to differences of opinion concerning your work. While you may be overly sensitive to criticism at first, over time you will come to understand its value in the greater context of your life. This does not necessarily mean developing a thick skin, but becoming aware of the criteria by which you are judged and developing your own system for judging the criticisms levelled at your work. Not every piece of art you produce will be considered successful in the eyes of others, but everything you create has the power to instruct you in your journey through art and soul. As you mature as an artist, you will learn to judge your work more objectively. This will help you decide which pieces ought to be exhibited publicly and which pieces are better viewed only as personal experiments or learning devices.

There are three things you need to consider as you prepare for public exhibition, and you ought to ask a few questions about each. The first is the choice of media. Since in visual art media represent at least part of the message, you can evaluate the success of your use of media in a given image. Does the image exploit your media in the best possible sense? That is, could this particular artwork have been produced just as easily using different media, or are the media you used integral to the visual statement? For example, in my previously described lithograph-collage entitled *Persona Distortions* (Gallery Image 5), I wanted to show the different personae of our personality as diverse expressions of a single unit. With the black drawing printed from an image drawn on a lithographic stone and coloured tissues printed from the same stone, I was communicating that there is something common to all personae. If I had redrawn the face several times in different colours (as originals), the symbolic value would not have been the same. In this case, the medium of lithography was essential to the statement. When you look at your images, you need to think about why you chose this particular medium to present this idea and whether your choice has contributed to the overall effect. Further, if you determine the medium to be a good one for the image, you can proceed to examine your use of it. If it is charcoal, are the tones adequately developed? If the image is watercolour, are the layers transparent? And so on. These questions will be answered as you look carefully and objectively at your handling of the medium.

Next, consider the *design* of your image. How have you used the visual tools of perspective, composition and light? Do these add to the overall effect of the image or are they inconsequential? As you mature in the artistic journey, you will become more conscious of these elements in the planning stages of your work. If, for example, you have produced an interesting image as an improvisation, such as the mandala in Chapter 10, you may want to reproduce it as a planned composition, recognizing that not everything provided by your intuition springs forth in perfect form. Drawing images from your unconscious, you can consciously shape them in a way that enhances the content, deliberately arranging the elements of line, shape, tone and colour in your composition to better express the intent of the intuition

that gave birth to it. Even images deemed to be successful at first can sometimes be improved when you combine your learned skills with your imagination. Of course, not everything can be improved upon – but most things can. Whether abstract or representational, elements of design can be evaluated.

Finally, consider the *message* you hoped to convey through your image. What are you trying to say with your image? Have you said it well? Is your use of symbolism, whether representational or abstract, appropriate to what you are trying to communicate? Might others read it differently, and if so, what effect will that have? Is there a message in the work that has universal application? Some of the best artworks tie together the personal and the universal, speaking to us on many levels. We are attracted to art when we identify personally with such themes. Whether a work promotes a feeling of harmony or discord, the realization of shared human experience draws us to it. Your best works will contain this quality.

Exhibiting

Remember my friend from Chapter 1 who likened exhibiting her artwork to standing naked in front of strangers? Do not be surprised if you find the prospect of public exhibition of your work a bit scary at first. You are, after all, exposing your most intimate thoughts for all the world to see. In doing so, you will generate one of three possible reactions – acceptance, indifference or rejection. And while it is obvious that acceptance is favourable, indifference is usually the most disturbing for an artist. Rejection at least implies some sort of reaction, indicating that we have stirred something within the viewer! Regardless of the reaction to your work, keep in mind the reason you are exhibiting it: to share your vision. Exhibiting your art gives you more opportunities to interact with others at the level of soul. Through the creation and exhibition of your art, you tell the world you have something to say and feel so strongly about it that you will risk their apathy or wrath. No matter what others may say about your work, take the chance.

Once you have decided to show your work to others, you will find many venues for exhibiting. Commercial and public galleries are not the only options for a budding artist – I have always been attracted to non-traditional venues for showing my work. In addition to exhibiting in galleries, I have mounted exhibitions for churches, hospitals, offices, commercial retail outlets of various kinds, restaurants and outdoor fairs (Figure 12.2). One of my favourite exhibitions took place in a gym. The images, which explored the outside world through the windows of a fitness facility, were displayed in the building from which they were painted on rough easels covered with sheets. It was great fun to watch people comparing the images to the physical objects that inspired them.

Regardless of where they are exhibited, you need to consider the suitability of your images to

Figure 12.2 Sometimes it is rewarding to exhibit artworks in non-traditional venues, like a church.

the venue. On one occasion I had my work censored by a commercial gallery because they objected to the nudes I included. More attention to administrative details prior to the exhibition would probably have prevented an embarrassing and uncomfortable situation before the opening. So, the next time I exhibited the same images, I took extra care to ensure that they would be displayed with dignity. Our artwork represents us to the people who view it. Whether they like or dislike it is not up to us, but how and where it is displayed is something we can control. As you think about the people who might be most interested in the kinds of works you are creating, find ways to put your images in their paths. For example, my first three books were created as mini-exhibitions, so that I could share my images and thoughts with people in ways that would be inexpensive and convenient.

The preparation for a specific exhibition depends on the nature of the work as well as restrictions of the venue. You will want to enhance the appearance of the image when you display it. Since traditional framing can be very expensive, it is always good when starting out to be on the lookout for new and innovative ways of presenting material. For example, works on paper should be protected by glass, but if they are hung where they cannot be touched or damaged in some way, it may be possible to display them without spending money on framing. No matter what venue you select for exhibiting, think about the conservation needs of each work. (Many useful books and web sites address these issues.)

Exhibiting your work completes a cycle in the art process. Not only have you learned how to use media to create visual images, you have considered what you want to say with them and shared them with others. But this is not the end. As in a spiral, you return to the same process, this time a little wiser because you have been informed by your experience. For example, going through the art classes presented in this book again will allow you to repeat your experience at a more advanced level: you will learn more about using different media, refine your vision and continue to share your results. This is the process involved in being an artist; and when you follow it, that's exactly what you are!

EXERCISE

Consider who would best be able to appreciate what you are working on in matters of art and soul. Seek out opportunities to share your work, selecting carefully the images that best exemplify your skill and ideas, then preparing them for others to see. You might begin by asking a few friends or business acquaintances over for tea as a way of introducing yourself as the emerging artist you are. Listen to their responses to your work, but do not follow their advice until you are convinced in your innermost being that it is right to do so. Remember that the journey of art and soul takes as long as your life lasts and that your work at any given moment reveals where you are only at that particular point. Be gentle with yourself, recognizing your gifts and allowing others to share in your insights as you progress. Finally, use the lessons in this book to practise what you have learned, beginning another level in the spiralling growth of your art and soul.

SHARING THE SOUL'S VISION

Theology of the imagination

Once, after I nervously read one of my poems as part of a church service, a woman from the congregation approached me to say thank you. She had been writing poems of her own for years but could not find the courage to share them. I do not know if the content of my poem was meaningful for her, but my act of sharing was. By sharing ourselves – and our art is part of who we are – we encourage others to share themselves. Our willingness to make ourselves vulnerable generates a similar willingness in others, and thereby a deeper communication as well as progress in human spiritual development. Sharing our soul's vision is also important to the continued growth of our own personal spirituality, much as exhibiting is to artistic development. Through the ongoing process of articulation, interaction with others and reflection, we are all able to progress.

Historically, artists from various religious traditions have expressed their understanding of transcendent reality through their art. I am sharing my vision of Christianity here in the hope that it might evoke a process of exploration, investigation, articulation and sharing in you, the reader. I believe that we are all called to be theologians – working out an understanding of God that makes sense to us. If we call ourselves Christian, we need to understand more particularly the role of Christ in our system of theological beliefs. While I have been sharing my understanding of religion in a more general way throughout the text, what follows represents the cornerstone of my beliefs as a Christian.

I will acknowledge at the start that my views do not always conform to the theology of mainline Christianity (Catholic or Protestant). While from one vantage point this fact may seem only another manifestation of tensions between perceptions and practices that are always present in religious traditions, such theological differences are not to be taken lightly. Wars have been (and continue to be) fought over them. It is my view that if our awareness of ourselves and of God is to grow, we must listen to each other in a spirit of openness. My journey through the Christian tradition has introduced me to a wide variety of practices, thus deepening my appreciation for ecumenism. Taking my cue from Gamaliel, the honoured leader of the Jewish community who came to the defence of the disciples when they were being persecuted after Jesus' death, I believe that ultimately it is God who will prevail, not a specific understanding of God (Acts 5:38, 39). Consequently, my interpretations do not reflect those of any specific Christian tradition or denomination; they are the result of many years of study and reflection through the lens of my imagination, and will no doubt be further honed as I continue in my spiritual journey.

Jesus of Nazareth

Jesus of Nazareth was born about two thousand years ago into a family of modest economic and social means. He surrounded himself with everyday people, sometimes called 'sinners,' 'outcasts' or 'publicans' in the Bible. He appealed to ordinary people with his unpretentious attitudes and unlimited compassion. According to what we know about him from the Gospels, he did not think or act like most people of his time, religious or secular. For example, he considered enemies to be as worthy of love as family, and thought that those who were least in the eyes of the community were first in God's eyes. Jesus lived his life close to his soul, reaching through it to the very heart of God. What he found, he mirrored with his own life: gratitude, simplicity, compassion, humility and love. He taught that by connecting with God directly, people find abundance instead of poverty, peace instead of war, joy instead of grief. His humility illustrates an ego fully transformed into the true self. He had many friends who hungered to hear his words and feel the acceptance of his unconditional love, but he also had influential enemies. Jesus of Nazareth saw himself not as a saviour but as a friend – someone who would willingly lay down his life for another not in a show of bravery but because of his mission to express God's love in the world. He was brutally murdered because he would not abandon or change his understanding of God to conform with accepted standards. He spoke about his death in advance to prepare his disciples (execution was the usual penalty for someone who criticized social and political authorities). He knew his death would serve as an important example of his message about God.

The Christian tradition holds that Jesus was fully divine as well as fully human. I have struggled with this idea, and sought an understanding of it that I can accept. I believe that Jesus was perfectly human, exhibiting the emotions, strengths and weaknesses we all share. He was given to bouts of anger; he became frustrated when his friends seemed to miss his point repeatedly; he cried out for God when he felt abandoned. The historical Jesus was just like us, except that he lived his life entirely from the perspective of his soul. While we know little of his formative years, what is written about the adult Jesus (which stands as Scripture for Christians) provides the example of one whose ego-centred desires had been completely replaced by the objectives of his soul. Jesus of Nazareth discovered, nurtured and expressed divinity through the connection to his soul. Through that process he was as fully divine as anyone in human form can be, while alive on this earth. The bridge between humanity and divinity represented by the soul was clearly revealed in him, and so he stimulates hope for us all. Because he was fully human, possessing nothing that we don't also possess, at least potentially, we can follow his example to discover divinity within ourselves (Galatians 2:20). The transcendence and immanence of Jesus' experience provides a Way for us to connect with and live the mystery of God.

The roots and wings of Christianity

While Jesus of Nazareth was an historical individual, the power of the theological concept of *Jesus as the Christ* is mythological. It is mythology that brings our theology to life. Myth, as I understand it, provides a story with which we can identify personally. Unfortunately for many of us, our Western mindset has made us think of myth as fiction, replacing metaphor with analogy, symbols with signs, and creativity with acquiescence.

The creative process helps to restore our relationship with mystery. Artists tap into mystery when they create their images, relying on metaphor and symbolism to stimulate the imagination of their viewers. Art punctuates insights with silence, providing a pathway to a different kind of knowledge that respects the individuality of the recipient. A myth, like a parable, is a story, complete with a beginning, a middle and an end; from it we gain insight as we unravel the stories of our lives. Unlike factual reports, myths open the door to our imagination and speak to us individually; our interpretations will differ as the experience we bring to them differs. According to Joseph Campbell, myth helps "put [our] mind in touch with [the] experience of being alive."[30] And being alive is the greatest of all mysteries!

Myth provides a guide by which to live the mystery of the divine–human connection. As we uncover our soul, which has always been with us – and which is connected to God – we bring the mystery of God's reality more fully into our everyday existence, becoming instruments of God's love in the world.

What follows is a version of the myth of Jesus as the Christ developed from the composite story of the life of Jesus in the Bible. As a myth, the story provides, as we will see, a basic structure for spiritual development in modern times; it also represents a specifically Christian version of the transition from unenlightened ego to true self, and shows that an 'imitation of Christ' is still possible for creative thinkers in modern times.

The way of Jesus

1. Birth

The story of Jesus as the Christ according to Matthew and Luke begins with a virgin birth that involves the fusion of human and divine energy. Our own spiritual story also begins with a birth, a reconnecting with our divine source, as we are awakened to see ourselves as participants in a divine–human relationship. Recognizing our divinity for the first time, perhaps in moments of heightened creativity, we feel stirrings prompting us to uncover what has been hidden within. Through this metaphorical birth, we begin to understand our physical journey as part of a greater spiritual reality and our life as an opportunity for the creative development of both.

2. Baptism

Jesus' baptism by John, as indicated by all four Gospels, initiates him into a community of like-minded people who recognize him as the Son of God. Likewise, after awakening to our divine connection, we will want to seek out those whose experience affirms our new way of seeing the world, a spiritual family from whom we can expect support and to whom we will be accountable. Baptism represents entrance into a creative and spiritual community where our gifts are accepted, nurtured and valued. It is a reciprocal experience of knowing and being known by God in the presence of others – a shared experience in which we acknowledge ourselves as God's children, consciously committed to promoting the soul's vision. A deeply profound commitment to God in the presence of witnesses, our own baptism, whether literal or metaphorical, is the covenant that reorients our lives from within.

3. Temptations

After his baptism, Jesus is led by the Spirit into the desert, where he is tempted for forty days. Matthew and Luke say that during this time Jesus doesn't eat and is hungry. When we are spiritually hungry, the unenlightened ego – our personal inner tempter, which the text calls "the devil" or "Satan" – promises to satisfy our cravings and in doing so distorts our vision of what life is really all about. While in the biblical story it may seem that the temptations are levelled at Jesus from the outside, essentially all temptations are inner conflicts as we struggle to overcome the misguided power of our ego. Just as Jesus combats his temptations with the word of God, we can overcome the illusions of our ego by maintaining our commitment to follow the path of our soul. Continually working with the positive and negative in our lives, as with the shapes in our images, our preference for arranging our lives according to the soul's vision will gain momentum, helping us to find the strength we need to resist the ego's temptations. We will not need to avoid direct contact with those temptations; they will simply become less interesting to us, like an inferior composition for a painting, as our attention is directed towards creating a new kind of order in our lives.

4. Teaching

After his temptations in the desert, Jesus calls his first disciples and, according to the Gospel of Luke, begins his teaching career – speaking as one having authority and performing miracles. Accepting his role as a channel between God's wisdom and power and the lives of those he teaches, Jesus allows his will to merge with God's. As we open ourselves to God's wisdom and miraculous power in our own lives, we too can become channels of divine love, allowing God's energy to flow through us. We do not need to wait until we are perfect before we begin teaching. Teaching begins as we humbly share with others our struggles and the insights we have gathered. Recognizing ourselves as both teacher and student, we consciously participate in creating a world order in which diversity of insight is valued – like an image in which all tones, textures and colours are used to create a fuller expression of reality. As Jesus used prayer to maintain his strength for teaching, we too can draw strength from God by engaging in regular prayerful acts – including acts of artistic creation – that keep us in touch with our soul.

5. Betrayal

In the Gospels, even though Jesus speaks words of wisdom and performs miracles before their very eyes, his disciples repeatedly misunderstand him and eventually all abandon him. Indeed, the betrayal by one of his own leads to his arrest, conviction and death. But Jesus does not blame others for what has happened to him. Rather, he accepts the consequences of their betrayal and continues firmly on the path of his soul, meeting the new challenges head on without complaining or becoming bitter. In the same way, much of what hurts us is the result of other people's actions. Following the way of Jesus, we can let go of our need to point fingers and cast blame, thus overriding the ego's defences and allowing us to stay in touch with our soul. And since even with this powerful connection to God we can no more control the thoughts and actions of others than Jesus could at the time of his betrayal, we must ultimately let go of our desire to do so. While we may not like the influence others have had on the direction our life has taken, our soul connection provides strength and direction in each new situation. By accepting betrayal in our lives as a given we can move forward despite it, arranging the raw material of our lives according to the objectives of our soul like an artist who paints marvellous pictures with his limited palette, finding myriad combinations as he applies his imagination to the task.

6. Death

According to the Bible, Jesus dies a painful, humiliating and public death. In the midst of a crowd – comprised of some who loved him and many who hated him – he suffers alone as life drains slowly from his body. His last words, according to the Gospels of Mark and Matthew, are "My God, my God, why have you forsaken me?" According to Luke, Jesus' final statement is one of self-submission, and the author of John's Gospel has him saying, "I am thirsty… it is finished." Understood mythologically, Jesus' death represents the public relinquishing of the unenlightened ego. Accepting that our self-interested ego still separates us from God, we acknowledge our spiritual thirst, and submit ourselves to God in order to quench it. The complete death of our egocentric desires is necessary for complete transformation. Like St. John of the Cross, we must learn to embrace our darkest hours, finding the light within ourselves that is only visible through the experience of darkness. As we allow God to become our primary light source, shining from within, we become better equipped to identify secondary sources of light in relationships and activities of our outer world – even when all around us remains in darkness. Jesus' death on the cross reminds us that our greatest strength comes from God, and that we obtain it through submission.

7. Resurrection

In the myth of Christ, death is not the end of life, but a pivot that changes its direction. While the Gospels agree that Jesus was buried after his crucifixion, they don't tell us when he was resurrected, only when his resurrection was discovered. Even then, his resurrection itself is not described, only its effects on others. His resurrection experience takes place in private. Metaphorically, we can understand Jesus' resurrection as the end of our own personal experience of 'three days in the tomb' and the beginning of a new way of being in the world. Our resurrection is a second spiritual birth, one more conscious than the first, marking the further emergence of our true self. When we are resurrected, the ego, in the form of the true self, is completely at the disposal of the soul. We are given a fresh opportunity to compose our lives consciously, responsibly and deliberately from the soul's perspective, finding a balance that allows us to turn our attention more fully to the divine vision.

8. Appearances

The appearances of Jesus after his resurrection, emphasized by all Gospel writers, are moments intended to edify and instruct others – which is reminiscent of the story of the Buddha, who does not enter Nirvana but, out of his great compassion, chooses to return to help others find the path of enlightenment. As our true self emerges, we become more aware of our public role as instruments of God's love. Our mission is not to separate from the world but to help transform it according to the soul's vision. As resurrected beings, we can share ourselves with others authentically – from the level of soul. Like Jesus on the road to Emmaus, we can help others to see what has been before their eyes all along. Unlocking the barricade between God's inflowing love and those around us for whom it is intended, we accept others as they are and offer ourselves in their service. Like artists experimenting in different media, we discover how our gifts can be used to give the best expression of God's love in each situation.

9. Ascension

The Gospels of Mark and Luke record Jesus' ascension into heaven, with the author of Mark stating further that Jesus takes his place at the "right hand of God" (Mark 16:19). Ascension is an important element in the practical application of the myth. It represents sustained resurrection – being continually conscious of God's presence in all areas of our lives. Through ascension we are brought close to God through our soul, able to draw continually on God's wisdom and strength.

As in the innermost mansion of St. Teresa's castle, or like Brother Lawrence, who found joy among the pots and pans in his kitchen, we see all of life – joy, pain and everything in between – through the eyes of our soul; we enter into the divine mystery as fully as possible in human form. Ascension reveals that God is all and is in all. The strength of our bond allows us to carry the awareness of God in our hearts regardless of our external circumstances; we no longer sense a separation between ourselves and God, but experience God's reality within: "I no longer live, but Christ lives in me" (Galatians 2:20). Ascension is the acceptance of the due process of God's mystery and our submission to it. It represents the final reconciliation of transcendence and immanence – the soul completely revealed in our daily lives, the living of life from that place where art and mystical experience are born. Prayer becomes a continuum linking us to God as each moment of our lives is gratefully received – a unique and precious treasure, regardless of its content.

10. Second Coming

Even after Jesus ascends into heaven, according to the biblical text, the story is not yet finished, the way not yet complete. The author of the Book of Acts tells us that Jesus will come again! Jesus' way demands that all find their soul connection to God. The process is not complete until everyone discovers and implements the perspective of soul into everyday reality. This means that the mind of Christ must be discovered again and again in countless ways as each of us realizes the life of God within and honours our responsibility to express the vision of our soul with our lives. Only then will Jesus' prayer that the kingdom of God be instituted on earth as in heaven (Matthew 6:10) become real. By informing and applying our intuition in the service of a greater reality, we contribute to a new world order, transforming the external world from within by expressing the love of God through our actions. Thus each of us participates in Jesus' second coming.

A living myth

Our spiritual journey, like our art, develops further and faster the more we understand the process and practise what we learn. Often we may feel we are not making much progress. But if we adopt the myth of Christ, we can be guided by reflection on its various stages as we seek direction for our continuing journey. Myth offers guidance for integrating spirituality with our everyday life. Like the balance adopted by artists who divide their time between observing and practising, we need to find a spiritual rhythm of introverted gathering and extroverted dispensing of God's energy. As in a cosmic breath, inhaling spiritually we absorb the love and presence of God; exhaling, we share what we have experienced with the world. Our private and public actions are thus united in a common pursuit. We establish a rhythm by which we are fed, so that we, in turn, can feed others, thus echoing Jesus' example of balancing prayer with preaching (Mark 1:35-38). Gallery Image 12, The Connection, illustrates this interdependence. The lithograph shows two concentric circles united by a green vine. The inner circle, representing our inner life, is yellow; the outer circle, representing our involvement in the external world, is blue. The green vine (resulting from yellow plus blue) extends inward and outward, thus representing balance and integration.

We cannot breathe in fully unless we have first breathed out fully. In spiritual breathing, to emphasize inhaling or exhaling at the expense of the other is to upset the natural balance of our soul. As we learn to adjust our lives so that our spiritual breathing is deep and regular, we will benefit not only ourselves, but all those we meet. We are God's breath in the world. While we cannot directly breathe spiritual life into anyone else, we can keep ourselves alive by developing spiritual practices that put us more fully in touch with our soul, giving us energy to help others do the same.

EXERCISE

In your journal, reflect on your life as a mysterious combination of divine and human energy. Consider the stages of spiritual development in the myth of Christ as they relate to your life. After reflecting on your journey thus far, write a personal creed that reflects your current beliefs. Simplify your answers into short sentences – the fewer words the better. Type or print your creed as a poem and attach it to your journal or pin it up in your studio. Incorporate it into your personal ritual, asking yourself each time you read it if it continues to express what you believe, and making changes as they become necessary. Keeping track of these 'creeds' and thinking about them from time to time will help you to better understand and deepen your journey in art and soul.

SELECTED BIBLIOGRAPHY

Albrecht, Renate. "Paul Tillich: His Life and His Personality." In *Religion et Culture*. Eds. Michel Despland, Jean-Claude Petit and Jean Richard. Quebec: Les Presses de l'Université Laval, 1987.

Anderson, Sherry Ruth and Patricia Hopkins. *The Feminine Face of God*. New York: Bantam, 1991.

Bibby, Reginald W. *Restless Gods: The Renaissance of Religion in Canada*. Toronto: Stoddart, 2002.

The Bible. *The New International Version*. Ed. Kenneth Barker. Michigan: Zondervan, 1985.

Bolen, Jean Shinoda, M.D. *Goddesses in Everywoman*. New York: Harper & Row, 1985.

Borg, Marcus. *Meeting Jesus Again for the First Time*. New York: HarperCollins, 1994.

——. *The God We Never Knew*. New York: HarperCollins, 1997.

——. *Reading the Bible Again for the First Time*. New York: HarperCollins, 2001

Briggs, John, and F. David Peat. *Seven Life Lessons of Chaos*. New York: HarperCollins, 1999.

Brother Lawrence. *The Practice of the Presence of God*. Old Tappan, NJ: Fleming H. Revell Company Publishers, 1967.

Brown, D. MacKenzie. *Ultimate Concern, Tillich in Dialogue*. New York: Harper & Row, 1965.

Campbell, Joseph. *The Power of Myth*. New York: Doubleday, 1988.

Cook, John. *The Book of Positive Quotations*. Minneapolis: Rubicon Press, Inc., 1993.

Coupar, Regina. *The Spirit Sings*. Nova Scotia: Gamaliel Publications, 1992.

——. *Echoes of the Remnant*. Nova Scotia: Gamaliel Publications, 1993.

——. *Light Among the Shadows*. Nova Scotia: Gamaliel Publications, 1995.

Crossan, John Dominic. *Jesus: A Revolutionary Biography*. New York: HarperCollins, 1994.

Davies, Paul. *The Last Three Minutes*. New York: HarperCollins, 1994.

de Caussade, Jean-Pierre. *Abandonment to Divine Providence*. New York: Doubleday, 1975.

de Mello, Anthony. *Sadhana: A Way to God*. New York: Doubleday, 1984.

Edwards, Betty. *Drawing on the Right Side of the Brain*. Los Angeles: J.P. Tarcher Inc., 1979.

——. *Drawing on the Artist Within*. New York: Simon and Schuster, 1986.

Ferris, Timothy. *The Whole Shebang*. New York: Touchsone, 1998.

Fiorenza, Elisabeth Schüssler. *In Memory of Her: A Feminist Theological Reconstruction of Christian Origins*. New York: Crossroad, 1994.

——. *The Power of Naming: A Concilium Reader in Feminist Liberation Theology*. Maryknoll, NY: Orbis Books, 1996.

——. *Bread Not Stone: The Challenge of Feminist Biblical Interpretation*. Boston: Beacon Press, 1995.

Flanagan, Sabina. *Secrets of God: Writings of Hildegard of Bingen*. Boston: Shambhala, 1996.

Fox, Matthew. *Creation Spirituality*. New York: HarperCollins, 1991.

——. *Original Blessing*. Santa Fe: Bear & Company, 1983.

Fromm, Erich. *Psychoanalysis and Religion*. New York: Bantam, 1967.

Furlong, Monica. *Merton: A Biography*. London: Darton, Longman and Todd Ltd., 1985.

Gilligan, Carole. *In a Different Voice: Psychological Theory & Women's Development*. Cambridge: Harvard University Press, 1993.

Gribbin, John and Mary Gribbin. *Almost Everyone's Guide to Science*. London: Weidenfeld & Nicolson, 1998.

———. *Richard Feynman: A Life in Science*. New York: Penguin, 1997.

Guerber, H.A. *The Myths of Greece and Rome*. New York: Dover, 1993.

Harvey, Andrew. *The Essential Mystics*. New York: HarperCollins, 1996.

Henri, Robert. *The Art Spirit*. New York: Harper & Row, 1984.

Hillman, James. *A Blue Fire*. New York: Harper, 1989.

———. *The Force of Character*. New York: The Ballantine Group, 1999.

Hozeski, Bruce. *Hildegard von Bingen's Mystical Visions: Translated from Scivias*. New Mexico: Bear & Company, 1995.

James, William. *The Varieties of Religious Experience*. New York: Penguin, 1985.

Jamison, Kay Redfield. *Touched with Fire*. Toronto: Maxwell MacMillan Canada, 1993.

Julian of Norwich. *Revelations of Divine Love*. Translator, M.L. del Mastro. New York: Image Books, 1977.

Jung, C.G. *Dreams*. Princeton: Princeton University Press, 1974.

———. *The Archetypes and the Collective Unconscious*. Princeton: Princeton University Press, 1990.

———. "Relation of Analytical Psychology to Poetry" in *The Portable Jung*. New York: Penguin, 1976.

———. *Psyche and Symbol*. Princeton: Princeton University Press, 1991.

Kandinsky, Wassily. *Concerning the Spiritual in Art*. New York: Dover, 1977.

———. *Point and Line to Plane*. New York: Dover, 1979.

Lao tsu. *Tao te Ching*. Boston: Shambhala, 1998.

Langer, Susanne K. *Feeling and Form*. New York: Charles Scribner's Sons, 1953.

Lauter, Estella. *Women as Mythmakers*. Bloomington: Indiana University Press, 1984.

Lonergan, Bernard J.G. *Insight*. San Francisco: Harper & Row, 1978.

May, Rollo. *Paulus*. New York: Harper & Row, 1973.

———. *The Courage to Create*. New York: W.W. Norton & Company Inc., 1994.

McNamara, William. *Christian Mysticism*. Warwick, NY: Amity House Inc., 1981.

McNiff, Shaun. *Art as Medicine*. Boston: Shambhala, 1992.

Merton, Thomas. *New Seeds of Contemplation*. New York: New Directions, 1972.

———. *Zen and the Birds of Appetite*. Toronto: McClelland and Stewart, 1968.

———. *Conjectures of a Guilty Bystander*. New York: Doubleday, 1966.

———. *Raids on the Unspeakable*. New York: New Directions, 1964.

Miller, Barbara Stoler (Ed.). *The Bhagavad-Gita*. New York: Bantam, 1986.

Newman, Barbara (Ed.). *Sister of Wisdom: St. Hildegard's Theology of the Feminine*. Los Angeles: University of California Press, 1989.

Newport, John P. *Paul Tillich*. Texas: Word Books, 1984.

Ostriker, Alicia (Ed.). *William Blake: The Complete Poems*. New York: Penguin, 1977.

Pagels, Elaine. *The Gnostic Gospels*. Toronto: Random House of Canada, 1989.

Pauck, William. "The Sources of Paul Tillich's Richness." In *The Future of Religions*. Ed. Jerald C. Brauer. New York: Harper & Row, 1966.

Peat, F. David. *Synchronicity*. New York: Bantam Books, 1988.

Progoff, Ira, (Trans.). *The Cloud of Unknowing*. New York: Bantam Doubleday Dell Publishing Group, 1989.

Rae, Eleanor and Bernice Marie-Daly. *Created in Her Image*. New York: Crossroad, 1990.

Rand, Ayn. *The Fountainhead*. New York: Free Press, 1985.

Robinson, James M. (Ed.). *The Nag Hammadi Library*. San Francisco: Harper & Row, 1988.

Roskill, Mark (Ed.). *The Letters of Vincent Van Gogh*. London: Collins, 1990.

Saint Augustine. *Confessions*. New York: Penguin, 1998.

Saint Ignatius. *The Spiritual Exercises of St. Ignatius*. Chicago: The Newman Press, 1951.

Saint John of the Cross. *Dark Night of the Soul*. New York: Doubleday, 1990.

Saint Teresa of Avila. *Interior Castle*. New York: Doubleday, 1989.

Schiffer, Fredric, M.D. *Of Two Minds*. New York: Simon and Schuster, 1998.

Schillebeeckx, Edward. *Jesus: An Experiment in Christology*. New York: Seabury, 1979.

Smith, Houston. *The World's Religions: Our Great Wisdom Traditions*. San Francisco: Harper SanFrancisco, 1992.

Stevens, Dr. Anthony. *Archetypes*. New York: William Morrow and Company, 1982.

Thomas à Kempis. *The Imitation of Christ*. London: William Collins & Sons, 1962.

Tillich, Paul. *The Courage to Be*. London: Collins, 1971.

——. *Systematic Theology*, Volume Two. Chicago: The University of Chicago Press, 1966.

Underhill, Evelyn. *Mysticism*. New York: Doubleday, 1990.

Von Franz, Marie-Louise. *Dreams*. Boston: Shambhala, 1991.

Walker, Susan (Ed.). *Speaking of Silence*. New York: Paulist Press, 1987.

Wilhelm, Richard (Trans.). *The Secret of the Golden Flower*. New York: Harcourt Brace, 1962.

Winter, Miriam Therese. *Out of the Depths*. New York: Crossroad, 2001.

Woodman, Marion and Elinor Dickson. *Dancing in the Flames*. Boston: Shambhala, 1996.

Woolger, Jennifer Barker and Roger J. Woolger. *The Goddess Within*. New York: Ballantine, 1989.

Zukov, Gary. *The Dancing Wu Li Masters*. New York: Bantam, 1994.

NOTES

1 Thomas Merton, *Raids on the Unspeakable* (New York: New Directions, 1964), 171.

2 Thomas Merton, *Conjectures of a Guilty Bystander* (New York: Doubleday, 1966), 156.

3 Merton, *Conjectures of a Guilty Bystander*, 158.

4 Alicia Ostriker (Ed.), *William Blake: The Complete Poems* (New York: Penguin, 1977), 506.

5 William James, *The Varieties of Religious Experience* (New York: Penguin, 1985), 380-382.

6 Evelyn Underhill, *Mysticism* (New York: Doubleday, 1990), 445.

7 Underhill, *Mysticism*, 75.

8 For more on quantum physics see Timothy Ferris, *The Whole Shebang: A State of the Universe(s) Report* (New York: Touchtone, 1998).

9 James Gleick. See *Chaos, Making a New Science* (New York: Penguin, 1987), 11-31.

10 John Briggs and David F. Peat, *Seven Life Lessons from Chaos* (New York: HarperCollins, 1999), 14.

11 John Dominic Crossan, in a lecture at the Atlantic Seminar in Theological Education, Truro, Nova Scotia, June, 2001.

12 James Hillman, *The Force of Character* (New York: The Ballantine Group, 1999), 36.

13 Thomas Merton, *New Seeds of Contemplation* (New York: New Directions, 1972), 34, 35.

14 Merton, *New Seeds of Contemplation*, 42.

15 Merton, *New Seeds of Contemplation*, 29.

16 See Saint Augustine, *Confessions* (New York: Penguin, 1998).

17 See Matthew Fox, *Original Blessing* (Santa Fe: Bear & Company, 1983).

18 See Marcus Borg, *Reading the Bible Again for the First Time* (New York: HarperCollins, 2001); also *The God We Never Knew* (New York: Harper Collins, 1997).

19 Saint Ignatius. See *The Spiritual Exercises of St. Ignatius* (Chicago: The Newman Press, 1951).

20 See Paul Tillich, *Systematic Theology, Volume Two* (Chicago: The University of Chicago Press, 1966).

21 See Saint John of the Cross, *Dark Night of the Soul* (New York: Doubleday, 1990).

22 Julian of Norwich (M.L. del Mastro, Translator), *Revelations of Divine Love* (New York: Image Books, 1977), 125.

23 John Gribbin and Mary Gribbin, *Richard Fenyman: A Life in Science* (New York: Penguin, 1997), 1.

24 John Cook, *The Book of Positive Quotations* (Minneapolis: Rubicon Press, 1993), 322.

25 Carl Jung, *The Archetypes and the Collective Unconscious* (Princeton: Princeton University Press, 1990), 292.

26 Jung, *The Archetypes and the Collective Unconscious*, 10.

27 See Wassily Kandinsky, *Point and Line to Plane* (New York: Dover, 1979), 38.

28 See Elisabeth Schüssler Fiorenza, *In Memory of Her: A Feminist Theological Reconstruction of Christian Origins* (New York: Crossroads, 1994).

29 Reginald W. Bibby, *Restless Gods: The Renaissance of Religion in Canada* (Toronto: Stoddart, 2002), 4, 72, 73.

30 Joseph Campbell, *The Power of Myth* (New York: Doubleday, 1988), 6.

INDEX

I invite you to visit my web site: www.reginacoupar.com

I also welcome your comments on the book by e-mail: artist@reginacoupar.com

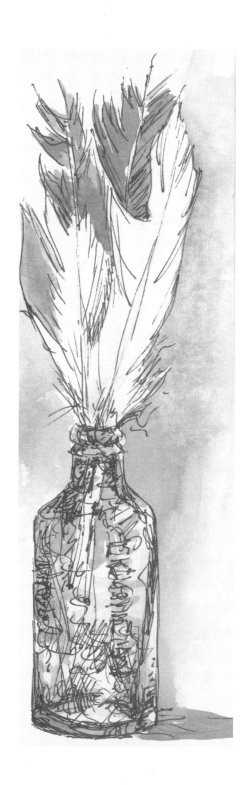

RECONNECTING
WITH MY CREATIVE SELF

Choosing My Soul's Path

Following My Soul's Path

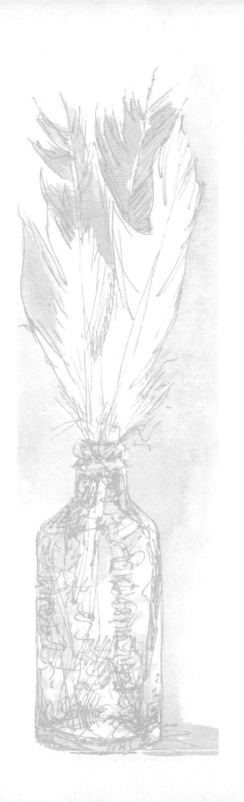

Affirming My Soul's Path

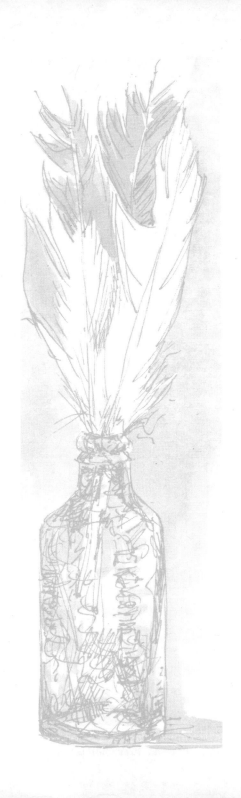

Illumining My Soul's Path

THE GALLERY

Birthing

The Parable of the Sower

3. ORDER

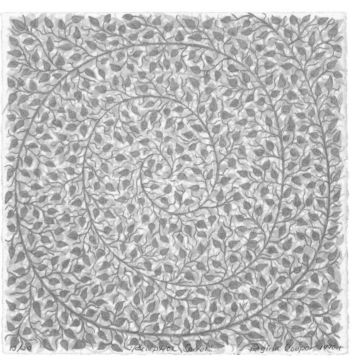

Perception Spiral

Ecclesiagenesis

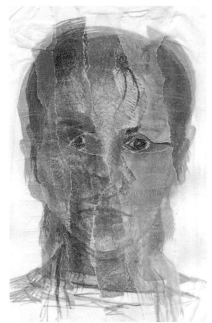

Persona Distortions

6. REVELATION

The Light of the World

The Web

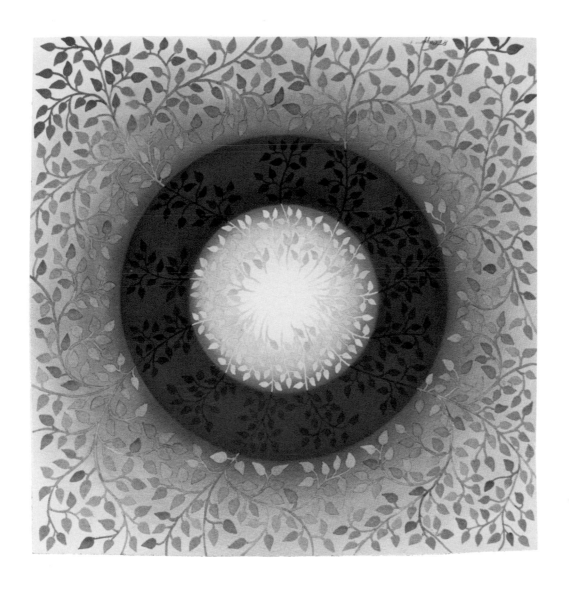

Dark Night of the Soul

9. MYSTERY

Atonement

10. Intuition

Mediator

The Mask

12. SHARING

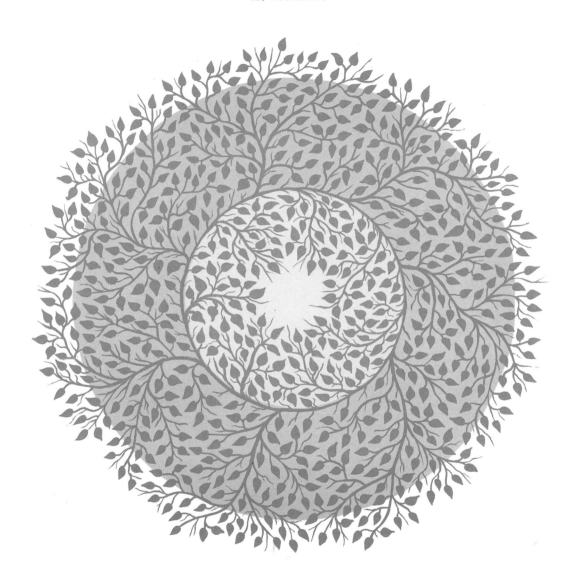

The Connection

FIGURES IN CHAPTER 5

Figure 5.1 The palette is laid out with small blobs of paint on the edges, with ample room being left for mixing colours.

Figure 5.2 Primary colours.

Figure 5.4 Tertiary colours added by mixing equal quantities of secondaries with their adjacent primary.

Figure 5.3 Secondary colours added by mixing primaries in equal quantities.

Figure 5.5 Complementary colours are located opposite each other on a colour wheel.

Figure 5.6 While these two barns have been painted in the same colour, the barn with the greener field seems redder. This illusion results from the juxtaposition of complementary colours.

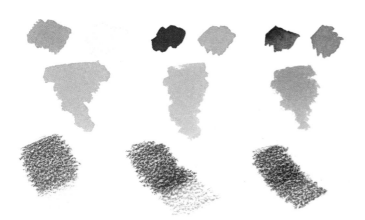

Figure 5.7 When mixed together, complementary colours produce neutrals. When layered, they subdue the intensity of their complement.

Figure 5.8 To experience the relationship between complementary colours, begin by staring intently at the red leaf, trying to blink as little as possible. Focus on the whole leaf, fixing your gaze so that your eyes do not wander about over the image. After a few minutes shift your gaze to a white wall and continue staring intently for at least 7 seconds. Be sure to give your eyes adequate time to adjust to the white wall. What you see on the wall should be the opposite or complementary colour of the leaf. The longer you stare at the leaf initially, the more defined its shape will appear on the wall.

Figure 5.9 A garden of diverse flowers with colours that might seem not to go together in other contexts are in perfect harmony in their natural setting. (Photo: Rose Caissie)